CHUCK,
IT'S ALL
ABOUT
RELATIONSHIPS!

Praise for *Heavy Hitter Sales Psychology*

"Breaking into the C-level executive suite is an absolute must for sales success today, and this book provides the strategic road map to open up one big deal after another."
    Scott Raskin, CEO, Mindjet Software

"This isn't just another book; it's an investment in your future. Whether you manage direct, indirect, inside, or major accounts sales, *Heavy Hitter Sales Psychology* breaks down sales psychology into simple techniques that work."
    Joe Vitalone, Vice President of Sales, Shoretel

"Most sales books provide rudimentary sales tips for beginning sales-people. *Heavy Hitter Sales Psychology* provides sophisticated sales advice for senior salespeople on how to penetrate the C-level executive suite."
    Chip Terry, Vice President and General Manager of Enterprise Solutions, Zoominfo

"Steve brings a whole new light to the golden rule of sales . . . People buy from people who understand how they are wired!"
    Gene Gainey, Senior Vice President of Sales, Learn.com

"This not your typical book on sales scripts; it is a lesson on how to use language to create relationships at the highest levels of organizations."
    Tom Furey, Vice President and General Manager, Standard Register

"Steve Martin brings a new level of thoughtfulness to the psychology of sales. Understanding your own linguistic profile and uncovering the 'bully with the juice' will help you achieve success in the ever-changing landscape of complex selling."
    Sam Adams, Senior Vice President of Sales, Picis

"A must-read for underdog sales organizations that have to compete against 800-pound gorillas."
    Benedetto A. Miele, Executive Vice President of Sales, Globoforce

"Now more than ever, you need an unprecedented understanding of the customer's perspective, motivation, and true intent. *Heavy Hitter Sales Psychology* provides the path to build more meaningful executive relationships that will separate you from your competition."
    Charley Knight, Vice President of Sales, Shaw Industries

"This book takes instruction regarding communication to a new level. Having trained with Dr. Milton Erickson, I am sure he would be unbelievably pleased."
    Dr. Constantine Callas, Chairman and Founder, Medata

"Star salespeople are not always cognizant of how they go about closing C-level deals. *Heavy Hitter Sales Psychology* does a great job describing the foundation and process that comes naturally to successful Heavy Hitter salespeople."
    Todd DeBonis, Vice President of Global Sales, TriQuint Semiconductor

"Steve's latest book is a good combination of highbrow science and tactical examples. Unlike most one-dimensional sales textbooks, *Heavy Hitter Sales Psychology* will keep your interest throughout."
    Garth Moulton, Vice President of Community and Cofounder, Jigsaw

"If you want to become a successful salesperson and rise above the competition, *Heavy Hitter Sales Psychology* is a must!"
    Mike Berlin, Vice President of Sales, Applied Voice & Speech Technologies

HEAVY HITTER SALES PSYCHOLOGY

How to Penetrate the C-Level
Executive Suite and Convince
Company Leaders to Buy

Steve Martin

TILIS Publishers
24881 Alicia Parkway, #E293
Laguna Hills, CA 92653
(866) 688-4547
www.tilispublishers.com

Ordering Information
Orders by U.S. trade bookstores and wholesalers. Please contact Cardinal Publishers Group: Tel: (800) 296-0481; Fax: (317) 879-0872; www.cardinalpub.com.
Orders for college textbook/course adoption use. Please contact TILIS Publishers: Tel: (866) 688-4547.

Cataloging-in-Publication Data
Steve W. Martin, 1960-
    Heavy hitter sales psychology : how to penetrate the c-level executive suite and convince company leaders to buy / Steve W. Martin.
    p. cm.
    Includes index
    ISBN 9780979796128
1. Selling—Psychological aspects. 2. Marketing—Psychological aspects. 3. Business communication. 4. Success in business. I. Title
HF5438.25 .M37366   2009
659.10688 20—dc22   2009930572

Printed in the United States of America
FIRST EDITION
14 13 12 11   10 9 8 7 6 5 4

Cover design: Kuo Design
Interior design and composition: Girl of the West Productions
Editing: PeopleSpeak

Contents

Introduction: How to Use This Book

This book is for senior salespeople, those who have been in the field for five, ten, and fifteen plus years. The goal is to help them accomplish the most difficult task in all of sales: penetrate the C-level executive leader's office and convince him to buy in the life-or-death meetings that determine whether the salesperson will win the deal.

I would like to thank the more than five hundred C-level executives whom I interviewed as part of the win-loss studies I have conducted on behalf of my clients. Listening to these senior leaders share their honest thoughts about how they made their decisions and why they selected the vendors they did was always fascinating. Throughout this book I have inserted their comments along with the title of the person who said them, as shown in the example below.

> Every salesperson is trying to get into my office and explain how their wonderful products will save me tons of money. Very few do because most don't understand what it takes to sit across the table from me.
>
> CHIEF EXECUTIVE OFFICER

I would also like to thank another very important group of people. As part of my preparation process for the keynote presentations and the sales training workshops I conduct, I have had the privilege of interviewing over one thousand of the top salespeople at some of the world's best companies. I never grow tired hearing the stories of how these Heavy Hitters defeated their archrivals by winning over executive decision makers.

Finally, I would like to offer you some words of advice about reading this book. First, fight the urge to "power read" through this book. Although reaching your destination as quickly as possible may be ingrained in your psyche, those who have been in sales for many years have come to realize that the journey is the destination. Slow down and read this book in chunks of ten pages or so at a time.

Second, write in this book. Highlight passages you find interesting. Make notes in the margins about tactics you plan to try. Bend the corners of pages that are important to you. Most importantly, complete the nineteen exercises. By doing so you will learn more not only about people you must persuade, but about yourself too. The exercises will help you internalize the concepts and apply them on your next executive sales call. Most assuredly, you will reap the rewards for doing so.

Part I

The Foundation of Selling to C-Level Executives

Your most important competitive weapon is your mouth and the words you speak. While you will frequently meet with lower-level and midlevel employees at companies whose business you're trying to secure, the rare conversations you have with C-level decision makers will directly determine whether you win or lose the deal. Therefore, it is critical that you understand how C-level executives think and how they communicate and that you are able to adapt your use of language to match C-level decision makers'. In part I we address *sales linguistics,* the study of how the customer's mind uses and interprets language during the decision-making process.

1

Comprehend

UNDERSTANDING SALES LINGUISTICS

> If you understand what I am trying to do—here's how I can help you
> in the short and long term, and here's how I have done it at other
> places—then there is a partnership quality to the relationship, not
> just a vendor and a supplier.
>
> CHIEF EXECUTIVE OFFICER

There's no such thing as reality; it doesn't exist. Most likely, you find this statement hard to believe. After all, you are a real person reading a real book. However, please allow me to explain why this is actually the case.

While absolute reality—the world as it truly is—does exist, no one is able to experience it. We don't know exactly what absolute reality is because we each experience our own individual version of reality. Your reality is based upon your conscious and subconscious minds' perception, and my reality is based upon my minds' perception. And since every mind is different from the next, people's perceptions of reality vary. Therefore, if everyone's interpretation of reality is different, reality doesn't actually exist.

Perhaps an analogy will help you better understand the concept of individual reality. Pretend for a moment that you are in an airplane en route from New York to Los Angeles in seat 9B. You're wedged between two larger passengers and quite uncomfortable because they are using both armrests. The passenger to your left in seat 9A is peacefully sound asleep, and you can hear his slow, deep breathing. The businessman to your right in 9C is concentrating on his laptop. He's making last-minute adjustments to the PowerPoint presentation he'll give tomorrow morning before catching a flight back to New York.

The retired couple sitting in front of you are poring over sightseeing maps of Los Angeles. They are chatting excitedly about attractions they plan to see. The young woman across the aisle in 9D has been immersed in her Stephen King novel for the entire flight. You peer into the first-class section and notice that the passenger in seat 6D is comfortably enjoying his fourth glass of wine. The woman behind you in 10C has complained to the flight attendant three times that the cabin is too cold. The college student in seat 8D is reading a science textbook. She looks as if she is on her way back to school after coming home for the holidays.

The reality is that all of these passengers are on an airplane heading for Los Angeles. However, each of them is having a completely different experience from the others. Each is in a completely different set of mental, physical, and emotional states. Just as each has an individual seat number, each has an individual reality. As a result, no one of them can experience absolute reality.

The same is true when you are meeting with a C-level executive. While both of you are physically present at the meeting, you each have a different mental orientation, level of attentiveness, and way of sensing the world. Therefore, the overall success or failure of a C-level sales call is determined by your ability to adapt yourself and your use of language to access the executive's reality. On the plane for example, you would start a conversation about the horror books you have read with the Stephen King reader, the sights to see in Los Angeles with the tourists, and your college experiences with the undergrad.

The airplane passengers will receive thousands of points of information through three different sensory channels during the flight—visual information from the eyes, auditory information from the ears, and kinesthetic information from the senses of touch, smell, and taste. Similarly, thousands of points of information are exchanged during a

C-level sales call. They are transmitted verbally and nonverbally, consciously and subconsciously.

As the mind continually records each point of information, it builds a model of the experience that will ultimately be summarized into a single memory. By the end of both the flight and the C-level sales call, each passenger and the executive will have a lasting impression that is good, bad, or indifferent. More often than not, the impression of such an event is indifferent, meaning the event was unremarkable and indistinguishable from previous similar ones. However, certain experiences stand out from the rest in a positive or negative way.

Having flown millions of miles during my career, I would have difficulty remembering the specifics of an average flight I took last month. However, I can easily recall the very bad and very good ones, like the flight to Chicago when we flew into a wind shear and it seemed the plane would crash or the time my wife and I sat alone in first class on the upper deck of a 747 on the way to Fiji. (We ate an entire plate of chocolate strawberries during that flight.)

Obviously, we want to stand out positively and be long remembered by the C-level executive. We want him to select us over our competition. To accomplish this, we must enter his reality. In this chapter we will focus on the inner workings of the mind. Once we understand how the mind works, we can communicate in the executive's terms and begin the process of defusing the stress of decision making. We can create a compelling message that separates us from the pack. Most importantly, we can change reality.

The tool set we use to change reality is language. The words you speak are a collection of symbols ordered to express your reality. Without language you really wouldn't exist. You wouldn't be able to share your ideas, display your personality, or express yourself to the world. You couldn't communicate your needs and desires to others, and the never-ending dialogue within your mind would stop. The words we speak truly define who we are. However, since we are talking all the time, we underestimate the complexity of communication and take the process for granted. We mistakenly assume other people speak in our language, but they really don't.

The Customer's World

Unfortunately, when most salespeople meet with prospective customers, they talk in only their own language and only about themselves. The subject of the conversation is me, me, me: my company, my product's benefits, and my product's features and functions. Because the meeting is so important and they're nervous, they understandably fall back on reciting their canned marketing pitch. When Heavy Hitters (truly great salespeople) meet with customers, they talk about them, them, them: their problems, their values, and their plans and desires. Most importantly, Heavy Hitters speak the customers' language. They naturally adapt their mental wiring to mirror the executives'.

You are wired to be right-handed or left-handed. Your brain is naturally wired in that way. You probably know that 90 percent of all people are right-handed. Most interestingly, this is one of the few traits that hold true for people all around the world, regardless of their culture.

Although the exact cause of right-handedness is not precisely known, it is generally accepted that it is associated with language specialization in the left hemisphere of the brain. One point validating this theory is that no populations of nonhuman species have a tendency toward one-handedness. Even studies of our closest biologically related animals—chimps, gorillas, and monkeys—reveal that while there may be an individual preference to use one hand over another, there aren't any population-level tendencies.[1]

But there's a huge difference between your mental wiring for one-handedness and your wiring for language. Although your tendency to prefer one hand was determined before birth, the words you choose to use are the result not only of your genetics but also of your life's experiences from childhood to the present.

In the previous example, everyone on the airplane flight had a different experience and would use distinctive words to label the experience. The first-class passenger might say it was "enjoyable," while others might say "miserable" or "uneventful." We use words as linguistic labels for very complex personal experiences. For example, words like "childhood," "marriage," and "success" can evoke very complicated feelings and memories.

Words are not the flat, black-and-white letters depicted in the dictionary. They are three-dimensional objects that contain feelings, sounds, and pictures when they are said or read. Even the shortest words can trigger small dramas within the mind because words are tightly intertwined with memories.

All the mundane and traumatic experiences of your life have determined the language you use—the surroundings where you grew up, the language used by your loved ones, where you went to school, your friends, your career, the amount of money at your disposal, and even your spirituality. Just as no one else on this planet has had these experiences, no one else speaks your precise language. Therefore, the language two people use to describe the same situation may be very different.

You and the C-level executive have accumulated unique sets of memories. The conversations you have together are quite complex because the language used by each of you comes from different worlds. They consist of verbal and nonverbal messages that are sent consciously and subconsciously. Ultimately, they are streams of information that are transmitted and received in completely different formats.

How People Receive and Transmit Information

During the first four years of your life, 90 percent of your brain's growth and development occurred.[2] Your mind evolved as it interacted with the world around you and recorded strange and exciting new experiences. You learned to speak by mimicking the people around you, and by the time you were five years old, your vocabulary was about two thousand words.[3]

In conjunction with your genetic wiring, your mind developed strategies to interpret the wide varieties of information you had to contend with. To remember what you had seen, you had to think in pictures to imagine or replay what you saw. To remember what was said, you had to recall sounds. You would repeat to yourself what you heard. To remember what you were doing, you had to form an association between your body and feelings.

Three channels of information continually bombard our brains with information: visual, auditory, and kinesthetic. You can't turn off your senses. You can't slow down your vision, turn off your sense of touch, or silence your hearing. Your mind has had to adopt a strategy to assess and prioritize incoming information. While you were born with a tendency to prefer one stream of information over another, during your childhood you adopted the channel processing strategy your mind uses today. Figure 1.1 represents how people receive and transmit different streams of information.

You've used your strategy for decades now. It is ingrained in your mind. Of the fifty thousand words you know, the majority of the words you use in daily conversation actually reflect your strategy. You favor certain channels of information and vary the use of words according to these channels. In addition, the language you use is intimately connected with who you are.

Creating long-term relationships between companies is based upon the process of communication between people, starting with you and the prospective customer. However, since we are communicating all the time, for the most part we become preoccupied with our side of a conversation. We use our own channels to speak without regard to the channels the customer may use.

Some people have a more dominant ear (the one you use when you talk on the telephone), a dominant leg, and even a dominant eye. To determine your dominant eye, take a sheet of paper and cut a hole

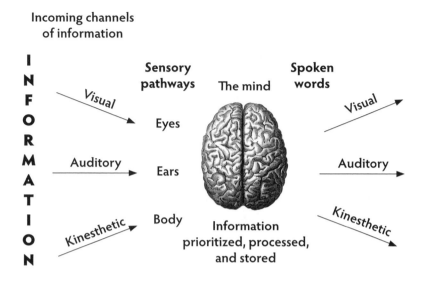

Incoming channels
of information

INFORMATION

Visual

Auditory

Kinesthetic

Sensory
pathways

The mind

Spoken
words

Eyes

Ears

Body

Visual

Auditory

Kinesthetic

Information
prioritized, processed,
and stored

Figure 1.1 How people receive and transmit information

about one and a half inches wide in the middle. Hold the paper out in front of you at arm's length and use both eyes to stare through the hole at an object that is at least twenty feet away. Now close one eye at a time. The object will remain in the middle of the hole when your dominant eye is open and will be covered by the paper when your weaker eye is open.

Similarly, people have a dominant, primary word catalog. A word catalog is the mind's method of gathering information, accumulating knowledge, and recording experiences based upon the visual, auditory, or kinesthetic senses. Your word catalog is also responsible for the association of psychological meanings to words. Your dominant word catalog might be visual, auditory, or kinesthetic. You also have a weaker, secondary catalog and, finally, a recessive catalog.

People process information with their word catalogs using pictures, feelings, or words, according to the strength of each catalog.

Because spoken language is the system we use to communicate our experiences, people describe their experiences and convey their thoughts in terms that match their word catalog wiring.

However, people do not use one word catalog exclusively. Instead, they use all three word catalogs. You have a primary word catalog, which is your "default" method for accessing your catalog of experiences. It is the catalog used most often. Visuals think in terms of pictures, Auditories in sounds, and Kinesthetics in terms of feelings. Your secondary word catalog is your next strongest method for accessing your catalog. Finally, your recessive catalog is your least used and least developed access method.

You can tell what people's word catalog wiring is by noting the adjectives and verbs they use in their conversations. An adjective is a word used to modify a noun, and a verb is an action word. However, some words can be used as either a noun, verb, or adjective, and this usage will significantly change the interpretation of the word catalog. The sentences in the left-hand column represent a visual, auditory, or kinesthetic usage, while those in the right-hand column do not imply any particular word catalog.

Don't *glare* at me.	The *glare* of the sun was intense.
Map out your account strategy.	Please hand me the *map*.
Please *watch* your mouth.	His *watch* is broken.
Focus on the problem.	The camera has automatic *focus*.

The italicized words in the sentences in the left-hand column are verbs that imply a particular word catalog. Although the same words are used in the right-hand column, they are used as nouns. As you know, a noun is a word that describes a person, place, or thing. In general, nouns do not imply any particular word catalog.

People with a primary visual word catalog will use visual keywords more frequently than auditory or kinesthetic words to describe their experiences. Here are some examples of visual keywords:

Beaming	Demonstrate	Frame	Imagine	See
Bleak	Diagram	Gaze	Light	Shine
Bleary	Diffuse	Glance	Look	Show
Blight	Disappear	Glare	Magnify	Sight
Blind	Discern	Glimpse	Map	Snapshot
Bright	Display	Graph	Murky	Spectacle
Brilliant	Distinguish	Hallucinate	Observe	Spot
Chart	Dreary	Hazy	Outlook	Stare
Clarify	Emit	Highlight	Perspective	Survey
Clear	Expose	Illuminate	Preview	View
Cloudy	Fade	Illustrate	Reflect	Viewpoint
Dazzle	Focus	Image	Scan	Watch

People with primary auditory word catalogs will use auditory keywords like these in their conversations:

Accent	Bark	Denounce	Note	Say
Amplify	Berate	Dictate	Paraphrase	Shout
Articulate	Bicker	Digress	Persuade	Slur
Ask	Blare	Discuss	Plead	Snap
Assert	Boast	Drone	Profess	Sound
Attune	Cajole	Edit	Promise	Speak
Audacious	Call	Giggle	Quiet	Spell
Audible	Chime	Hum	Rave	Talk
Backfire	Chord	Implore	Recap	Tell
Back-talk	Crunch	Loud	Retract	Vague
Banter	Cry	Noise	Ring	Yell

People with primary kinesthetic word catalogs will use kinesthetic keywords like the following:

Ache	Catch	Hard	Pique	Smile
Bash	Chafe	Heart	Plug	Smooth

Bask	Chew	Heavy	Post	Spit
Bat	Choke	Hit	Press	Squash
Bend	Chop	Hold	Pull	Sticky
Bind	Clinch	Impact	Push	Stink
Bit	Cough	Impress	Queasy	Strike
Blink	Crawl	Irritate	Rough	Taste
Boot	Draw	Kick	Rub	Thaw
Bounce	Feel	Leap	Scratch	Throw
Bow	Friction	Mark	Sense	Touch
Breathe	Gnaw	Move	Sharp	Walk
Caress	Grab	Nip	Smell	Weigh

How Are You Wired?

What is your primary word catalog? Here's an exercise that will help you understand how you are wired. Print out the last ten business e-mails you sent to colleagues within your company and the last ten personal e-mails you sent to friends or family. Write the letters *V* *A* and *K* across the top of a piece of paper. In the left column write "Work," "Personal," and "Total." The chart should look like figure 1.2.

You are now ready to perform a "VAK keyword count." Examine the e-mails and circle each occurrence of a visual, auditory, or kinesthetic word. Remember to circle the word only when it is used in the context of an action or description ("you *light* up my life," not "please

	V	*A*	*K*
Work			
Personal			
Total			

Figure 1.2 VAK keyword count chart

turn the *light* on"). As you circle the words, add a tally in the appropriate column. The chart may look something like figure 1.3 when you are done.

	V	A	K
Work	III	ⅣⅥ I	III
Personal	ⅣⅥ	ⅣⅥ ⅣⅥ	ⅣⅥ IIII
Total	ⅣⅥ III	ⅣⅥ ⅣⅥ ⅣⅥ I	ⅣⅥ ⅣⅥ II

Figure 1.3 Sample results of a VAK keyword count

Did you notice a difference between the tallies from your work and personal e-mails? Most likely, the language in your work e-mails is more androgynous and technical; therefore, the counts will be lower. I like to joke that this is because most communication in the business world is in fact "senseless." Were the counts evenly dispersed or clustered under one catalog? In the example above, the person's word catalog wiring is primary auditory, secondary kinesthetic, and recessive visual. You can do a similar exercise with the e-mails you receive to determine a sender's word catalog wiring.

Determining the C-Level Executive's Word Catalog Language

Although nouns do not usually imply any particular word catalog, there are exceptions to this rule. When a person's communication is dominated by nouns that can be associated with one of the word catalogs, this is a good indication of that person's wiring. For example, if an e-mail had a pervasive or repetitive use of nouns such as "photograph," "picture," or "maps," this would provide additional clues that the person is a Visual. If someone continually referred to conversations they were part of, this would suggest they were an Auditory.

Other nuances about VAK keywords are helpful when you want to determine someone's word catalog. The more stressful or tense a situation is, the more likely people will communicate in their primary word catalog. People also tend to lie in their secondary or recessive word catalogs.

I have spoken at the sales meetings of hundreds of companies. In order to secure the speaking or training engagement, I have to contact and convince one of five C-level executives to buy: the CEO, the president, the vice president of sales, the chief marketing officer, or the chief operating officer. This is my exact target market.

Before I even consider sending an e-mail or letter, I first study the language used by the executive I am trying to reach. I'll search the Web for video and magazine interviews, company videos he has appeared in, articles he wrote, entries on his blog, letters he may have written to customers or employees. I'll analyze any language sample that will help me understand how he is wired.

I will also conduct VAK counts when I speak with him in person or over the phone. I'd suggest you do this by bringing a notebook to your next meeting or keeping one by your phone. Whenever you meet with someone, perform a VAK count to determine the primary, secondary, and recessive word catalogs of the person you are talking with. You don't have to count for the entire meeting or conversation, just until you have a basic understanding of the person's wiring. Better yet, take along your manager or associate to a meeting and have him conduct the count so you can concentrate solely on your presentation. The manner in which your manager or colleague speaks to the executive and whether your colleague emphasizes visual, auditory, or kinesthetic words will indicate the executive's wiring to you.

Another trick is to place customers' business cards inside your notebook and write the VAK counts directly on them (in tiny print). Later, you can review the cards and refresh your memory about people's wiring. The results of your VAK counts will be fascinating. You will begin to be able to identify people's word catalogs in a very short time. You will also spot patterns and similarities between people who share the same word catalogs.

Your ultimate goal is to become aware of VAK keywords automatically without any handwritten counts. You want the process to become a natural part of listening so that, for example, when a customer is explaining his company's needs, you hear not only his content-level words but also the VAK keywords. Therefore, I suggest you start conducting VAK counts for all customers you meet with (and even others). Obviously, it's important to know how everyone within a prospective account is wired. Also, people tend to hire people that are similarly wired. In this regard, meeting with the vice president of application development may help you better understand how the CIO he reports to is wired.

VAK Keyword Count Patterns

As you begin to perform VAK keyword counts, you will notice some patterns developing. Figure 1.4 shows VAK counts for three speakers, each of whom made a forty-five-minute presentation. Interestingly, their VAK counts were representative of the three major types of VAK count patterns: balanced, strong secondary, and dominating primary.

	Visual	*Auditory*	*Kinesthetic*
President/CEO	20	17	14
Vice President of Engineering	16	20	2
Product Manager	5	34	4

Figure 1.4 Sample VAK keyword counts

The president has a visual primary catalog along with strong auditory and kinesthetic catalogs. This is a very balanced pattern. This wiring suits him well in his position. As president, he is responsible for the vision of the company, and it makes sense to have a Visual in that role. Other responsibilities of the president are company communication and consensus building. His well-developed auditory and kinesthetic catalogs help him to naturally accomplish these two tasks with people who are not visually wired.

The vice president of engineering has an auditory primary catalog and a strong secondary visual catalog. His kinesthetic recessive catalog is almost nonexistent. The nature of the vice president of engineering's position is both analytical and visionary. He has to be able to give specific direction to the programming teams in order to build products. Since the communication framework by which this is done is a functional specification (a detailed description of the product in the form of words), having an auditory primary catalog helps.

Meanwhile, he has to chart the product road map; therefore, having a strong visual secondary is desirable. Since the vice president of engineering is immersed in the technical specification language (the precise, androgynous, nonpersonal language that uses technical operators to modify general words), a strong kinesthetic catalog is not necessarily needed in this position and, in fact, could even be a detriment.

The product manager has a primary catalog that is so overwhelmingly dominating that the secondary and recessive catalogs are very rarely used. This pattern is called a "dominating primary." In this example, the person has a dominating auditory primary catalog. A dominating catalog could be visual or kinesthetic just as well.

This person's role is primarily technical. One of his main job functions is to create detailed technical collateral, such as white papers, data sheets, and technical content for the company's Web site. Having a strong auditory primary catalog is helpful in accomplishing these tasks.

In addition to the VAK keywords, catch phrases, descriptions, and clichés also reveal a speaker's word catalogs. Some individuals use an unusually high number of clichés, for example. These people tend to be strong Auditories, and they actually say a cliché to themselves first before repeating it out loud. In fact, Auditories tend to spend more time listening to themselves speak than do Visuals and Kinesthetics because the volume of Auditories' internal dialogues is higher.

Sayings, descriptions, and clichés may be used by people with any primary catalog. However, usually a phrase is used more often by people with one particular catalog. For example, "sizzling hot" is most likely to be said by Auditories. They hear the sizzling sound. Upon hearing this phrase, Visuals might picture a grill with something sizzling on it, and Kinesthetics might think of a finger actually touching the grill (particularly if they have burnt themselves in the past).

Sayings and Clichés

Let's do another exercise. Below is a list of sayings and clichés. After each phrase, mark a *V* for visual, *A* for auditory, or *K* for kinesthetic. If you think a phrase has multiple interpretations, write the order of what you believe is the priority usage. Here are some examples:

"music to my ears," A   "from their perspective," V
"tough nut to crack," K, A   "that's alarming news," A

The answers follow, but don't look at them until you finish the entire list. Also, it's okay to write your answers in the book.

"keep your fingers crossed"   "armed to the teeth"
"down to the short strokes"   "iron out the problem"
"we'll keep pinging him"   "barking up the wrong tree"
"ducks in a row"   "look them in the eye"
"we'll hammer it out"   "banging the phones"
"coin rattling down the pipe"   "see how the smoke clears"
"die a slow death"   "bury the hatchet"
"level playing field"   "a little bird told me"
"hit the nail on the head"   "ear to the ground"
"bite the bullet"   "that's a new twist"

"between a rock and a hard place"
"look a gift horse in the mouth"
"X marks the spot"
"talk it through"
"chip on his shoulder"
"flying off the shelves"
"clear as a bell"
"bang for the buck"
"talk the talk"
"in the cross hairs"
"apple of your eye"

"echoes what I say"
"close-knit"
"after my own heart"
"crunch time"
"quit your bellyaching"
"newly charted territory"
"smoke and mirrors"
"carry the flag"
"kick them when they're down"
"that resonates with me"
"crocodile tears"

Based on my experience, here is the most likely usage of these phrases matched to the word catalog:

"keep your fingers crossed," K
"down to the short strokes," K
"we'll keep pinging him," A
"ducks in a row," V
"we'll hammer it out," K, A
"coin rattling down the pipe," A
"die a slow death," K, V
"level playing field," V, K
"hit the nail on the head," K, V
"bite the bullet," K
"between a rock and a hard place," K
"look a gift horse in the mouth," V
"X marks the spot," V
"talk it through," A
"chip on his shoulder," K, V
"flying off the shelves," V
"clear as a bell," A, V

"armed to the teeth," K, V
"iron out the problem," K
"barking up the wrong tree," A, V
"look them in the eye," V
"banging the phones," A
"see how the smoke clears," V
"bury the hatchet," K
"a little bird told me," A, V
"ear to the ground," A, K
"that's a new twist," K
"echoes what I say," A
"close-knit," K
"after my own heart," K
"crunch time," K, A
"quit your belly aching," A, K
"newly charted territory," V
"smoke and mirrors," V

"bang for the buck," A

"talk the talk," A

"in the cross hairs," V

"apple of your eye," V

"carry the flag," K, V

"kick them when they're down," K

"that resonates with me," A

"crocodile tears," K, V

Speaking Characteristics

Many salespeople pay attention only to the words a customer speaks. They don't pay attention to the person's speaking characteristics—the tone, tempo, volume, and patterns of words. In addition to keywords, you can determine a customer's primary word catalog by his speaking characteristics.

Auditories are actually talking to themselves and tend to speak in repetitious patterns. The pattern could be melodic or more like Morse code. The Morse code–type pattern tends to be monotone. Certain words are enunciated in the pattern. In the following examples, all the "dot's" are enunciated in a similar way, and all the "dash's" are accented in a different way:

- We are committed to your satisfaction.
  (Dot . . . dot . . . dash . . . dot . . . dot . . . dash)
- We guarantee high performance and availability.
  (Dot . . . dash . . . dot . . . dash . . . dot . . . dash)
- Some Auditories speak in a monotone voice.
  (Dot . . . dot . . . dot . . . dot . . . dot . . . dot . . . dot)

Other Auditories have speech patterns that are more melodic. Their sentences are more wavelike; that is, the ends of their sentences will vary in pitch, tone, or even pronunciation from the beginnings.

Auditories tend to be very proficient masters of the technical specification language, the nonpersonal, androgynous, technical talk used in the customer's industry. Auditories tend to not "leak" or show their word catalogs through the use of VAK keywords as much as Kinesthetics or Visuals. However, when their secondary catalog is kinesthetic, more VAK keywords will be embedded in their conversations. Auditories also tend to quote what they have been told by others. They will also quote themselves in their conversations.

Here are more examples of auditory sentence structures:

- "Our meeting went great. Bob told us, 'We did a great job and everyone is excited to work with us.'"
- "The meeting was going really well and then 'Boom, boom, boom,' we were asked some really tough questions."
- "And I started to ask myself, 'Are they still a partner of ours?'"

The speech pattern of a Visual is quite different from that of an Auditory. Strong Visuals are being bombarded with pictures inside their brains. As a result, they have a difficult time keeping the pace of the words being said synchronized with the pictures being created in their minds. This condition is somewhat analogous to a computer's CPU (central processing unit) having to wait for the mechanical movements of the disk drive to be complete before it can further process any information. As a result, strong Visuals are constantly trying to speed up the mechanical process of speaking. Therefore, they usually talk faster than Auditories or Kinesthetics. Here are examples of sentence structures of strong Visuals:

- "WE ARE COMMITTED TO YOUR SATISFACTION."
- "VISUALSHAVEALOTTOSAYANDASHORTTIMETOSAYIT."

To Visuals, words are an interruption of the pictures or ideas in their minds. They have to get them out of their internal dialogue as fast as possible because thoughts are constantly getting stacked up. Therefore, they speak with energy and a sense of urgency.

In presentations they tend to speak even faster. Their stream of speech may be interrupted only by the necessity to breathe. Have you ever heard someone insert "um's" in every other sentence? Visuals tend to do this more than Auditories or Kinesthetics. These filler words are basically used as a checkpoint to synchronize the images in their minds with their spoken dialogue. The um's are also said at the same speed and tone as the other words.

Conversely, Kinesthetics say "um" much slower and in a deeper tone than the other words they speak. Their um's are actually synchronized with their feelings, and this takes extra time. You also may notice them looking down when they say "um." Meanwhile, the Auditories' um's are not enunciated any differently and blend in with the rest of the sentence. However, Auditories tend to use um's as a part of their editing process to ensure the words they are saying are politically correct. The um provides them additional time to choose their spoken words with more precision.

Visuals tend to talk not only faster but also louder. Visuals are painting a picture for their audience. When they are telling their story, they are trying to make the language represent all the detail and complexity of a picture. You've heard the saying "A picture is worth a thousand words." For Visuals, it's true, and they have to communicate all of the thousand words to convey the picture they are seeing. Therefore, Visuals are the most talkative too!

Having to "always" communicate a thousand words at a time creates a lot of energy. When Visuals are making presentations, they will move back and forth across the stage. Auditories will stand in one place or a small space, and Kinesthetics will shift their weight back and forth. Visuals' arm gestures are more exaggerated since they are illustrating a picture with their bodies. They'll outstretch their arms as far as they can horizontally (so that they resemble a cross) to make their point. Kinesthetics are more likely to make the same point by holding their hands vertically (with one hand over the head and one hand at the waist). Auditories hold their hands closer to their bodies and will use arm gestures sparingly.

While making a PowerPoint presentation, Visuals will point at the screen frequently and may use an index finger like a flashlight. Kinesthetics will extend an arm, using the entire hand or palm to point. Auditories will most likely point an arm (in the locked position of a push-up) straight in front of the body or from the shoulder horizontally. You will notice that Visuals' arms are held higher on the body or over the head. Kinesthetics will cradle or hold themselves with their arms and hold their arms lower, at the waist.

Most people wrongly assume that people with a kinesthetic primary catalog are overly emotional, introverted, or extroverted. This may or may not be the case. Kinesthetics simply catalog their experiences in terms of feelings. However, people who are strongly kinesthetic will reflect this in their speech patterns, and in turn their personalities will be affected.

Kinesthetics tend to speak slower than Auditories and Visuals. Their speech is slower because they are frequently checking their feelings while they speak. Their speech pattern may also be frequently accentuated by their breathing, which is deeper than that of Visuals and Auditories. When speaking to a group, they tend to talk directly to a single person in the audience, unlike Visuals, who will constantly scan the audience. When talking about issues, Kinesthetics are more likely to associate a person with the issue or task at hand.

Strong Kinesthetics tend to be more dramatic in their speech patterns. They commonly insert pauses and use voice inflections. Unlike Auditories with their Morse code patterns, Kinesthetics are "feeling" the words they are speaking. Their tone of voice tends to be lower because they are constantly validating and comparing their feelings with what they are hearing and saying.

Here are examples of sentence structures of strong Kinesthetics:

- "*We* are committed to *your* satisfaction!"
- "I *enjoyed* meeting with *you*."

Every communication with Kinesthetics is personal. The emphasis is on the words "we," "your," "I," "enjoyed," and "you" because they directly correlate with the Kinesthetics' feelings. For example, their interpretation of "we" is actually "me and my company," and their interpretation of "you" is "you and your company." These words represent very personal feelings, so their enunciation is likely to be slower or in a lower tone than the other words in the sentence. Kinesthetics' speech has other patterns. For example, Kinesthetics' voices will tend to rise at the end of sentences or fall and trail off.

The language Visuals, Kinesthetics, and Auditories use reflects the different ways they define their own reality and interact with the real world. Since every company purchase decision usually includes a cross section of Visuals, Kinesthetics, and Auditories, it's obviously important to be able to communicate in each channel.

Keep in mind that people with certain word catalogs communicate better with each other than other combinations. For example, strong Visuals and strong Kinesthetics naturally communicate together better than strong Visuals and strong Auditories. Auditories naturally communicate better with Kinesthetics than with Visuals. Kinesthetics have an intrinsic communication advantage since they are always in touch with their own feelings and are sensitive about the feelings of others. This consideration is incorporated into their communication process.

If you are talking with executives who are wired exactly as you are, you are already mirroring them. Most likely, these are people you naturally communicate with and who are the easiest for you to sell to. However, it takes skill and effort to communicate with someone who has a primary catalog that is the same as your recessive catalog. Ultimately, you want to become a "communication chameleon" who can adapt to any word catalog.

If you are a Visual talking to a Kinesthetic, slow down and speak in terms of feelings; this will naturally lower your voice tone and decrease your volume. If you are a Kinesthetic talking to a Visual, speed up and speak in terms of pictures; this will naturally raise your voice tone and increase your volume.

Auditory salespeople face more of a challenge than Visuals or Kinesthetics in presenting their thoughts to customers. If you are an Auditory, you must make a conscious effort to watch the people you are talking to in order to make sure they are grasping what you are saying. What sounds good to you may not look good to a Visual or feel right to a Kinesthetic. Good advice to Auditories is to stop listening to yourself talk and make sure you are hearing what the customer is saying.

Conversely, Visuals and Kinesthetics should adopt auditory speech characteristics when they are speaking. Just as a chameleon changes colors to match its surroundings, your goal is to change your speaking mannerisms to match those of the person to whom you are speaking. To establish rapport we need to mirror the way customers communicate and enter their world, not make them enter ours.

Rapport Is Harmonious Communication

At the foundation of all sales is a relationship between people. Great salespeople have an innate talent to build such relationships by creating rapport so that the customer feels at ease and enjoys their company.

Rapport is a special relationship between two individuals based upon harmonious communication. To establish rapport with C-level executives you should start by mirroring their language. Create imagery for the visual customer, tell stories to the auditory customer, and speak with feelings to one who is kinesthetic.

Finally, keep in mind that people alter their communication styles when they are part of a group. For example, a group of employees meeting with their CEO will probably speak quite differently when he is in the room than after he leaves. They will speak not only in a more professional tone using carefully chosen words, but also with an entirely different frame of mind. Similarly, the CEO will speak very differently when conversing with a group than in private with a trusted lieutenant.

Conclusion

Everyone lives in his or her own world. The world you experience is not the real world but rather your perception of the world. The way in which you perceive your world is intricately connected to the language you use and how you sense your surroundings. You use your senses to define everyday experiences for storage in your brain. Your word catalogs are the storage-and-retrieval mechanisms used to access these experiences. They are also responsible for the words you select to communicate your world to others.

Hallmark, the world's largest greeting card maker, conducted extensive city-by-city research recently to determine which Valentine's Day card sold the most. The results of the study surprised the researchers. They expected to find geographical preferences for different cards, but one card was the top seller in every city across the nation.

The card's designer, Marcia Muelengracht, said she was not at all surprised about the card's success: "I cut to the chase—what I would want to give and what I would want to receive. A guy wants to say he still loves her. A gal wants to know he still does. She wants to get goose bumps. He wants to think he'll get lucky."[4]

On a deeper level, the card was able to successfully connect with the word catalogs of the readers who would ultimately buy it. It makes sense that a card you would give to someone you love dearly would be written using primarily kinesthetic words. An article gave this description of the card: "The card's face is a deep red foil, with 'For the One I Love' across the top in black script, a large picture of a red rose in the center, and a thick black ribbon cutting through the middle. Inside, it simply states: 'Each time I see you, hold you, think of you, here's what I do . . . I fall deeply, madly, happily in love with you. Happy Valentine's Day.'"[5]

Developing rapport by connecting with customers is a top priority in every conversation with C-level executives. In this regard, your most important competitive weapon is your mouth and the words you speak. Knowing which word catalogs executives use and speaking to them in their language will help them fall in love with you and your solution.

> The vendor we chose has a group of smart, dedicated, customer-oriented people. To a great degree, I don't think their products and services are different from their competitors'. They distinguish themselves with their people.
>
> VICE PRESIDENT OF SUPPLY CHAIN

2

Communicate

THE SEVEN DIFFERENT LANGUAGES C-LEVEL EXECUTIVES SPEAK

> Their salespeople have an order taker mentality. They are not a value-added layer. Even some of the most senior people on our account tend to not come to me with strategic thoughts or ideas for the future but come to me and say, "What do you need today?"
>
> EXECUTIVE VICE PRESIDENT OF WORLDWIDE OPERATIONS

Every day, you speak and listen to thousands of words. Through the words you speak, you are able to explain your ideas, recount your past experiences, and share your personality with others. Since the communication process comes so naturally, you assume you are understood. However, the most important words you speak during the entire year are those you say to C-level executives during the make-or-break meetings that determine if you will win a deal.

Most of the time, you probably don't think about the specific meaning of the words you are using. Since the words are so integrated with your being, they just seem to happen. However, your words represent your attitude, outlook, and perspective about life. But language doesn't consist solely of spoken words, it has an entirely nonverbal dimension as well.

In chapter 1, we learned how we organize the world according to the information received by our senses (sight, hearing, touch, taste, and smell) and use language as the method to describe what we have experienced. The language we use is dependent upon our word catalogs, and each person has a primary, secondary, and recessive catalog that determines how his or her brain processes and stores information.

In this chapter, we are going to take the next step in understanding the C-level communication process. You will learn how you can actually "watch" the mechanical movements of the brain as it accesses a particular word catalog and how this enables you to identify an executive's wiring. Once the catalog is identified, you can adjust your communication style to build rapport using the executive's own language.

Your brain is infinitely more complex than any computer. It's an intricate architecture of more than one trillion cells that control all of your body's components. These components include the nervous system, muscular system, respiratory system, digestive system, and circulatory system. These systems are also responsible for gathering data via the senses.

The brain has three major parts: the cerebrum, cerebellum, and brainstem. From a sales perspective, we are most interested in what is happening within the cerebrum. The cerebrum controls our voluntary functions, such as body sensations, learning, emotions, and pain.

Two hemispheres make up the cerebrum. The right side controls the left side of the body. The left side controls the right side of the body. This cross-management occurs because the nerves connecting to the body cross the spinal cord. The cerebellum coordinates our movement and keeps us in balance. The brainstem controls our automatic functions, such as breathing, heartbeat, and circulation.

If you are right-handed, you have a dominant left side of the brain. If you are left-handed, you have a dominant right side of the brain. Your brain is wired a certain way. You were born with this wiring and you cannot easily change it.

While it is interesting to know the parts of the brain and understand their physiological functions, it's far more important to understand the seven different languages the C-level executive's mind creates.

1. *Word catalog language.* The mind's method for receiving and interpreting information based upon the three sensory channels—visual, auditory, and kinesthetic.
2. *Internal dialogue language.* The never-ending stream of communication inside the mind that represents honest, unedited, and deep feelings.
3. *Physical language.* Also known as body language, the nonverbal communication that is constantly being emitted by the executive's body posture.
4. *Intersecting activity language.* Interests, hobbies, and personal pursuits by which the executive displays his personality, beliefs, and values.
5. *Technical specification language.* The androgynous, nonpersonal, and technical communication that is based upon the nomenclature and technical terms of the executive's industry.
6. *Business operations language.* The language that is specific to the daily running of the executive's business and his role in the organization.
7. *C-level language.* The most powerful trust-based language by which the executive explains his personal needs, desires, and plans along with the strategy by which he hopes to fulfill them.

Let's address each of these seven languages in further detail.

Word Catalog Language

The deepest level of meaning occurs inside the mind's word catalog. This is where words are decomposed into their base objects of a picture, sound or feeling and associated with complex psychological meanings. While your lexical dictionary defines the basic meaning of words, your word catalog links that meaning to associations from past experiences.

Your word catalog has been profoundly influenced by your life's experiences, which are unique to you. These experiences, both good and bad, have shaped your perception of the world. Through your senses, you are constantly adding to your cumulative knowledge of how your world functions. As you accumulate new experiences, they are edited and influenced by your history. As a result, it is accurate to say that every person functions in his or her own unique world. Your world is your own personal reality. You use your word catalog to classify your experiences and describe your world to others. For example, the word "childhood" can evoke either positive emotions or bad memories, depending upon how you cataloged your childhood experiences.

As we discussed in the last chapter, most people use one word catalog more frequently than the others. Visual customers describe their experiences in visual terms and are likely to say, "I see what you mean," "Looks good to me," or "Show me how it works." Auditory customers will say, "Sounds great," "Talk to you later," or "Tell me how it works." Kinesthetic customers might say, "Feels right to me," "We'll touch base later," or "I can't get a handle on how it works."

People use all three catalogs in different amounts and priorities. For example, a person might use visual words 60 percent of the time, kinesthetic words 25 percent of the time, and auditory words only 15 percent of the time. And the strength of each system and the order in which the systems are used can profoundly impact a person's ability to persuade.

When you sleep, your mind can create vivid dreams. You can be transported back to your childhood to relive an experience that is stored in your long-term memory, or you can replay yesterday's sales call that resides in your short-term memory. Although they are just dreams, they seem equally real.

Similarly, when you are awake, you are constantly accessing your short-term and long-term memory. However, it is much easier to access your short-term memory. Accessing your long-term memory is harder and slower. Much like a computer's disk drive, it requires some "mechanical" movements. Short-term storage is accessed "electronically" and is therefore unobservable; however, access to long-term memory can be seen. Amazingly, by observing people's eye movements, you can follow the mechanical movements of the brain that happen when they access their long-term memory. By watching their eyes move, you can determine if they are making pictures in their mind, listening to themselves speak, or experiencing feelings. From this information, you can determine their word catalog wiring and the primary language they use.

When remembering pictures, people will move their eyes up to the right, keep their eyes straight while defocusing their pupils, or move their eyes up to the left (figure 2.1).

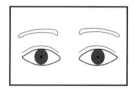

Figure 2.1 Visual word catalog eye movements

When remembering sounds, people will move their eyes straight to the right, down to the left, or straight to the left (figure 2.2).

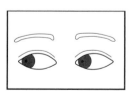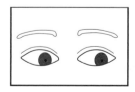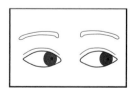

Figure 2.2 Auditory word catalog eye movements

People will move their eyes down to the right when remembering feelings (figure 2.3).

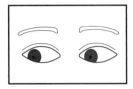

Figure 2.3 Kinesthetic word catalog eye movements

Take a minute and complete the following eye movement exercise. Try to hold your eyes in each position for at least ten seconds. After each eye movement, make a mental note on whether the position was more comfortable than the others.

- Up and to the right
- Up and to the left
- Straight to the right
- Straight to the left
- Down and to the right
- Down and to the left

What happened? Did some movements feel strained while others were easy? Suppose that in the analysis of your e-mails you performed earlier, your VAK count indicated that you have a visual primary, kinesthetic secondary, and auditory recessive wiring. Most likely, the auditory eye movements were noticeably more uncomfortable to make than the others. If your VAK count indicated that you are wired with an auditory primary, kinesthetic secondary, and visual recessive, then the visual movements were most likely harder to do.

Eye movements reflect the inner workings of the mind. Let's suppose people are asked, "What was the best day of your life?" Visuals may start searching their memory by looking for stored pictures before finally deciding on a specific day, such as the day their first child was born. To search their memory bank of pictures, their eyes would move up to the right, move up to the left, or look straight ahead with the pupils defocused. Once retrieved, the picture could then trigger the feeling they had of holding the baby for the first time. Their eyes would move down to the right to get the feeling. Finally, to re-create the entire experience, their eyes may move down to the left or straight to the right or left to actually recall the sound of the baby crying.

Have you ever tried to have conversations with people who would not look at you? Perhaps they tilted their heads down and stared at the ground during the entire discussion. Maybe they turned their heads slightly to the right or left so they seemed to be looking at something behind you. Or they could have cocked their heads back, as if they were looking at the sky. These are examples of people who have an exceptionally strong or dominant primary catalog. These people have a single catalog that is so controlling that their heads become an extension of their eye movements. If their heads tilt down and to the right, that indicates they are dominant Kinesthetics, while people who always tilt their heads up are dominant Visuals. When people tilt their heads down and to the left or laterally away from you for the majority of your conversation, you can assume they are dominant Auditories. The person you may have thought of as being "shifty eyed," or untrustworthy, may actually just be an Auditory.

While some people will make very obvious eye movements, other people's eye movements are very subtle and consist of quick glances away from you. Some people have to blink to think. They have to close their eyes for a second to retrieve information. In this case, you will be able to see the bulge of their pupil and iris on the eyelid as the eye moves. The main point here is that you have to pay close attention and look for subtle movements as well as obvious eye movements.

When people search their long-term memories they will quite often perform a "search loop." Their eyes will initially go to their primary system, then their secondary, then their recessive system and repeat the pattern. Their eyes will look like they are going around in circles. They are simply trying to find a mental tag (by sifting through different pieces of information) that will help them bring back the entire memory.

There is also a very rare group of people that I call "Masterminds." One out of one hundred people have the uncanny ability to instantly recall exceptionally detailed autobiographical memories and past personal experiences even though they may have occurred decades before. I surmise that they have more neural pathways that enable their superior memory. Even though most of the Masterminds I have ever met have been Visuals, they don't seem to make any eye movements at all.

Calibrating Eye Movements to Determine Truthfulness

A polygraph machine measures the body's response (breathing, heart rate, and temperature) of a subject to determine if the person is answering questions truthfully. At the beginning of a polygraph test, the administrator asks a certain number of questions known to be true, such as the subject's name and social security number. These questions calibrate the response of known answers to the machine's measurements.

Similarly, you can calibrate eye movements of individuals by watching their responses to known answers. By doing this, you can establish a baseline measurement of their truthfulness. For example, here's how you can sequence questions during a meeting with a C-level executive to ascertain whether or not he is telling you the truth. Based on your VAK count, you know he is auditory primary, kinesthetic secondary, and visual recessive.

SALESPERSON: How long have you been evaluating solutions?
C-LEVEL EXECUTIVE: (*Eyes left, momentary pause.*) Well, we started last . . . November.

Analysis: Since the evaluation started over ten months ago, this question was a date-dependent event stored in long-term memory.

SALESPERSON: When do you plan to roll out the first systems?

C-LEVEL EXECUTIVE: (*Eyes straight, not defocused, instantaneous answer.*) Our plan is to be up and running by the end of Q2.

Analysis: This is another date-dependent question. However, the answer was in short-term memory. This is probably an important project date, and it is always on his mind.

SALESPERSON: Where will the first system be implemented?

C-LEVEL EXECUTIVE: (*In a search loop, eyes left, down to the left, up to the right.*) Probably . . . Los Angeles.

Analysis: This question may have caused him to search for an answer. He was actually making his best guess as the decision is not final.

SALESPERSON: What other companies are you talking to?

C-LEVEL EXECUTIVE: (*Eyes straight, not defocused.*) We are looking at Acme, Beta Company, and ABC Company.

Analysis: The answer resided in short-term memory. He's probably talking to all the vendors on a regular basis.

SALESPERSON: Does one of the solutions sound better than the rest?

C-LEVEL EXECUTIVE: (*Eyes up to the right.*) No, they all sound the same.

Analysis: This answer is incongruent communication. His eyes were in the visual position as he spoke auditory words.

In the preceding example, the first four questions established the baseline measurements. The decision maker's eyes moved to the left when he accessed his long-term memory. They were straight and centered (not defocused) when he accessed his short-term memory. Any eye movements outside these two ranges must be evaluated in context with the answer.

We can assume that the answers to the first three questions were truthful. The third answer was his best guess. Based on the nonpolitical content of the question, this would be an appropriate assumption. The answer to the fourth question, about which companies he is evaluating, should be in short-term memory. If his answers "Acme, Beta Company, and ABC Company" were given extemporaneously at a quick tempo, then you could assume he was being truthful. If he went into a thirty-second search loop to produce the other vendors' names, he was editing his response, which is another form of incongruence, and this requires further investigation. If you observe very complex eye movements for seemingly simple questions or no eye movement for questions for which you would expect movement, then you need to investigate further to ensure the person is being truthful.

The fifth question is the interesting one. The five questions were purposely sequenced in this order. The salesperson wanted to know if the playing field was level or one vendor was favored. His goal was to find the truth. The first four questions established the baseline to set up the fifth question. While the first four questions provided valuable information about the sales process, they also gave the salesperson a chance to calibrate the answers to the customer's word catalog. The answer given to the fifth question was most likely a lie because it was incongruent communication.

In congruent communication, a person's words and thoughts corroborate each other and the *entire* body is in alignment when the message is delivered. However, the executive contradicted himself while answering the fifth question. His eyes went up to the right to his visual recessive catalog. This is the first incongruence. Based on the previous questions, we would have expected that his eyes would go to either short-term memory (straight, not defocused) or long-term memory (straight left). Since his eyes went to the visual position instead, it can be assumed he was "imagining" or creating an answer.

The second incongruence is that the visual eye movements did not match the content language he used. "No, they all sound the same" is an auditory statement. However, when he said this, his eyes were in a visual position. The two incongruencies suggest that there is mental conflict and this person is not telling the entire truth. This type of incongruence happens all the time during sales meetings. Most salespeople rely on their intuition to tell them they are being misled. With this methodology, anyone can develop the same skill by tracking eye movements and matching these movements to spoken words.

Internal Dialogue Language

Every waking hour, a stream of communication is going on inside your mind. You are always talking to yourself. This conversation is an unedited, honest discussion that represents your deepest feelings. The second language is the internal dialogue layer, or simply the "internal dialogue."

When people are being totally honest, they repeat their internal voice word for word without editing. People also abandon the editing process during times of great emotions: when they're very sad, extremely mad, or ecstatic or they're experiencing any other intense feelings. When you are consumed with your emotions, you don't have the wherewithal to plan what you are going to say. The words are spoken in the same instant that they are created within the mind.

Usually, the words being spoken externally are a subset of the internal dialogue. In between is an editing process to filter the precise statement. Most C-level executives are seasoned politicians who are always severely editing the words they speak. Figure 2.4 illustrates this editing process.

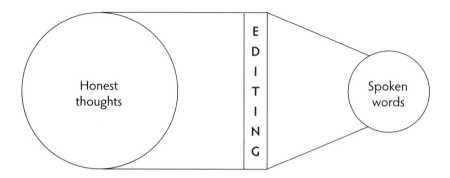

Figure 2.4 Spoken words as a subset of the internal dialogue

You can't turn off your internal dialogue. It's always there, always working consciously. It's also being affected by subconscious memories of past experiences. When you make a sales call, you are not talking to people. You are talking to their internal dialogue. Understanding this is crucial to becoming a Heavy Hitter.

During the sales call, your internal dialogue is at its loudest. It is constantly communicating, telling you what to say next and how to respond to questions. It also monitors the rapport being established with others. Unfortunately, many salespeople are too busy listening to the conversations inside their heads to empathize with customers' problems and situations.

Even though empathy is a core human emotion, not everyone is equally empathetic. Empathy is now thought to be a genetic trait determined by your DNA makeup. An estimated 15 percent of the U.S. population are "empaths," people born with the trait of high sensitivity.[1] If you are not a natural empath, use the "pause-to-check" method to improve your listening sensitivity. After every few sentences you say during a sales call, pause for a moment and check with your audience. Specifically, check for nuances in their facial expressions and how they are holding their bodies. Do you think they are more or less engaged? Why? It's okay to stop and say, "Are you still with me?" or "I hope I didn't confuse anyone."

Physical Language

The third language is the physical layer, which is also known as body language. Body language can be very subtle or more powerful than the actual words being spoken. Body language is unique in that it is a three-dimensional language. The response on the outside of our bodies represents what's going on inside our minds. Our posture indicates our comfort level in any particular situation.

Understanding the nuances of body language is a tricky proposition. First, you cannot assume that each body movement means the same thing for everybody. For example, I worked with an individual who moves his right foot constantly during every meeting. This is his "rapport posture," or the position he assumes when he is in a receptive state. He is very different from someone who shows impatience by moving in the identical way. Second, the way to understand the meaning of a physical movement is by observing the movement over time. The time period could be as long as an hour or as short as a few minutes. The ability to recognize and interpret a person's body language can help you validate a person's word catalog language.

You can learn a lot from someone's handshake. Here are some observations. Kinesthetics tend to shake hands a little longer than Visuals and Auditories. Dominant Kinesthetics will put their other hand on top of the handshake or pat the other person on the shoulder or arm. Visuals tend to shake hands with a faster up-and-down movement. Recessive Kinesthetics tend to not make eye contact when they shake, almost as if they want to end the unpleasant process as soon as possible.

Save an imprint of the handshake from the beginning of the meeting and compare it with the handshake at the end of the meeting. Was it more sensual or colder? Longer or shorter? Did the amount of direct eye contact change? Was there more than one handshake? Did the person pat you on the back or touch you in some other way during the latter handshake? Handshakes provide instant feedback about how a meeting went. Like a kiss with your lover before boarding a plane, the longer and more emotional, the better. From now on, be conscious of handshakes.

Hand movements will vary based on a person's word catalog. Visuals and Kinesthetics will use hand movements while speaking much more frequently than Auditories. The position of the Visuals' hands will be high in context to their bodies, usually at the chest or above. They will use their hands to point to things. They want to make sure you see whatever it is that is important to them. The fingers of their hands are usually straight or pointed out. They have no problem extending their arms and hands as far as they can because they want you to see the "big picture." They will use their hands as an imaginary marker to help draw a picture of the content they are trying to communicate. Visuals' hand movements will be quicker because they are exploding with thoughts that must be communicated quickly.

Kinesthetics will make "deep" hand gestures while they communicate their feelings. That is, their gestures will be lower on their bodies in accordance with their feelings on a subject. The fingers of their hands will be in a closed or interlocked position. They will touch and hold their bodies while they speak. They may use their hands to cradle their heads or use their arms to hug their bodies. Their hand movements tend to be slower and more deliberate than Visuals' or Auditories' because formulating feelings takes more time than creating pictures or assembling words.

Auditories listen to themselves speak. This alone is a full-time job; therefore, they will use fewer hand movements. When they do use them, they tend to keep their hands closer to their bodies. Another term for this is "dinosaur hands" since their arms are being held like the arms of a *Tyrannosaurus rex*. Their hand gestures will tend to be at the middle of the body, lower than Visuals' hand gestures but higher than Kinesthetics'. Their hand movements also tend to keep time with their voice tempo.

You may not have noticed this, but people actually breathe quite differently from each other. Obviously, people breathe at a different pace depending on whether or not they are performing a physical activity. The aspect of breathing that we are interested in, however, is the changes in breathing patterns while customers are in their normal state (when most business meetings take place), and these changes can be quite subtle. If a customer is wearing a suit or jacket or if glancing at the customer's chest would be considered inappropriate, breathing patterns can be observed by watching people's shoulders rise and fall as they inhale and exhale.

Different breathing paces can be observed by watching different areas of the abdomen. Some people breathe fast and some slow. Some people have a repetitive rhythm to their breathing: deep breath, pause, deep breath, pause. Some people's breaths are quick and shallow. Visuals tend to breathe shallower and higher in the chest, while Kinesthetics breathe deeper and lower in the belly. Auditories' breathing is somewhere in between.

How someone breathes is really not that important. What is important is trying to spot a change in a breathing pattern. A change is a signal that a person's internal communication state has changed and the level of rapport has fluctuated. This is valuable information to help identify a customer's state of rapport. People experiencing rapport are relaxed and their breathing reflects this.

Intersecting Activity Language

The fourth language is the intersecting activity language. All people have outside interests, hobbies, and personal pursuits by which they display their personalities, beliefs, and values. Think about all the potential non-business-related subjects you can discuss with your customers:

raising kids	the cost of living	home ownership
cars	computers	dating and marriage
college	food	professional sports
traveling	dieting	music
movies	airplanes	toys
humor	astronomy	clothes
pets	poetry	religion
art	gardening	the economy
antiques	body piercing	billiards
investments	horses	karaoke
books	beer	firearms
television	origami	cigars

Each intersecting activity topic listed above also has a unique content language. In order to have a meaningful conversation about an intersecting activity, you need to understand its language. For example, a conversation about stock investing requires an understanding of terms such as "price earnings ratio," "market cap," and "stock shorting." If you are talking with someone about dieting, being able to discuss the Atkins or Zone diet makes your participation in the conversation credible. Through the use and understanding of these common terms, rapport is established.

Heavy Hitters always employ a strategy to find personal intersecting activities they have in common with their prospective customers. By doing so, they develop rapport with the *entire* person, not just the *business* person—building a personal friendship that sets them apart from the competition.

Technical Specification Language

The fifth language is the technical specification language. Every industry has developed its own language to facilitate mutual understanding of terminology and an exact meaning of the words used throughout the business. These abbreviations, acronyms, and words form one of the primary languages your customers speak. Whether you are selling airplanes, computer chips, telephone equipment, or real estate, you need to know the terms and nomenclature of your industry. For example, if you sell telephone systems to businesses, you need to understand what PBX, PDC, and ACD mean.

Technical specification languages have four major characteristics. First, unlike normal day-to-day language, words within a technical specification language have very narrow meanings. The language is precise and exact. For example, "100 Mbps" means "100 megabits per second," not 99 or 101. Second, the meaning of general words can be completely changed by the addition of operators. For example, a general term like "car" completely changes in meaning when "sports" or "luxury" is added in front of it and keeps changing meaning when additional operators such as "BMW" or "Jaguar" are added. Third, the language is completely androgynous. In general, no reference is made to feminine or masculine characteristics. Finally, the language is usually nonpersonal. After all, it's referring to products, not people.

Unfortunately for salespeople, the technical specification language usually is adopted by customers as the default standard for all of their communication. This presents salespeople with a significant problem. They are trying to create a personal relationship with the buyer. However, the buyer is communicating in an androgynous, nonpersonal, technical language. More importantly, given the use of this unusual language, salespeople must somehow decipher the underlying meaning and intent of the customer's words. In addition, the technical content of the language is the yardstick by which a customer's technical peer group (the team selecting a product) measures a person's relevant knowledge. Outside of formal titles, it's another way members of the peer group will establish a hierarchy. It's also how they will validate the sales team's value to them. Conversely, it is how the sales team members will present their product's features and the technical reasons for selecting their product.

This is one of the primary languages that C-level executives use to communicate with their subordinates and instruct them what to do. For example, the CIO may instruct the vice president of infrastructure that he would like to "Replicate the SAP IBM server data in New York to the NOC in Los Angeles." Obviously, a computer salesperson who doesn't understand these terms will have a difficult time winning the company's business.

Business Operations Language (What Executives Do)

The sixth language is the business operations language. This is the language executives use to run their organizations. A popular misconception is that you have to be a subject-matter expert to speak effectively with a C-level executive. For instance, you have to know financial accounting standards inside and out before you should even think about meeting with a CFO, you have to be a shop-floor control expert to meet with the vice president of manufacturing, or you must be an expert on corporate branding to hold an important conversation with a CMO.

While having a deep domain area expertise is the ideal situation, in reality all C-level executives perform the same basic duties associated with running a company. These duties fall into "create" and "control" categories. The business operations language consists of these create and control descriptions. Executives are either creating something new or controlling an ongoing process.

CEO: Creates corporate direction through top-level business goals.

Controls which departmental initiatives will be undertaken to accomplish these goals.

VP of Sales: Creates revenue through customer relationship strategies.

Controls sales force behavior through compensation plans and sales forecasts.

CFO: Creates the financial plans to run the business.

Controls money through budgets, accounting practices, and company policies.

Here's a partial list of create and control tasks that senior executives must fulfill.

Create

Prepare and present the fiscal budget.

Provide forecasts.

Implement new programs and policies, and provide their general administrative direction.

Develop and execute departmental best practices.

Sign financial agreements and long-term contractual agreements.

Provide justification for all recommendations and decisions on capital expenditures.

Conduct new business development activities to promote growth or decrease costs.

Foster departmental and company communication.

Build positive relationships with customers, the press, trade associations, and industry organizations.

Develop and maintain relations with employees, customers, and the community.

Maintain responsibility for the selection, appointment, and retention of key management personnel.

Control

Administer the management of daily operations.

Analyze operating results versus established objectives.

Take appropriate steps to reverse unsatisfactory results.

Work closely with other departmental executives to ensure the company is functioning smoothly.

Supervise budget performance throughout the year.

Ensure that the growth of the company is in accordance with identified goals.

Maintain the desired quality of products, customer service, and professionalism.

Ensure that the company is in compliance with federal laws and local regulations.

Operate the organization in a profitable manner.

Provide oversight of and make recommendations for business initiatives.

Resolve all departmental business and human relations problems.

Ensure that the company's policies are uniformly understood and administered by subordinates.

Establish standards for managerial performance.

Recommend staffing and compensation changes within the organization.

Approve all personnel promotions and staff reductions, and oversee the hiring/firing processes.

Conduct periodic performance and salary reviews of key personnel.

In the boom times of the '90s the business emphasis was on creating—creating larger companies through mergers, creating new products to take advantage of the Internet, and creating revenues by expanding sales forces. In a recession, the business operations language is all about control—controlling costs and doing more with less money, fewer people, and fewer company resources.

Certain features and functions of your solution are associated with create and control mode tasks. It's time to stop reading and complete an exercise. List ten create aspects and ten control aspects of the solution you sell. Go ahead and write in the book, or list your ideas on a piece of paper.

Create	*Control*
1	1
2	2
3	3
4	4
5	5
6	6
7	7
8	8
9	9
10	10

Congratulations. If you completed the exercise, you now officially know how to speak the business operations language.

C-Level Language
(What Executives Want to Do)

The seventh and most important language is the C-level language. While the business operations language is a process-based language about what executives do on a daily basis, the C-level language is a personal language based upon what they want to do in the future. It's the language associated with the human nature of leading a group of people to accomplish a specific objective. The C-level executive's duties include many aspects beyond create and control processes. The job description below illustrates some essential C-level attributes:

C-Level Executive Officer Job Description

The individual must be a visionary leader who has the ability, skills, and knowledge to take the business into the future. He must instill in the staff a passion and understanding of the business philosophies as they relate to serving customers and the company. This individual will have expertise in the areas of leadership, communication, team development, and coaching, as well as situation assessment skills. He must possess the ability to motivate or influence others as a material part of the job, requiring a significant level of diplomacy and trust. The individual will be an innovative, proactive leader who can analyze trends and develop ideas for all areas of the business and for process improvement. This individual will assess the present business and after evaluating the findings will strategize on new ways to improve operations. He must be able to develop, recommend, and set business-related goals for the company's strategic direction.

The C-level language is the most significant language spoken on executive sales calls. It's the language of strategic planning because it provides the executive's personal motivations for pursuing a project, the internal politics of the organization, and really the executive's real goals.

The C-level language has two variations. Companies and the executives who run them have a natural need to protect their images. The "public" C-level language is spoken when the executive is toeing the company line about why he is doing what he is doing. This is the official version for public consumption versus the off-the-record truth. When he's speaking the public C-level language, he is telling you the same thing he is saying to your competitors.

The "confidential" C-level language is spoken when the executive treats you like a confidant and shares his personal reasons why he is initiating a project and what he hopes to personally gain when it succeeds. Like a close friend, he discusses his private matters and problems with you. However, he will speak the confidential C-level language to only one of the salespeople competing for his business. He doesn't want to run the risk of having his true motives publicly known.

Quite often, salespeople mistake the public C-level language for the confidential C-level language. In the following exercise, try to determine whether each statement below is the public or confidential C-level language.

1. "Let me be honest with you: if this project doesn't succeed, we'll probably have to cut two thousand jobs at our Dallas operation."
2. "The strategic goal of this project is to improve our workforce efficiency during the next twelve months."
3. "Our win rate is decreasing and the CEO keeps pointing his finger at me, telling me to fix it now."
4. "Our goal is to increase sales by 10 percent, and this will require great changes to the company."
5. "Our employees act like they work for the post office. Our new CEO and I are on a mission to change this antiquated monolithic organization into a state-of-the-art customer-driven company."

The odd-numbered sentences were examples of the confidential C-level language. They were personal revelations that would not typically be shared with someone who wasn't trusted. They revealed the executive's off-the-record opinion, personal dilemma, and ulterior motives, as well as the stress he is under. They aren't statements that would be made in public for everyone to hear. They would be said only to the salesperson who was trusted. The even-numbered sentences were examples of the public C-level language. They're generic statements that could have been said to all the salespeople because they aren't personally revealing.

In order to achieve your ultimate goal of speaking the confidential C-level language, you must be able to speak in each of the seven C-level languages summarized in figure 2.5. By doing so, you will establish credibility and trust, and use common languages that are at the foundation of meaningful communication.

Whether you are talking with a CEO or a receptionist, the first step of communication is to check comprehension, whether or not the spoken words can be found in the personal dictionaries that are kept inside your listener's minds.

The Lexical Dictionary: Did I Understand You?

Your lexical dictionary determines your word comprehension. The average person's dictionary contains about fifty thousand words. However, all words are not equally persuasive. General words such as "performance," "reliability," and "quality" by themselves are not influential. Additional operator words, words that improve the persuasiveness of general words, must be added to influence a customer's mind. Adding "nine hundred pages per hour" to define "performance" adds a comparison-point meaning. Adding "one hundred thousand hours mean time between failures" to specify "reliability" helps makes the word more convincing. Believability is improved when "lifetime guaranteed replacement" is associated with "quality."

It is important to note that sometimes the terms your marketing department believes are so important and persuasive actually detract from your credibility. I have reviewed more than one hundred

C-level language	The most powerful trust-based language by which the executive explains his personal needs, desires, and plans along with the strategy by which he hopes to fulfill them
Business operations language	The language that is specific to the daily running of the executive's business and his role in the organization
Technical specification language	The androgynous, nonpersonal, and technical communication that is based upon the nomenclature and technical terms of the executive's industry
Intersecting activity language	Interests, hobbies, and personal pursuits by which the executive displays his personality, beliefs and values
Physical language	Also known as body language, the nonverbal communication that is constantly being emitted by the executive's body posture
Internal language	The never-ending stream of communication inside the mind that represents honest, unedited, and deep feelings
Word catalog	The mind's method for receiving, interpreting, and transmitting information based upon the three sensory channels—visual, auditory, and kinesthetic

Figure 2.5 The seven different C-level executive languages

corporate PowerPoint presentations in the past year alone. Not only do they all look the same, they all use the same general words to describe their companies' unique advantages, such as "powerful," "reliable," and "scalable." Product claims based upon these words by themselves are not persuasive.

New words are continually being added to your lexical dictionary. For example, you may not know the meaning of the word "amorphous." However, you can derive its meaning when you hear it used in a sentence such as "The customers gave a vague and amorphous answer when asked when they would make a decision." Operator words work much in the same way. They allow you to introduce new concepts to customers by deduction. For example, when you say "Our multiprocessor architecture results in performance that is three times faster than the competition's," the customer deduces that "multiprocessor" is advantageous.

New words are also continually introduced into the English language. They pass through periods of introduction, adoption, and then widespread use, when they are subject to "linguistic inflation." For example, the word "green" as it refers to environmental friendliness is in a period of linguistic hyperinflation and is quickly losing its value. At the end of an overused word's life cycle, its meaning is deadened from the word's excessive use. This is what has happened to the words "powerful," "reliable," and "scalable."

After your lexical dictionary has defined a word, personal meaning is associated with it. For example, your lexical definition of the word "children" might be "kids between two and twelve." In your mind, children are not teenagers or babies. Your mind then tries to derive personal meaning from the word "children." If you have children, you might immediately think of your son, your daughter, or all your children. You might think of a child playing or even a schoolroom. Thus, another level of personal interpretation occurs.

The deepest level of meaning occurs inside the mind's word catalog where it is associated with psychological meaning. While your lexical dictionary defines the basic meaning of words, your word catalog links that meaning to your past experiences. For example, you may have felt a sense of pride when you thought about your children and a specific memory such as a school graduation ceremony or sporting event they competed in.

Conclusion

Famous Swiss psychiatrist Carl Jung is credited as being the creator of the word association test. He would present his patients with 100 test words, one at time, and tell them to respond with the first word that came into their mind. He used the test to determine patients' intellectual and emotional deficiencies based on whether they repeated the test word (woman: woman), responded with an opposite meaning word (woman: man), defined the test word (sky: air), provided an association (car: fast), or made a personal judgment (politician: bad). He believed that a single word could trigger a complex psychological response.

We connect with people through the words we speak and the way in which we say them. However, the words we use are complex three-dimensional objects that don't mean the same to everyone.

Let's do a word association exercise. For each of the following words, what is the first thought that comes to mind?

- Dog
- Cat
- Sports
- Church
- Marriage

If you have a dog, you probably thought of your dog. A picture of your dog may have come to mind, and you may have said your dog's name to yourself. If you are a "cat person" who dislikes dogs, you probably wondered how anyone could like those drooling, unruly beasts. Conversely, the word "cat" evoked positive feelings. The word "sports" may have caused you to think about the sport you played in school because words are anchored to our memories. The word "church" could elicit many different responses, ranging from a sense of purpose to resistance to authority, depending upon your orientation. Meanwhile, marriage is to some a blessing; to others, a dream; and to the unlucky, a nightmare. So the word "marriage" is likely to evoke your feelings based on your experience.

All of these words have something in common. In order to be understood, they must be interpreted into something meaningful:

familiar thoughts and terms. This process occurs in steps: determining the lexical meaning of a word, translating the word into personal meaning, and finally, forming a psychological impression determined by how the word is cataloged.

My dog's name is Gizmo. He's named after the main character in the movie *Gremlins* who was both adorable and mischievous. That's what I personally think of when someone mentions the word "dog." What dog did you think about? How strange that a little word like "dog" can carry so much meaning.

> Their salespeople need some type of a more senior-level executive overview, something that resonates with high level executives. Senior executives only have two seconds to look at something and figure out if it matters. Our top executives still aren't sure what their product does. I think they assumed it is a bleeding-edge product, and they are not risk takers.
>
> SENIOR VICE PRESIDENT OF E-COMMERCE

3

Calibrate

> This was a huge decision for our company, a huge purchase we
> would have to live with for many years. I was worried we wouldn't
> get it right.
>
> CHIEF EXECUTIVE OFFICER

Are you unhappy with some aspect of your looks? Are you satisfied with the amount of money you have in the bank? Do you regret some of the choices you have made in the past? Do you want more from life? A sincere response to each of these questions is typically much deeper than a yes or no. This is because three separate elements within you are constantly active, always on guard, and driving you to become better. They are your mind, heart, and soul.

Anyone who has to make a decision—whether you are asked about your looks or a customer is asked to buy a product—will have internal conflict. The first type is the mental conflict based upon the honest, never-ending discussion we are always having with ourselves in our minds. This internal dialogue might argue that we have critical flaws and shameful inadequacies. Conversely, it will also seek to protect our fragile psyches by reiterating positive statements. Both of these types of mental conversations will draw upon bad or good memories to validate our negative or positive perceptions of ourselves.

The second type of conflict is between the head and the heart. While our rational intellect relies on information, our emotional being, the heart, has been shaped by a lifetime of interactions with people who have loved us, hated us, or ignored us. It is based upon needs, wants, desires, and hurts. In essence, our heart pulls us in the opposite direction from our head.

Finally, somewhere deep inside, is conflict based on our spiritual idealization of ourselves. Our soul has a vision of personal perfection. Unfortunately, in the business world it is difficult, if not impossible, to measure up to the soul's aspirations. In one sense, the soul's vision is like a mirage on the horizon in the desert—it disappears as we approach it. Even though we make forward progress toward our soul's aspirations, we never reach that oasis of self-contentment.

Whenever a decision must be made, these forces of the mind, heart, and soul are activated. Therefore, all decision makers face inner turmoil. Should I purchase the trendy new sports car or the less expensive, reliable family car? Should I make a long-term financial investment or take a dream vacation? Even the decision to buy a doughnut or a bran muffin for breakfast creates conflict. Every decision involves mental contention because an ongoing battle is raging between our rational intellect, our emotional being, and the compass of ideals that guides us through life.

This conflict produces stress, and nowhere is this stress greater than in the C-level executives who must decide whether or not to buy from you. With every major purchase decision a company leader makes, his career, reputation, and livelihood are on the line. Recognizing that this stress exists is the first step toward becoming a Heavy Hitter. Understanding how to defuse customer stress and create stress for the competition is one of the secrets of Heavy Hitters.

The dictionary defines stress as "mental tension resulting from factors that tend to alter an existent equilibrium."[1] In other words, stress alters a person's mental state, causing that person to behave differently than he or she would normally. It may cause a self-assured person to become nervous, a quiet person to become more talkative, or an even-keeled person to become agitated.

C-level executives will go to great lengths to reduce the stress of buying. They might list their needs in documents that are hundreds of pages in length. They might hire consultants to verify that they are making the right decisions. And they'll conduct lengthy evaluations to test prospective products, talk to existing users of the products, and complete pilot testing to ensure the products work as advertised—all in an effort to eliminate their fears, reduce their uncertainties, and satisfy their doubts.

However, C-level executives are never 100 percent sure they are purchasing the right product. Regardless of their confident demeanor, on the inside they are experiencing fear, uncertainty, and doubt. In fact, fear, uncertainty, and doubt are at the core of every sales cycle. They play a key role in determining the winner of the deal. Fear, uncertainty, and doubt create stress. Therefore, all salespeople need to understand this lowest common denominator of human decision making—they need to understand the nature of stress.

When Strangers Meet

Meeting new people is stressful. Let's pretend we are surveying guests at a party and watching strangers meet for the first time. If you watch strangers meet at a party, you'll notice that they are on guard. When strangers met in olden times, the first task was to decide whether or not the other person was a threat. Therefore, people shook hands to determine if the other person was carrying any weapons.

In the modern times of today, we don't necessarily have to worry that strangers are a physical threat. More often, we have to worry that they are a psychological threat. Therefore, we try to ascertain whether a stranger is in a dominant, equal, or submissive position in comparison to our position. Next, we try to find out what we have in common by discovering intersecting activities. Finally, we try to classify the relationship into a familiar pattern so we can decide how we should behave and whether we should invest more time with the person. Figure 3.1 illustrates the process of meeting a stranger.

Figure 3.1 The process of meeting a stranger

The instinctual comparison of dominance tends to occur quickly when people meet. Just as packs of animals instinctively establish a hierarchy so that the group can function more efficiently, people are naturally inclined to seek structure in group environments. Therefore, they create mental pecking orders to understand their place in complex social settings such as parties and sales calls.

But what makes someone dominant? Dominance can be the result of a diverse set of attributes. When two people talk at a party, one person may be better looking, more intelligent, funnier, wealthier, or better respected or have a quality that the other person lacks, such as kindness, generosity, humility, aggressiveness, assertiveness, or selfishness. Even a trait that is perceived as negative by society can make someone dominant. For example, how do you act when you see a tattooed, leather-clad motorcyclist in the rearview mirror when you are driving?

When meeting someone new, people experience varying amounts and types of stress depending on whether they perceive themselves to be dominant, equal, or submissive. A person who feels inferior to someone else is under much more stress than a person who feels dominant. The stress manifests itself in different ways. How differently would you feel about meeting Bill Gates versus meeting the counterperson who serves you coffee? Most likely, you would be far more nervous when meeting one of the richest men in the world. However, if you have a secret crush on the counterperson, your behavior would be quite different than if you had little interest. You would be in the submissive position because you'd want to be liked.

While some dominant people will surround themselves with submissive people, most dominants want to associate with people whom they perceive as equals. Equals converse with relative ease.

This is a critical point. One of your most important goals when meeting with a C-level executive is establishing yourself as an equal. That's one of the main reasons why you need to speak the technical specification language, the business operations language, and the C-level language described in the previous chapter.

You may have noticed at parties that people naturally coalesce into small groups of equals. These groups are segregated from each other by an attribute. It might be age, attractiveness, where they live, what they do for a living, or even the nature of their personalities. These people are equals because they share an intersecting activity.

The natural course of party conversations is for the strangers to try to find out what they have in common. Through intersecting activities, people display their personal interests, character, and temperament and express their value systems. Intersecting activities create shared bonds and reduce the level of stress involved in meeting someone new.

Intersecting activities play an equally important role in sales calls. Regardless of whether the salesperson or the customer initiated the meeting, the first intersecting activity is the sales call itself. It is the first point in common between the salesperson and the customer.

Heavy Hitters use the first intersecting activity (the sales call) to find *personal* intersecting activities. By doing so, they develop rapport and begin the process of building a personal friendship. In essence, they try to relieve the stress caused by the typical dominant-submissive meeting between a customer and a vendor by turning it into a conversation between equals.

The intersecting activities Heavy Hitters talk about are quite diverse—the local professional sports team, golf, wine, cars, movies, or any hobby. Usually, these first conversations are on "safe" topics, with little risk that someone's revelations will create controversy, because the goal is to reduce stress, not create more of it.

In sales calls with C-level executives, dominance is always initially on their side since they have the ultimate say over whether any relationship will be created. However, this dominance is based upon the situation, not personal attributes. In a different social setting, the salesperson might be truly dominant because he is more charismatic, athletic, witty, and so on. However, the salesperson can establish dominance over C-level executives.

At the root of true dominance is the "Better Person Syndrome," which is based on the theory that people will naturally gravitate toward people they feel are better than themselves in some way. In this respect, the Better Person Syndrome helps explain the old saying that opposites attract. For example, my wife has many qualities that I admire. She is far more patient and kind than I'll ever be. I am attracted to these qualities.

The theory also applies to sales. When C-level executives are choosing between two similar products, they will not always buy the better product. Rather, their tendency is to buy from the salesperson they believe is the better person. So while one salesperson may have a slightly better product and be more proficient in explaining its features and functionality, in the end the customer will buy from the person who has the personal attributes the customer most admires. (Obviously, if one product is light years ahead of another, then the Better Person Syndrome is neutralized.)

Some executives will gravitate to a friendly and responsive salesperson. They admire and respect these qualities. Others might enjoy being around an aristocratic salesperson in cufflinks and a monogrammed dress shirt. Perhaps these executives behave and dress in a similar way and have some deep-seated desire to be like him. Because people admire different qualities in other people, every sales call is unique.

Your dominance in any setting is dependent upon the submissiveness of the person you are talking with. It is not a measure of how easily you overpower the person. Rather, it depends on the traits that the other person respects, admires, or does not possess. For example, a C-level executive may be submissive to a salesperson's industry expertise, technical aptitude, or product knowledge. Many executives become submissive when they perceive a salesperson to be better looking, more charismatic, or more enthusiastic than they are. For instance, I know several vice presidents of sales who will hire a good-looking salesperson with average sales skills over a great salesperson who is not so attractive.

Most C-level executives tend to gravitate to salespeople who are similar to themselves. They want to be surrounded by competent, successful people. However, opposites attract as well. For example, very meticulous, no-nonsense executives sometimes bond with lack-adaisical, carefree salespeople who are their exact opposites. These executives seem to be hypnotized into a submissive position. One of the best salespeople I ever knew was the most unorganized, lackadaisical, smart-mouthed goof-off I ever met. However, a certain cross section of executives absolutely adored him because he always said exactly what was on his mind in the most politically incorrect way. Surprisingly, the executives he bonded with were usually straight-laced, button-down CFOs and CIOs. I think they found his uniqueness intoxicating compared to the personalities of the staff members they had to deal with daily.

Now it's time to do a quick exercise to help you discover what makes you dominant in customer meetings. The list below includes just a few of the wide range of dominant traits that people respond to submissively. As you read the list, think about when you used one of these attributes to put yourself in a dominant position over a lower-level person at a recent account you won. Recall not only the account but the specific person who responded to you submissively and followed your lead.

Athleticism	Humor	Product knowledge
Attractiveness	Hyperactivity	Professionalism
Business knowledge	Industry expertise	Sales acumen
Charisma	Integrity	Sense of humor
Cleverness	Lackadaisicalness	Seriousness
Compassion	Negotiation skills	Straightforwardness
Curiosity	Open-mindedness	Technical aptitude
Eloquence	Optimism	Thoroughness
Empathy	Organization	Thoughtfulness
Enthusiasm	Passion	Tolerance
Friendliness	Persistence	Trustworthiness
Honesty	Pessimism	Wholesomeness

Now repeat the same exercise while thinking of the seniormost executive you met with at the same account. Were you able to establish dominance? If so, was there a difference in your dominance and the attribute you used when compared to your meetings with the lower-level person? Remember, even a trait that is typically associated with weakness can be used to establish dominance.

You probably have used a wide range of attributes, depending upon the customers you have met with. That's a fundamental trait of Heavy Hitters. They behave in a way that makes them dominant, even if that means they must behave submissively. For example, empathetically listening to a C-level executive describe his problems is submissive behavior, but it will enable you to establish a dominant position with him later. Only by knowing his goals, objectives, frustrations, and fantasies will you be able to explain how you can address them with your solution. In reality, you will be in a dominant position because you will control his happiness. Now all you have to do is convince him of it (a topic we'll discuss later).

Obviously, a salesperson who can employ a wider range of dominant traits can sell to a wider range of customers. Knowing which trait to draw upon is determined by your sales intuition. For instance, in one account a salesperson might display an optimistic attitude in order to instill optimism in the evaluators. He might say to an executive, "I've worked with many other customers with the identical problem. They have been able to solve the problem within a couple of months of implementing our solution with far fewer resources than you have to dedicate to this project." In this example, the salesperson has become a dominant source of hope to someone in pain. In another account the same salesperson might display outward pessimism and say "I am not sure you have the wherewithal to implement our solution," forcing the executive to explain why he believes he can implement the solution successfully. In both circumstances the salesperson has established dominance.

As the sales cycle progresses, a salesperson's goal is to gain dominance over a submissive customer. While dominance is commonly associated with brute force, this is not the case in sales. It's simply how people judge others. They are sensing whether their position will be superior to yours, relatively equal, or inferior in some way. In turn, this impacts what they say as part of the conversation and the way they behave. Relaxed dominant people are free to speak and do as they like. Anxious submissive people speak guardedly and are forced into restricted behavior.

As we have seen, once strangers establish who is dominant, they search for what they have in common. Next, each person tries to characterize the relationship by placing it into one of the categories of relationships he or she is familiar with.

We all have many different types of personal relationships. We have friends, family, coworkers, and neighbors. When we meet someone new at a party, we decide if we like the person and whether he or she might become a friend or is more likely to remain a distant acquaintance.

This classification also happens on sales calls. However, each customer may have an entirely different perception of your character. For example, you may be characterized as a friend by one customer and an acquaintance by another. You could be a little brother to an older customer or a big brother to a younger one. You could be thought of as a father, lover, uncle, cousin, or even an enemy.

Let's do another exercise. Take a moment and think of the last three accounts you won. Write down the characterization that best describes your relationship with your main contact at each account. Most likely, this was a lower-level or midlevel employee in the account and your relationship can be described in close family terms. Then write down the characterization that describes your relationship with the seniormost executive you met during the same sales cycle in that account. Here are some possible characterizations:

Acquaintance	Employee	Lover
Aunt	Father figure	Mentor
Best friend	Friend	Mother figure
Big brother	Girlfriend	Nephew
Big sister	Godparent	Neighbor
Boss	Grandchild	Niece
Boyfriend	Grandfather	Son
Buddy	Grandmother	Soul mate
Childhood friend	Husband	Stepchild
Cousin	In-law	Stepparent
Coworker	Little brother	Stranger
Daughter	Little sister	Uncle
Deadbeat	Loser	Wife

Were the characterizations different? Were you a lot closer to your main contact than the senior executive? This is very normal because you probably had a lot fewer interactions with the senior executive and you probably behaved quite differently around him. You may have played it safe and been extremely cautious because you didn't want to ruin the deal.

Now try the same exercise for the last three accounts you lost. You'll probably find quite a difference in the way you characterize the relationships. You also probably had a lot fewer interactions (or even none) with the C-level executives in these accounts than in the accounts you won. While it's perfectly normal to act conservatively in accounts where you are far ahead of the competition, playing it safe when you're behind is a mistake. You must take chances on the one or two occasions you have the opportunity to meet with the senior executives. In fact, when you do meet with one of them, a primary objective should be to establish a stronger personal relationship (as a son, father figure, wife, etc.) that supersedes the relationship the executive has with the salesperson of the leading vendor. Besides, since you have nothing to lose, why water down your own unique selling style and your effervescent personality?

When I ask salespeople what role they take in C-level executive meetings, the majority of say "Consultant." Unfortunately, every salesperson competing for a deal is trying to be a consultant. You need to establish a stronger relationship. Some may consider this advice counterintuitive and risky. However, as part of your planning for a C-level executive meeting, I recommend that you actually identify the familial relationship you wish to achieve with that person ahead of time.

I remember a critical meeting I had when I was twenty-eight with the founder and CEO of a $600 million company who was almost twice my age. It was November and I was trying to close this biggest deal of the year before year-end. From a features and function standpoint, my solution was comparable to my main competitor's. However, it cost about 20 percent more. In the short meeting, the CEO beat me up badly on price and a laundry list of other objections he had about our proposal. Even though I was totally intimidated, I pushed back on some of his comments to the point where I became emotional about one comment in particular that I felt was totally unfair.

While no significant agreements came out of this meeting, the most important moment of the entire eight-month sales cycle happened as I got up to leave his office. The CEO smiled at me and said I was "meshugana." I asked him what he meant and like a father talking to his son, he explained that it was a Yiddish term for someone who is a little bit crazy. At that moment I knew I would win the deal, and we signed a $2.7 million contract in December. In hindsight, I think the CEO saw himself in me. It's funny how you remember sales moments like this even more than two decades later.

Depending upon your background, you may want to be the trusted father figure, the up-and-coming son, or the soul mate the C-level executive is searching for. Whatever it is, don't be solely a consultant. Never forget the old saying "Consultants are a dime a dozen."

When I was younger, my goal was always to be thought of as a son by the C-level executives I met with. Why? Because I wanted them to give me advice and feel good about giving their business to someone they truly were fond of. Now that I am older and have written several books, I want the C-level executives I speak with to consider me a father figure if they are younger or their brother if they are about my age. Also, I still don't mind when someone treats me like a son.

It is human nature for all customers to categorize you into a familial or friendship relationship. Knowing whether you are a customer's submissive little brother or a dominant mother figure and knowing when to act like a buddy or be a mentor plays an important role in the sales cycle. When executives treat you like they would a loved one, that's a great sign that you will win the deal. Conversely, you are in big trouble if everyone in the account treats you like the weird uncle.

Dominant and Submissive Conversations

A sales cycle is the formalized exchange of information between a customer and a salesperson. However, each party has different goals. Customers are trying to *gather* information about the salesperson's company, product, and customers. Their main goal is information assessment. Whether formally or informally, they have developed and prioritized their needs. They need information in order to measure the fit of the salesperson's solution.

The salesperson wants not only to *present* information about his company and solution to sway the customer to buy but also to *uncover* information about the politics and biases inherent in every selection process. Gathering, presenting, and uncovering information results in interactions between customers and salespeople that can be thought of as circular vignettes.

Vignettes are small dramas, short interchanges between a customer and a salesperson. Usually they focus on one topic or one conversational theme. They are considered circular because every vignette will come to an end and close as the topic of conversation is exhausted. During each vignette, the salesperson is either in a dominant position, in control, or in a submissive position, trying to regain control.

Vignettes typically change when the subject changes or when an implied agreement on the current topic of discussion is reached. The implied agreement may or may not mean that the issue is resolved. Often, it is an agreement to move on for the sake of time. Unfortunately, unresolved vignettes don't go away by themselves and almost always come back to haunt salespeople later.

A sales call is a collection of these circular vignettes. Since the use of PowerPoint is so pervasive in sales presentations today, most vignettes last as long as one slide or a series of several slides (one to five minutes). A typical sales presentation will begin with individual vignettes about the company's history, milestones, and customer references before moving into vignettes explaining specific technical features of the product.

Every sales call will have several critical vignettes that determine whether the call is a success or failure. While every vignette will close, the issues associated with some vignettes will remain open. Heavy

Hitters know that unresolved issues will come up again later in the sales cycle, usually when they least want an objection. Therefore, they always try to address these awkward points early. They want them out in the open. They want to know whether an issue will inhibit the purchase of the product, and they want to know as soon as possible.

Similar to a tennis match, a C-level sales call is a psychological rally between the executive and you. Unfortunately, all C-level meetings start with you in the submissive position. You can move to a dominant position only if you establish rapport and can successfully answer the executive's questions and concerns. Once in the dominant position, you have earned the right to ask about the dynamics of the decision process. You can ask questions to get a better understanding of the knowledge, credibility, and influence on the decision process that your main customer contacts have. However, you will quickly move back into the submissive position when the executive uncovers a weakness with your company and solution or asks a question you can't answer. We'll talk a lot more about the questions senior executives ask and the questions you should ask them in the third part of this book.

Choosing the moment to take control of a vignette is critical. For example, after you have proved the legitimacy of your company and product, you can change the subject and ask sensitive questions about the decision-making process. To do so earlier would alienate the executive and violate business etiquette. Although the conversation may seem natural and free flowing, your goal is to maintain dominance by guiding the interactions to topics you feel will positively influence the executive's perception of your solution.

Throughout the course of a sales call or presentation, the relationship between the customer and salesperson is continually being recalibrated. Dominance shifts from one side to the other and the familial characterization of the relationship can change quickly. A salesperson who thought he had found his soul mate at the beginning of a sales call could be quickly disappointed when he learns that the executive is really in love with another vendor.

Fight or Flight

Sales is a profession based upon pressure: pressure from sales management to make your quota, pressure from competitors who are trying to defeat you, pressure you place on yourself to be number one, and pressure to perform well on every sales call. Pressure upon the salesperson during C-level sales calls has a profound impact. It creates an emergency situation that triggers the body's fight-or-flight system. Here are a few of the physiological changes that happen to a salesperson who is making a stressful executive-level sales call or conducting the critical presentation he hopes will land him a big deal:

- The eyebrows instinctively rise and the eyes widen. The iris muscles of the eye contract causing the pupils to dilate. These actions enhance vision so that maximum visual information about the perceived threats can be sent to the brain.
- The brain's cortex interprets the visual information it is receiving and transmits messages to the brain's hypothalamus. The hypothalamus activates the adrenal gland, which instantaneously releases adrenaline into the bloodstream. The hormone adrenaline activates the body's emergency response systems.
- The heart pumps at up to twice its normal rate. Breathing quickens so that the lungs can supply more oxygen to the blood. Oxygen-rich blood is sent to the brain for clearer thinking and to muscles for quick reactions. The stomach stops digestion so that blood can be diverted elsewhere in the body. The liver releases sugar reserves for a quick boost of energy, and the bladder sends a message that it wants to be emptied so the body can flee faster.
- On the outside of the body, perspiration forms as sweat glands are activated to reduce the body heat caused by the increased flow of blood. The mouth widens so that air can be taken in faster than through the nose. The face loses color and appears ashen as blood is diverted for more important uses.

The increase in bodily activity corresponds to the escalation of mental activity as well. The salesperson's internal dialogue speeds up, jumps from subject to subject, and second-guesses itself. "Are they with me?" "What should I say next?" This tension and fear are exposed in some salespeople's speech. They talk too fast, repeat themselves, stutter, or under extreme stress completely forget what they were going to say.

The irony of this situation is that the salesperson must project a calm, cool, collected presence to customers at all times. To do otherwise would increase customers' stress levels. Nervousness and agitation may be misinterpreted and convince executives that the salesperson has something to hide. Verbal faux pas may be thought of as incompetence. Think about your last visit to the dentist. What would your reaction have been if the dentist had seemed nervous, agitated, or flustered before he or she started to work on your mouth? You would have been scared and had a very stressful appointment.

All Buyers Are Liars (Even C-Level Executives)

Recently, a salesperson told me about an e-mail from a prospective customer that left him devastated. The customer questioned the validity of the salesperson's product, his company's capability, and his professionalism. The e-mail cited a laundry list of reasons why he and his company were inferior. Obviously, the customer wouldn't be buying his product.

The most distressing part of the e-mail questioned the salesperson's acumen. It detailed how his presentation to the selection team had been ill-received and went on to describe how the team's requests for information weren't responded to for days and even weeks. To make matters worse, the customer sent copies of this e-mail to the seniormost executives at his own company and numerous people within the salesperson's company. The e-mail closed by saying "I hope you will take this feedback constructively and look for ways to better meet the needs of your customers." However, the e-mail had a major problem. None of it was true.

Stress causes decision makers to act very differently than normal. It essentially forces them to lie. Customers will not only say things they don't mean but mean things they don't say. Therefore, a fundamental premise of all sales calls is that whether inadvertently or on purpose, customers will always lie. This includes C-level executives too.

Now this may seem like a harsh statement; therefore, it requires further explanation. First, we need to define the different types of lies customers tell because some are more destructive than others. Of course, customers tell fibs and falsehoods that contradict the truth. Other times, they'll simply withhold important information from you, which in itself is a lie because they haven't told you the entire truth. Worst is when they are giving a competing salesperson proprietary, privileged information that they are not sharing with you.

Lying often occurs subtly, for example, when customers overemphasize the importance of a certain feature or present an irrelevant step in the decision-making process as a red herring to throw you off the scent of the truth. Sometimes, customers will strictly adhere to their selection process guidelines, never giving any more information to you than they say they're allowed to give. Usually, each of these types of lies is intended to hide their personal bias toward another competitor.

In the case of the hapless salesperson who received the damaging e-mail, the lie was sent to keep the salesperson out of the account. The decision maker had wanted another solution from the start of the sales cycle and sent the e-mail to prevent the salesperson from further pursuing the account. It was a blatant attempt to ruin the salesperson's credibility and reputation so he couldn't talk with any of the C-level executives in the organization.

However, sometimes customers lie for an entirely different reason. Their lying is actually an act of benevolence. Customers will lie to protect a salesperson's feelings. When you are meeting face to face with someone, human nature dictates that the other person will try to avoid confronting or disappointing you. Most people don't enjoy hurting or humiliating others. So when a sales call ends and the salesperson asks, "Will we win the business?" most customers will give an optimistic answer. They don't want to let down or embarrass the salesperson, so they'll tell a lie for momentary relief. However, the truth will be revealed later—usually when the customer avoids the salesperson's follow-up calls.

Remember, executives will like some salespeople and dislike others. They will instinctively try to keep any conversations with the disliked salespeople at a business level in order to protect themselves. They'll rebuff the attempts from the disliked salespeople to befriend them. Meanwhile, they will reveal much more about themselves to their favorite.

The Stressed-Out C-Level Executive

Stress is inherent to the work environment. In a recent nationwide survey of workers, 50 percent said they were under a great deal of stress and 77 percent claimed job burnout.[2] Whether it's due to an unrealistic workload, tight project deadlines, or an overbearing boss, workplace stress profoundly affects the physical and psychological states of employees. Emotional distress manifests itself physically in the form of ulcers, migraines, high blood pressure, and even premature aging.

From a psychological perspective, stress causes people to act out of the norm. It shortens attention spans, increases aggression, escalates mental exhaustion, and encourages poor decision making. Therefore, it's important to understand the three main sources of executive-level stress: informational stress, peer pressure stress, and corporate citizenship stress.

Informational Stress: Is the Information Being Presented Truthful?

We live in very skeptical times in which information presented by experts and authorities is continually challenged and constantly debunked. In fact, the mantra of the '60s to "question authority" has now become our society's default behavior. Every institution is under attack by skeptics. Our society is naturally skeptical of the motives of and information from our government, politicians, sports heroes, religious leaders, and business leaders because in recent years, leaders in all these areas have engaged in misinformation, unethical behavior, and the abuse of power.

Not only do we question information, but we expect it to be a half-truth at best. For example, do you believe the new car you purchase will get the same miles per gallon (mpg) as the window sticker indicates? Probably not. But what may surprise you is how far off the number actually is. A recent *Consumer Reports* study showed that the Jeep Liberty actually got 11 mpg versus the 22 mpg it was supposed to get. A Honda Civic was touted as getting 46 mpg in the city but in reality produced only 26 mpg. A Chevy Trailblazer was supposed to get 15 mpg but could muster only 9 mpg in city driving.[3]

The report went on to explain the reason for the huge discrepancies. Cars are not actually tested on the road but in a garage on a treadmill-type machine. Hills, wind resistance, and anything else that may decrease mileage, like air conditioning or driving above 60 miles per hour, are avoided.

However, the "question authority" mantra is even far more extreme mantra when applied to salespeople. It is actually "question everything; believe nothing!" In addition to being subject to the general cynicism of our society, most executives have had negative experiences with salespeople. Their doubts and suspicions about the integrity of the sales profession have been proven true. Whereas our court system is based upon the presumption of innocence until proven guilty, to executives, salespeople are guilty until proven innocent. Therefore, customers are always in the stressful position of separating fact from fiction. Meanwhile, even the most ethical salesperson carries the stressful burden of proving he's not a crook.

Peer Pressure Stress: How Do My Colleagues Perceive Me?

Peer pressure is a powerful influencer of group dynamics, and a recent study of fourteen hundred music listeners proves this point.[4] The participants were divided into two groups of seven hundred and told to listen to forty-eight new songs on an Internet site. The members of one group remained independent and did not share their opinions with anyone, while the other group was segregated into eight "social groups" where opinions were freely shared.

In one instance, a song that was ranked in the middle (at the twenty-sixth position) by the independent group was placed at the number one position by one of the social groups. Another social group ranked the same song last. According to researcher Peter Hedstrom of Oxford University, "Popular songs became more popular and unpopular songs became less popular when individuals influenced one another, and it became more difficult to predict which songs were to emerge."[5] This study proves that not only does peer pressure influence the outcome of group decision making, but it makes it harder to predict.

From an organizational point of view, three types of pressure occur in organizations: upper-level pressure from managers and executives, horizontal peer pressure from those who function at the same organizational level, and lower-level pressure from employees who are constantly evaluating their manager's actions. Managers create performance pressure because they continually assess subordinates by how well they perform their jobs and run their departments. They are the judging eyes of the company. Peers create competitive pressure because all are striving to progress in their careers and move upward in the organization. Subordinates create validation pressure. They are continually seeking proof of their manager's ability because the power of their department and the progress of their careers are tied to the business and political acumen of their leader. In essence, they want to know if they have hitched their wagon to the right horse.

C-level executives are extremely worried about what the board of directors thinks of them (upper-level pressure). They also are continually thinking about how the other members of the senior leadership team feel about them (horizontal peer pressure). And of course, they want their employees to respect them as well (lower-level pressure).

Whether from above, below, or the same level in an organization, coworkers are continually evaluating the behavior, success, and failures of those tasked with the decision-making process. Obviously, this exerts pressure on executives to make the right decision.

Corporate Citizenship Stress: Is It in the Best Interest of the Company?

Beginning in childhood and throughout your entire schooling, you were probably taught to love, honor, and respect institutions like your school and our country. Most likely, you rooted for your school at sporting events, recited the Pledge of Allegiance, and knew the words to patriotic songs and maybe even your alma mater's fight song. Not only is this way of thinking about our institutions ingrained in us, but it's part of our wishful thinking because it is associated with many positive sentiments and memories.

However, the desire to believe in our institutions is diametrically opposed to the tendency to question authority. While executives inherently want to do what's in the best interest of the company and to be good corporate citizens, the fundamental dynamic of corporate-employee loyalty has changed. Business is a "survival of the fittest" world where employment is never guaranteed and loyalty goes unrewarded. Therefore, executives feel continual pressure to put their individual needs before the company's.

Achieving the company's goals sometimes contradicts the selfish wants and desires of senior leaders. Other times, it contradicts the desires of colleagues, subordinates, and superiors, causing more and more stress. With so many different types of stress, it's no wonder that customers dread the vendor selection process.

What Senior Executives Dread

People dread making decisions because every decision activates fear, uncertainty, doubt, and stress. Today's executives dread the number and similarity of options they must evaluate. While they have more choices than ever, competing products share the same basic features, functions, and benefits. If no single vendor stands out above the others, executives tend to base their final decision on their emotions and esoteric intangibles instead of widely known facts.

Executives also dread having to verify the information presented by vendors. While salespeople believe all buyers are liars, executives believe everyone in sales tells tall tales. Salespeople will exaggerate, describing a product's benefits as greater than they really are and talking about larger-than-life results their product cannot deliver. Executives know it's their responsibility to discount such claims and validate that the facts are as they have been represented. They are the watchdogs of their organizations, and this is a tremendous responsibility.

People who have been traumatized by a stressful event will suffer from posttraumatic stress disorder. They may have recurring nightmares, continually replay the event in their minds, or suffer from depression. Conversely, executives can suffer from "pretraumatic stress syndrome," whereby the stress of making a selection traumatizes decision makers.

Executives dread uncertainty. They anticipate they will have problems with every purchase. They fear the worst. For example, an executive selecting a contractor for a long-awaited building project fears it will run over budget and behind schedule. Executives selecting a complex computer system fear they will face technical difficulties and the system will be hard to use. An executive implementing new manufacturing machinery fears unforeseen production-line problems. All these executives fear that when all is said and done, they will be no better off than they were before they made the purchase.

> It's a pain in the ass to switch vendors. It's a pain in the ass to analyze whether you should or not.
>
> VICE PRESIDENT OF PURCHASING

Finally, executives dread the pain of selecting between vendors. Recent research of brain scans suggests that the anticipation of pain is equal to the actual pain itself. In the study, participants were given choices about the strength and duration of an electric shock as well as how long they would have to wait before it would be applied to their foot. Would they rather have a medium-strength shock in seven seconds or one in twenty seconds? A mild shock in twenty-two seconds or a strong one in four seconds? The results of the study were surprising. Volunteers almost always chose to take the shock with the shortest waiting time when the strength was the same. In other words, people wanted to get painful experiences over with as soon as possible. They dreaded waiting for pain.[6]

This study of foot shocks helps explain an important aspect of customer buying behavior. Customers often engage in long, protracted selection processes even though they have already made up their minds about which product they will buy. Although they would not admit it, they are only searching for the minimal information necessary to further validate their initial choice.

One vendor almost always has an unfair advantage going into the formal evaluation process because the final decision is made very early in the sales cycle. Dethroning the chosen vendor is an extremely tough task, and all the other vendors jump through the customer's sales process hoops for nothing. Because the customer is motivated to shorten the wait and end the pain of making a selection as quickly as possible, he informally makes a decision early, even though it may not be formally announced until months later.

Certain conditions exacerbate this situation—for example, one vendor is the clear market leader or the competing products are nearly identical. Under these circumstances, executives face little risk of choosing the wrong product so they can quickly settle on a favorite. Obviously, if customers have used one of the products, they know what to expect. The old cliché "We choose the devil we know over the devil we don't know" describes what they tend to do. Figure 3.2 illustrates factors that influence when customers are likely to make their decision.

Decision likely to be made before the selection process begins	Decision likely to be made during the selection process
The market has a dominant leader. Competing products are similar. The customer has previous product familiarity.	The market has several significant players. Competing products have tangible differences. The customer has no previous product familiarity.
The customer is motivated to eliminate dread.	*The customer seeks to shorten the period of dread.*

Figure 3.2 The impact of dread on C-level executive decision making

Executives are stressed out. They don't know whom or what to believe. They are under immense peer pressure, and they are torn between doing the right thing for the greater good of the company and acting in their best personal interest. This inner turmoil manifests itself during the selection process, which executives dread. To make matters worse, the vendors increase the pressure by injecting claims of their superiority and accusations about their competitors' inferiority.

> It sorts itself out pretty fast—those who will and won't make it with us. We are a big company, so there's always a tendency to go with the big players. Who are your proven big-time customers? What resources do you have to get something fixed?
>
> CHIEF OPERATING OFFICER

FEAR and FUD

The sales cycle has a natural condition. One vendor is almost always preferred going into the selection process. However, customers are in a predicament. They still want to collect information from the other vendors to be 100 percent certain they are selecting the right vendor. Or they may want to complete the evaluation process to show others within or outside their organization (management, colleagues, consultants, or government agencies) that their evaluation was thorough and fair.

As a result, they offer the other (losing) vendors a "customer placebo." The customer placebo consists of false information and all the types of lies described earlier. This is an entirely different kind of fear from the kind that salespeople experience—this is false evidence appearing real, or FEAR.

Many customers will say anything to please the lagging vendors, who have no chance of winning, and often present false buying signs that they are more interested in the products than they actually are. Unfortunately, these vendors continue to spend additional resources and time on the account when a decision for one vendor has, for all intents and purposes, been made already.

As the sales cycle progresses, these vendors then try to escalate FUD (fear, uncertainty, and doubt) in the customer's mind about the wherewithal of the competitors' companies and the capabilities of their products. For example, competitors will try to sabotage one another with facts such as unfavorable performance metrics, missing functionality, and tales of unhappy customers.

In turn, the attacked competitor will provide the customer with believable information that contradicts the original attacks. Therefore, the sales cycle naturally disintegrates into a "he said–she said" type of quarrel. This can leave company leaders not only confused but sometimes in "analysis paralysis" due to receiving too much contradictory information. This scenario helps set the stage for no decision to be made. The bickering tends to turn off potential buyers. Do you like watching people argue? Probably not.

But the biggest problem in the sales cycle is not FEAR or FUD. It's that the difference between products is extremely small. Compounding this problem is that everyone is presenting the same message to the customer. Take a moment and visit the home page of your company's Web site and those of your two biggest competitors. You'll see that the words and claims are interchangeable. Because all the competing products share the same basic features, functions, and benefits, the final decision to purchase is based upon the C-level executive's preferences and how he has exerted his influence on the decision-making process.

Conclusion

Psychological influences on people in group environments can be quite profound. At a cocktail party, for instance, people are more self-conscious about their looks when they meet someone who is better looking than they are. People feel inferior when they meet someone with great wealth. People feel like underachievers when they are introduced to someone who is famous. The undertones of dominance and submission exist every time strangers meet and permeate your interactions with senior-level executives.

The process of buying evokes fear, uncertainty, doubt, and stress in the C-level executive's mind. Senior executives seek to relieve this stress as soon as possible, often by making a selection very early in the sales process.

In this chapter we also reviewed an elemental premise of all sales calls—whether inadvertently or on purpose, the customer will always lie. Customers lie for many different reasons: as an act of favoritism, to protect themselves, and even to benevolently attempt to protect a salesperson's psyche.

Lying is an innate part of the sales cycle and should be accepted as such. C-level executives will misrepresent the truth and say what they think the salesperson wants to hear. They'll say what they don't mean and mean what they don't say. They'll tell you they like your solution when they really don't and withhold important information from nonpreferred salespeople.

A recent study about sexual activity reveals how common it is to lie. In a survey of 2,065 heterosexual nonvirgins with a median age in their late forties, women reported an average of 8.6 lifetime sexual partners, whereas the men claimed 31.9 partners.[7] Are these numbers to be believed?

Psychologist Norman Brown at the University of Michigan doesn't think so. According to Brown, the women were more likely to undercount and the men were prone to exaggerate. He said about the participants, "They gave an answer and then two minutes later admitted they had lied."[8]

One can surmise that peer pressure to give a socially acceptable answer played an influential role in their lying. And peer pressure is an equally important influencer in the final purchasing decision every C-level executive makes.

I am going to be honest when I say this: we'll try to use "legitimate" ROI [return on investment] information where we have it. But you have to be somewhat pragmatic, when you hang your hat mainly on ROI because you frequently create an exercise of fiction, people looking around to create numbers versus what feels right. It comes down to the confidence in the person presenting it.

CHIEF MARKETING OFFICER

Part II

Penetrating the C-Level Executive Suite

The toughest task in all of sales is penetrating the C-level suite and securing meetings with these busy executives. Think about it for a moment: the same executives you are trying to reach are continually hounded by your competitors and hundreds of other salespeople at the same time. Therefore, you need a linguistic strategy that enables your message to rise above all others, a tactical plan of execution, and impactful psychological suggestions that compel executives to take action and meet with you. In this part we address the grand strategy to penetrate the C-level executive suite and successfully message to company leaders.

4

Control

> While we put together a cross-functional team to identify our needs and come up with a recommendation, it wasn't too surprising that their recommendation came out the way I had envisioned it in the first place.
>
> CHIEF FINANCIAL OFFICER

Sales, like soldiering, is unlike most other professions. While doctors save lives, teachers build lives, and police officers protect lives, salespeople are on a mission to actually destroy the lives of their enemies. Salespeople are verbal warriors who seek to crush their enemies emotionally and psychologically. As salespeople, we want our competitors to question whether they are working for the right company, to lose faith in their sales skills, and even to second-guess themselves about whether they belong in this profession at all. Our goal is to annihilate the competition. Customers are the weapons we use to accomplish this mission.

Customers do not provide us the opportunity for face-to-face fights with our enemies in person. Rather, our enemies' destruction is based upon having customers choose us over our competitors. Rejection is a real killer. It obliterates faith, dreams, and careers. Rejection can stamp out a salesperson's soul just as a bullet can snuff out the life of a soldier.

Defeating our enemies and winning the war is based upon the indirect strategy of winning over customers. The objective of our battle is to win the trust, respect, and friendship of another human being, thereby causing our adversaries' demise. The victor builds the strongest customer relationship, manages the selection process better, and outmaneuvers his enemies over the customer's political landscape (the various decision makers involved in the selection process). The champion outsmarts, outhustles, and outwits the losers. Most importantly, the victor wins over the C-level executives and convinces them to buy.

The Concept of the Metaphor

You just read a description that equates the professions of soldiering and selling. This is a persuasion technique known as a metaphor. Metaphors are stories, parables, and analogies that communicate ideas by using examples that people can relate to and identify with. Metaphors enable complex concepts and theories to be explained in a simple, understandable, and interesting manner. In addition, a metaphor is a single story that can convey many meanings. Using metaphors is a nonthreatening way to make skeptics more receptive to your message.

The three different types of metaphors are educational, personal, and action based. Educational metaphors are analogies that help explain new concepts using common terms or everyday situations. When you make a drawing of your product's architecture to show the customer how it operates, you're using an educational metaphor. The story you tell about how one of your customers is successfully using your product is an example of a personal metaphor. Action-based metaphors use physical movement to communicate additional meaning and highlight important concepts. For example, a product demonstration is actually an action-based metaphor for how a customer can use your product. Site visits and reference calls with existing customers are action-based metaphors intended to get prospective customers to simulate product ownership.

Reciting your product's long list of features, functions, and business benefits will not persuade the customer to buy. Customers are naturally skeptical of salespeople, and C-level executives are the most skeptical of all. Using stories, parables, and other metaphors is a powerful, indirect method of persuading them to buy. In this chapter I use a variety of military metaphors to explain complex concepts involving grand strategy and how to destroy the competition by penetrating the protected fortress, which is the C-level executive suite.

Grand Strategy, Battles, and Battlefield Maneuvers

All wars can be broken down into three elements: grand strategy, battles, and battlefield maneuvers. The grand strategy is the overall approach to winning the war. In sales, the grand strategy should always be based upon an approach to influence the people, selection process, and politics of the customer's decision making. In other words, we want to build a personal relationship with the customer that's deeper than the competition's, change the selection process to better suit us, and influence the politics of how the decision is going to be made by winning over the senior executives making the decision. The grand strategy is accomplished by executing a series of battles (sales calls, presentations, demonstrations, and so on). Finally, the smallest element of war consists of battlefield maneuvers (such as phone calls, letters, and e-mails)—specific actions intended to move a salesperson to the next battle.

Although battlefield maneuvers are typically small steps, they can have a great impact on the deal. For example, let's say a customer is looking at a competitor's product and hesitates to meet with you. A battlefield maneuver might be to e-mail the customer an industry article that rates your product better than the competitor's. After reading the article, the customer may decide to let you present your solution. The idea is that you have to maneuver into position to fight the first battle.

Battlefield maneuvers prevent you from standing still, getting stuck at a certain stage in the sales cycle, or being pinned down by an opponent's tactics. These maneuvers are usually based upon a direct approach. Figure 4.1 illustrates the interrelationships between the grand strategy, battles, and battlefield maneuvers.

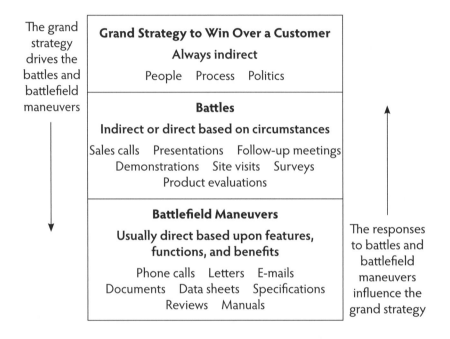

Figure 4.1 Grand strategy, battles, and battlefield maneuvers

The sales cycle is a sequence of battles or action points, such as sales calls, presentations, demonstrations, surveys, and site visits. However, each party participating in these battles has different goals. Your competitors are trying to eliminate you from the next battle. Meanwhile, you are a suitor, trying to court a customer into forming a long-term relationship, akin to a marriage. You try to accomplish this goal by scheduling battles to explain your product's features and benefits and the merits of your company. These events give you opportunities to befriend and win over the customer.

Customers have a different set of goals. Relationships are expensive and involve investments of valuable time and money. Customers have to spend time to determine whether a product's characteristics are as they have been represented. They have to spend time evaluating other suitors to determine whether they are picking the best possible partner. They have to spend time learning to use the new products they select, implementing them, and most likely, fixing product problems. In addition, customers have to acquire the solution and pay ongoing fees for support. They want to make sure they are selecting the best partner and have found their "soul mate." Your battlefield maneuvers may include facts and other proof points that put the customer's mind at ease and move you to the next battle, the next step in the sales cycle.

During a long sales cycle of several months or more, it's easy to focus on individual battles and lose sight of winning the war. The sales cycle is reduced to a series of battles without an overriding grand strategy. We become fixated on the next battle, proceeding from the initial call to the sales presentation, from the presentation to the demonstration, and from the demonstration to the product evaluation. Usually, the salesperson who experiences an eleventh-hour defeat fought in this "battle du jour" (battle of the day) manner without a grand strategy. The moment you work on an account without a grand strategy, you relinquish account control. Worse yet is when the details of the battles—where, when, and how they will be fought—are out of your control because they are determined exclusively by the customer or even a competitor. If you find yourself in this position take a step back and ask yourself these questions:

1. What is my grand strategy? Did I take time to create one in the first place?

2. Am I confusing battlefield maneuvers or my involvement in a sequence of battles with a grand strategy?
3. Is the customer or competition dictating when, how, and where the battles will be fought?
4. Who is selling highest in the deal? That is, who is meeting with the C-level executives?

You should continually ask yourself these four fundamental questions.

"Direct" Brute Force versus "Indirect" Psychology

Your competitors seek to destroy you. They have educated themselves about your products and sales tactics, and they're focused on defeating you. Fortunately, most of them believe in the use of brute force and think the best way to defeat you is by direct frontal attack. They'll say your products are subpar and your company is incompetent. In reality, however, an indirect strategy based upon the psychology of winning over the hearts and minds of customers carries the day.

The language salespeople use is usually provided by their marketing departments. However, the marketing departments at most companies don't truly understand what salespeople do. To those departments, selling is a series of steps that prospects are guided through. These steps are based on the logic of purchasing a product, and the marketing team's job is to provide the tools to move prospects to the next step. This is the "direct" brute force method of selling. We march into the customer's office and proclaim how great our company and products are.

Marketing departments almost always believe in using the direct strategy exclusively. They mistakenly think that customers' decision-making processes are completely unbiased and purely rational. As a result, they crank out data sheets, white papers, press releases, and other forms of company propaganda.

Meanwhile, salespeople must work with the unpredictable part of the process: people. Their job is to formulate an account strategy based upon the people they are trying to sell to. They are more like clinical psychiatrists who have to understand their customers' deepest thoughts and show how they can solve problems solely by the words they speak. However, the language they need to use depends upon the type of enterprise deal they are trying to close.

Renewal, Persuasion, and Creation Enterprise Sales Cycles

The nature of enterprise sales is that the deals are large, the decision process is complex, and great personal rewards are possible for individuals who can close deals. But what exactly is an "enterprise" sale? It has four major characteristics. The first characteristic is the size and complexity of the product. If you sell big-ticket products such as computers, machinery, commercial real estate, telecommunications, or airplanes, you are involved in enterprise sales.

The second characteristic is the complex nature of the sales cycle. It is a process that involves multiple people, or multiple groups of people, who in varying degrees make the purchase decision. The decision is made over a period of time that is typically measured in weeks or months.

Third, the size of the deals is large. A deal can be either one large single purchase or a steady stream of future revenue. Sales may involve material items such as electronics and equipment or the creation of new ideas, license agreements, and partnerships.

Finally, C-level executives are involved in every enterprise deal. They may be actively involved during the selection process or may be the ultimate decision maker who approves the evaluation team's recommendation. During tough economic times they have an even more significant role: to decide whether or not to approve any enterprise purchase at all!

The three basic types of enterprise deals are renewal, persuasion, and creation deals. Renewal deals involve selling more products and services to existing customers or trying to close a multiyear contract that is coming up for renewal. Persuasion deals are extremely competitive customer evaluations that usually involve the customer creating a request for proposal (RFP) or similar document. In these deals you are usually competing against your archrivals. Finally, in creation deals you target and penetrate a new account, trying to get the customer to use your products for the first time with the hope that the customer will make a much larger purchase in the future. Figure 4.2 shows the three different enterprise sales cycles.

Each enterprise sales cycle requires a different sales strategy. In renewal deals the goal is to execute a "sales virus" strategy where the salesperson is continually spreading out to meet everyone within the customer's organization across all departments and at all levels. Persuasion deals are quite different because they are based solely on the transmission and receipt of information. In essence, they are response-based deals where the customer is comparing the answers to their questions. Therefore, all the salespeople involved in the deal are continually saying to the customer, "We are the best because . . . " Creation deals are just the opposite. They are hypothesis sales based upon establishing trust where the salesperson says to the customer, "We can help you do X better. Let us come in and prove it!"

> We started to try a few things with them on a smaller scale. We didn't know enough about them or how well they provided it to jump in with both legs. If you prove one project works, we'll trust you with the next one and the next one.
>
> VICE PRESIDENT OF MARKETING

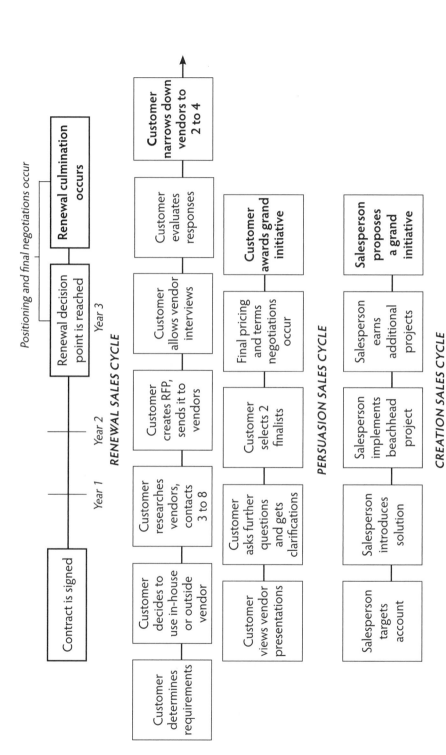

Figure 4.2 Renewal, persuasion, and creation enterprise sales cycles

Positioning and final negotiations occur

Contract is signed

Renewal decision point is reached

Renewal culmination occurs

Year 1   Year 2   Year 3

RENEWAL SALES CYCLE

Customer determines requirements

Customer decides to use in-house or outside vendor

Customer researches vendors, contacts 3 to 8

Customer creates RFP, sends it to vendors

Customer allows vendor interviews

Customer evaluates responses

Customer narrows down vendors to 2 to 4

Customer views vendor presentations

Customer asks further questions and gets clarifications

Customer selects 2 finalists

Final pricing and terms negotiations occur

Customer awards grand initiative

PERSUASION SALES CYCLE

Salesperson targets account

Salesperson introduces solution

Salesperson implements beachhead project

Salesperson earns additional projects

Salesperson proposes a grand initiative

CREATION SALES CYCLE

The persuasion sales cycle has two critical moments. The first is the vendor interview. This is one of the few chances you'll have to develop relationships and uncover the political structure of the account. Asking questions is an excellent way to demonstrate your knowledge. Questions are actually metaphors that show your expertise and the competency of your company.

The most important moment is the vendor presentation. Why? Because this is one of the few moments during the entire sales cycle when C-level executives are present. In most cases, it is your only opportunity to win them over. Therefore, your presentation has to be persuasive, to differentiate you from the competition, and to be flawlessly executed. (We'll talk a lot more about the presentation and how to ask executives questions in the final part of the book.)

Unfortunately, I have some very frightening news to share with you based upon hundreds of interviews with C-level executives. Approximately 30 percent of the time the winner of the persuasion sales cycle was determined before the "official" selection process started. Another 45 percent of the time, customers had already made up their minds about whom they were going to buy from about halfway through the process. That means, 75 percent of the time, customers had made their decision by halfway through the process. Only 25 percent of the time did customers make their final decision at the end of the selection process. Therefore, if you are not clearly in the lead at the midpoint of the selection process, the odds are that you are going to lose. Figure 4.3 illustrates this point.

Here's another frightening fact. In almost every case, the decision wasn't even close between the top two choices. Even though customers had made up their minds, they still caused all the other salespeople to jump through a series of hoops for nothing, wasting their valuable time, resources, and mental and emotional energy. Here are some quotes from C-level executives about when they made up their minds during the persuasion sales cycle:

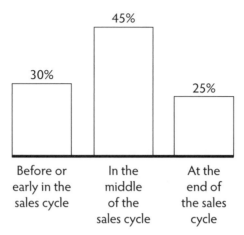

Figure 4.3 When persuasion sales cycle customers made up their minds

"The company that we were leaning toward at the beginning came out on top."

CHIEF INFORMATION OFFICER

"There was a company that I liked at the beginning, and we were just not going to give it to them. So we went through the whole procedure, making sure all the boxes were checked off by a panel of people."

CHIEF FINANCIAL OFFICER

"Our favorite came through."

CHIEF TECHNOLOGY OFFICER

"Based on a number of factors, yes, we had a favorite vendor going in, and they won."

CHIEF EXECUTIVE OFFICER

"It became apparent quickly that it would be a two-horse race, and we knew who would win."

CHIEF MARKETING OFFICER

"We wanted ABC Company after we narrowed it down from four to two."

CHIEF OPERATING OFFICER

The creation sales cycle is quite different from the renewal and persuasion sales cycles. It is hypothesis sales where the salesperson proposes he can improve some aspect of the company's operations or profitability. The salesperson's goal is to win a "beachhead deal" and get the customer to start using his company's product or to start a small project to validate the solution. The hope is that this project will successfully culminate with a big purchase. The creation sales cycle is primarily based upon establishing trust. Unlike the persuasion sales cycle, which is based upon persuasive words, the creation sales cycle is based upon completing actions that create trust, building respect, and forming alliances with employees who will promote the solution within their organization.

Charting Your Sales Cycle Position

Regardless of which type of enterprise sales cycle you are working on, the single most important goal is to penetrate the C-level suite and meet the seniormost executive involved in the decision-making process. This is not an easy task. The metaphor I like to use to describe the level of difficulty is that of a warrior who has to penetrate a fortress. This fortress is designed to protect the C-level executive from you and keep you out of his office.

In every account, salespeople will find themselves in one of five distinct positions, depending upon the amount of information they have acquired and the level of rapport they have developed with the prospective customer. These positions are fortress, reconnaissance, escalade, *coup de main*, and retreat.

Your position correlates to your competitiveness in the account. If you are in the lead, meeting with the C-level executives in charge of the selection, you are inside the security of the fortress. In the position of reconnaissance, you have rapport or relationships with lower-level personnel but not enough information about the deal from the C-level executives. Conversely, in the escalade position, you have information but no relationships at all. In coup de main, you are behind in the account and lack both relationships and information. When you have little chance of winning, you are in retreat. Figure 4.4 shows all of these positions.

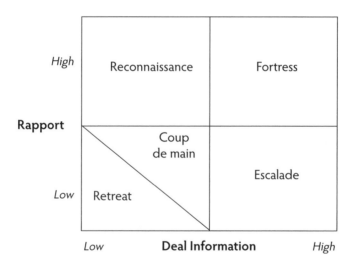

Figure 4.4 Charting your position

This figure can help you determine your bearings in an account. The vertical axis indicates the amount of rapport you have with a customer. For example, in a brand-new account you would have low or no rapport. A high-rapport account would be one in which you have personal friendships with senior members of the customer's selection team. The horizontal axis indicates the amount of truthful information being shared by the customer. This is your assessment of the quantity and quality of the information you are uncovering. It also includes any unique privileged information you are receiving that others aren't.

Fortress

The ultimate goal is to be securely inside the fortress. In the fortress, you have established rapport and have developed relationships with the company's C-level executives. They speak the confidential C-level language with you and provide you proprietary information that the other vendors aren't receiving. Only one salesperson can be in the fortress at any given time. All the others are attacking from outside the walls. Sometimes a salesperson can stay inside the executive fortress from the beginning to the end of the sales cycle. Other times, the focused attack of all the other vendors will weaken the salesperson's position, letting someone else overtake the fortress.

Inside the fortress, an interesting paradigm shift occurs in the salesperson-executive relationship. Because of the C-level relationships that have been established, the executives begin working with the salesperson as a long-term partner while they are still in the sales cycle. For example, when problems arise about the functionality of the product, the executives work with the salesperson to find an acceptable solution. This shift, from being treated like one of the vendors to becoming part of the customer's team, is very noticeable. If you are the salesperson in the fortress with the executives at this point, you have won the deal and should update your forecast accordingly.

Reconnaissance

The term "reconnaissance" is derived from the French word *reconnoître*, which literally meant "to recognize."[1] Reconnaissance is the act of observing the enemy—its strength, position, and movements—in order to gain information for military purposes.

In the position of reconnaissance, you have established rapport with lower-level personnel but have not been able to meet with the executives in charge. Therefore, you have a low level of information about their perception of you, if they prefer another vendor, or whether the deal will happen at all. For example, you may have painstakingly developed relationships with midlevel managers and lower-level personnel of the accounts payable group in the finance department of a Fortune 100 company. However, because of the finance department's immensity and bureaucracy, the accounts payable members are unsure if the CFO will approve their project. Therefore, even though rapport is high and the accounts payable group has identified specific business needs, the knowledge of whether a deal will be closed is lacking.

Escalade

Attacking a fortress was deadly business in medieval times, and the quickest way to take a castle, by escalade, was also the deadliest. Attackers would escalade, or scale the walls, using ladders. The success of the escalade was determined by speed and numbers. The ladders had to be set up quickly and in such great quantity that the defenders couldn't repulse them all. To impede an escalade, archers were stationed on top of the castle walls, water-filled moats surrounded the castle, and the walls had specially constructed openings from which defenders could drop boiling oil or molten lead on would-be attackers.

In sales, escalade techniques are based upon using information to infiltrate the fortress position and thereby establish executive-level relationships. The information could be your knowledge of the customer's industry, information about the customer's archrival, facts about the vendor who is in the fortress, or even unflattering details about how the selection process is occurring. (For example, you could tell the leader of the selection team that certain committee members are ignoring important criteria.)

A friend of mine gave me a great example of an escalade tactic. He had been trying to sell to a parts manufacturer without success. The senior-level executives simply weren't interested in meeting him and didn't want to hear about his company. However, one of my friend's other customers was a Fortune 100 company they had been trying to do business with, and when he offered to take the senior-level executives and introduce them to the executives there, he received an enthusiastic response. A few months later my friend closed his first $500,000 order with the previously unreceptive customer.

Coup de Main and Retreat

The bottom left-hand quadrant is where the salesperson has little information about the deal and little rapport with anyone inside the account. At the beginning of every new sales cycle, salespeople find themselves in this unenviable position. Their immediate priorities are to collect information and start the process of developing relationships in the hope of moving into the position of escalade or reconnaissance. Their ultimate goal is to be positioned inside the fortress.

Time is a salesperson's ultimate enemy. As the days and weeks slip by and no discernable movement toward the fortress quadrant takes place, the salesperson's anxieties grow. Finally, the internal turmoil creates a sense of urgency that forces the salesperson to take one of two extreme actions: a coup de main or a full retreat from the account.

According to the *United States Department of Defense Dictionary*, a coup de main is a "swift attack that relies on speed and surprise to accomplish its objectives in a single blow."[2] A coup de main is a sudden, unexpected make-or-break strike against the enemy. The term literally means "to strike with one's fist." In many ways a coup de main is an act of desperation, a lashing out against enemies or a conscious decision to bypass all established selection processes and customary sales etiquette to break out of a losing position.

It's natural to assume that the retreat position is the worst position to be in; however, this is not necessarily the case. Being in the retreat position actually is a double-edged sword. Because they have given up hope of winning the deal, salespeople in retreat won't spend any more time, resources, or mental anguish on it. In reality, the two most desirable positions to be in when the final selection is made are in the fortress or in retreat. All the salespeople in the other positions have wasted their time.

Battlefield Tactics Based on Position

Salespeople move from position to position as the sales cycle progresses. Moving from the coup de main to the escalade or reconnaissance position marks forward progress in the deal. Conversely, salespeople could experience setbacks that move them back to the coup de main position or dictate their retreat from the account.

The constant attack from competitors might weaken the leader's fortress walls over time and send him to the escalade position. A key executive contact might suddenly leave the company or be reassigned, forcing the salesperson from the reconnaissance position. A salesperson in the escalade position might never be able to establish anything more than a cordial relationship with the customer while his counterpart in the fortress enjoys a true friendship with the CEO. This may force him to try a last-ditch effort to win with a coup de main.

A variety of battlefield tactics can be employed by salespeople in each account position. These tactics are directed either at the vendor in the fortress to lessen his leadership position at the customer to improve the salesperson's position in the account. While a variation of each tactic can be used in any of the five account positions, each tactic is placed in figure 4.5 in its most commonly used location.

Fortress Tactics
Fortress tactics are based upon using your unique customer relationship and information advantage to stave off competitors and hold your leadership position. Here are some examples of fortress sales tactics.

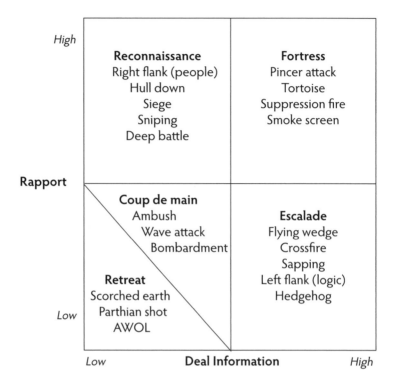

Figure 4.5 Tactics to penetrate the executive fortress

Pincer Attack   In sales, the two pincers that crush your opponents are C-level relationships and information. When C-level executives like you personally and believe your product to be best (whether true or imagined), you are placed in the advantageous position of being able to control and edit the information flowing to and from the other vendors. This lopsided combination of executive friendships and information superiority are pincers that crush the competition. No tactic is more effective than the pincer attack.

Tortoise   When Roman legionnaires attacked a walled city, they would use their shields in a formation known as a tortoise to protect themselves from arrows and missiles being hurled at them. The soldiers in the first row held their shields in front of them, the side rows held their shields to one side, and the rest of the soldiers held their shields above their heads so that the formation resembled a tortoise's shell.

In the sales equivalent of the tortoise tactic, advocates within an account form a shield to protect you from the slings and arrows of your competitors and from naysayers within the company. The strongest of these shields is provided by a senior executive—president, CEO, COO, or vice president—who is backing your solution. Regardless of your advocates' direct involvement in the selection process, the private opinions of these powerful people work behind the scenes to ward off known rivals and unseen internal detractors.

Suppression Fire   The goal of suppression fire is to hold the enemy in check at its current position by firing as many rounds of ammunition as possible toward the enemy forces. Although the suppression fire is highly unlikely to kill the enemy forces, it will cause them to stay behind cover and eliminate their ability to attack.

The sales suppression fire we seek to create forces our adversaries to answer uncomfortable questions about their products, companies, and reputations. We want the seniormost executives to interrogate them about their faults on our behalf. At other times, we want to influence the sales cycle such that the customer creates unnecessary and unimportant steps that keep the other vendors busy.

Smoke Screen   Both salespeople and customers employ smoke screens to hide behind during the sales cycle. Salespeople schedule meetings to discuss product functionality when in reality they are using these meetings to discern the personal biases of decision makers. They provide customers with detailed information or technical specifications about their products' strengths in order to divert attention from the products' known weaknesses. During a meeting, they present the illusion of being calm and collected when they are really scared and nervous.

Executives hide the truth as well. In fact, the entire selection process is a smoke screen designed so that vendors never know exactly where they stand. Executives believe that creating this uncertainty is the best way to gain leverage over the vendors and ensure they receive the best attention, information, and most importantly, price.

Perhaps the greatest smoke screen of all is the RFP. Almost all RFPs are created with a favorite vendor in mind. Think about it for a moment. In order to create an RFP, the customer must have investigated the solutions that are available, studied the market position of each vendor, and most assuredly, met with certain vendors. Therefore, it's not surprising that most RFPs include criteria that resemble one vendor's feature set or ask questions that the RFP creators know will cast particular solutions in a bad light. While all the responders put forth their best efforts to answer the RFP, in reality it is a smoke screen that has been laid down collectively by the seniormost executive in charge of the selection process and the favored vendor to camouflage the true nature of their relationship and the fact that the favorite already occupies the fortress position.

Reconnaissance Tactics

Reconnaissance tactics are all based upon relationships—taking advantage of existing midlevel and low-level relationships within an account to penetrate the executive fortress.

Right Flank (People)   Heading into battle, armies are organized into formations. A division of ten thousand men might consist of two brigades, each composed of two regiments. Regardless of size, every formation has a left flank, center, and right flank. Perhaps the most common military tactic is to attack a formation at a flank, away from its center strength.

The right-flank sales tactic is associated with the people involved in the decision process. It is named after the right hemisphere of the brain, which is dominant for facial recognition, spatial abilities, and visual imagery. A right-flank movement is focused on finding "coaches" within an account. Coaches are individuals who seem to like you, are receptive to your position, and appreciate your company. For example, when you ask your coach to set up a meeting to help you establish a relationship with a more powerful executive decision maker, you are performing a right-flank maneuver.

Hull Down   When a tank participates in a battle, it is frequently positioned behind the crest of a hill or within a man-made ditch so that only the turret and cannon are exposed. The gunner can then fire away at enemy targets while the tank remains safely hidden.

Salespeople employ the hull-down tactic by enlisting a member of the selection team or other key influencer to disseminate positive information about their solution and negative information about competitors to C-level executives while they remain hidden in the background.

Here is a very simple example of a hull down. You see the CEO of the company you are trying to close a deal with having lunch with an industry consultant. You walk up to their table and tell the CEO that your product is the best solution on the market and that his company should buy it. What would his response be? Most likely he would be skeptical at the very least. But let's suppose you'd asked the consultant beforehand to casually recommend your product to the CEO over lunch. The CEO's response to your pitch would be the opposite.

Siege   The siege tactic is an attrition-based strategy for conquering a fortress or city. A siege is both a conventional and a psychological operation. Daily supplies are blocked, causing shortages of basic necessities, while the stress of being surrounded and under threat of imminent attack weakens the defenders' resolve to hold out. Laying siege to a fortress or city is usually not the first choice of action by any military commander because it ties up large numbers of troops and other resources for long periods of time. Rather, it is a last resort after other battlefield tactics have failed.

In one sense, all salespeople lay siege to the accounts they are working on. However, many salespeople are experts at employing the siege strategy in a less conventional way. Contrary to common sense, they actually hound the customer into meeting with them and purchasing their solution. They will not abandon the account or leave it alone until the customer relents. Relentless, unapologetic hounding and stalking of lower-level personnel, midlevel managers, and company leaders are central to the siege tactic.

Sniping   Snipers are hated by infantries of all armies for good reason. From their well-hidden positions, snipers evoke fear. A single sniper can pin down an entire platoon and inflict many casualties.

In sales, not everyone on the customer's selection committee will be enamored with you and your solution. People will eagerly voice their opinions in the selection process. Usually, the venting of opinions, both good and bad, about your product will result in a healthy debate that is necessary for the committee to reach a consensus. However, occasionally an individual may be so ardently opposed to you and your company that that person must be taken out of the selection process altogether. The tactic to use in this situation is sniping.

The most effective sales sniping involves lying in wait for the perfect moment to discredit and take out a detractor. Let's assume, for example, that a member of the selection team has consistently harangued you during the sales process about your product's lack of a particular capability. In reality, his adamant opposition is just a red herring (an irrelevant topic presented to divert attention) to hide his personal bias toward another competitor. Meanwhile, after meeting individually with the other selection team members, you discover this capability isn't considered crucial. When you meet with the entire selection team again, you will want to get this issue out on the table and talked about openly so that the detractor is essentially "sniped" by the other committee members.

Recently, a software salesperson told me one of the best examples of sniping I have ever heard. The salesperson had been trying to penetrate an account for over a year and the CIO would not meet with him. So he had one of his best friends, who was an information technology recruiter, recruit the CIO to work for another company.

Sometimes sniping can get very personal. For example, a lower-level employee who is voicing opinions against you must be removed from the sales process. Taking advantage of your relationships with executives, you attack the subordinate's credentials, credibility, and capabilities. You instill fear in the executives that the project will be unsuccessful with this person on the team.

Usually, sniping is very uncomfortable to do. At times during customer meetings, you must dominate detractors and silence their opposition in order to maintain your momentum. While we tend to become more emotional when we are challenged, the most effective sniper remains calm. Whether you use a logical argument to contradict a detractor's claim, give a customer example to repudiate an antagonistic statement, or expose the ridiculousness of the objection itself, a composed response is far more effective than an emotional one.

Deep Battle   During the cold war, in anticipation of a Russian attack in central Europe, the U.S. military developed the military doctrine referred to as "deep battle." Deep battle synchronized the actions of ground troops fighting on the front to air operations simultaneously attacking the rear, deep in Russian territory.

Deep battle is an appropriate sales tactic when you sense a selection committee is aligned against you and fear its recommendation to senior management. The goal of deep battle is to use a spy—a friend on the inside—to introduce you to the ultimate and final C-level decision maker, who exists in every account. (We'll talk about the "bully with the juice" and the "emperor" in detail in the next chapter.) You want a chance to plead your case in person.

Since you need to bypass the evaluation steps laid out by the selection committee, you must have excellent intelligence to execute deep battle. If the tactic is successful, you will have neutralized the selection committee's power and have a chance to win the deal. If the tactic fails (which is often the case), you will have alienated the committee and therefore lost. However, knowing you have lost the deal is actually a blessing in disguise. Controlling your destiny, as opposed to bowing to the demands of a biased committee, will save you from wasting precious time and effort on an account where you just can't win.

Escalade Tactics

Escalade tactics are based upon information and logic, and their purpose is to create a psychological advantage. They can be used to appeal to the customer's deductive reasoning or effect fear, uncertainty, and doubt in the customer's mind.

Flying Wedge   The flying wedge is a concentrated battle formation focused on one point. The attacking force forms into a triangle to breach the enemy's line at a single spot. Once a gap is created in the enemy's lines, the formation expands and pushes out in different directions.

Here's a sales example of the flying wedge. Let's say you have advantageous benchmark information that shows your product is faster than your opponent's solution, which happens to be in the lead. At every possible opportunity, you harangue the senior decision makers about the implications of poor performance, the technical differences between the products that cause poor performance, how much unnecessary equipment would need to be purchased to rectify the performance problem, and the business impact of poor performance.

You continually hammer upon performance in order to create an opening, a wedge or gap between the leader and the customer, where you can begin to spread your company's story and your product's benefits to the decision makers.

Recently, I worked with a company whose software used newer relational database technology instead of the older flat file systems of their major competitor. The term "relational database technology" is in nearly every paragraph on every page of the company's Web site, and the salespeople recite this mantra over and over at customer meetings. When I interviewed some senior executives of accounts the company had recently won, they all said relational database technology was the key reason their product was selected.

Crossfire   In sales, the crossfire tactic involves using other people to help you win a deal. It may include other members of your company, such as your technical system engineer, sales manager, or business partners, who have a vested interest in your winning. You fire away at the competition together. It's a logic-based sales tactic designed to cause doubt in the customer's mind about another vendor's capabilities while bolstering your position.

It's extremely important that you bring along the right people from your company to executive-level sales calls. For example, if the executive is a technical genius, be sure to bring your technical mavens along with you to provide matching firepower.

Sapping   Another word for tunneling is "sapping" and sappers dig tunnels underneath their enemies to launch surprise attacks. Perhaps the most effective sales example of sapping is telling a prospect about the competition's customers who have dumped their products and switched to yours. Even a competitor who is safely in the confines of the fortress can have the lead position sapped from beneath him when the senior executives hear such enormously destructive stories. It's one of the best ways to remove a competitor from the fortress.

Left Flank (Logic)   While the right-flank tactic is based upon people, the left-flank tactic is based upon logic and information. Flanking to the left refers to the tactic of changing the customer's selection criteria or raising a critical issue the customer is unaware of. It is named after the left side of the brain, the part that is analytical and invokes rational reasoning and deductive logic.

The right- and left-flank tactics work together. For instance, a meeting can be set up under the guise of one topic when the goal is really to gain access to a specific senior executive (right flank) and influence that person to change the logical selection criteria (left flank).

Hedgehog   The hedgehog is a defensive tactic used offensively. Military units will employ a hedgehog defense scheme to protect a large area from attack when they don't have enough manpower to defend it conventionally. Soldiers are spread out into carefully placed positions and dig in, or "hedgehog." When the attackers encounter hedgehogs, they naturally funnel into the open spaces between them. While the attackers believe they are making progress, they are now subject to fire from other hedgehogs.

An effective hedgehog defense in sales is to spread out and lengthen the selection process to create more time to reach the senior executives. Contrary to the common-sense thinking that it is always best to shorten the sales cycle, sometimes it is necessary to make it longer by inserting steps the customer didn't think about or ask for.

Slowing down the sales cycle can create problems for the vendor in the fortress. Offering to complete a detailed on-site study of the customer's business, inviting the customer to make site visits to other installations, and taking the customer on a tour of your corporate headquarters are great examples of hedgehogs. These hedgehog events allow you to demonstrate your expertise, and they give you additional time to build the personal relationships you need to win.

Coup de Main Tactics

Coup de main tactics are risky and dangerous tactics and have a tendency to backfire. Therefore, keep them in reserve until late in the sales cycle when you are so far behind your competitors that you have nothing to lose.

Ambush. In the wild, a predator ambushes its prey by making a surprise attack from a hiding place. As simple as this may sound, military ambushes are quite complex and require careful planning to succeed. The ambush location must be a place the enemy passes predictably, and it must offer concealment and an easy escape route.

In sales, the ambush of competitors is just as complex. Which competitor are we out to ambush? What type of ambush will we execute? Will we lie in wait until that competitor makes a statement we know we can clearly contradict and ruin their salesperson's credibility? Will we take the initiative and instill fear and doubt in the senior executive's mind? Or will we take a consultative approach as the executive's trusted advisor and set a trap?

How will we carry out the ambush? Are we going to tell the executive about a new, unreleased product; provide third-party objective opinions; or disclose negative information about a competitor based upon our own experiences? When will the ambush occur? Will it be during the big sales presentation on the third PowerPoint slide or in an informal meeting with the executive? Who will execute the ambush? Will it be the salesperson, his manager, his presales engineer, or all of them together? Finally, what is our backup plan and what countermeasures will we take if our ambush fails?

These are just a few of the questions that need to be answered before attempting one. Above all, a successful ambush requires detailed planning.

Wave Attack During the Korean War, the Communist army frequently fought United Nations forces using the wave attack. It would send wave after wave of poorly equipped soldiers straight at the UN positions in a direct attack. The North Korean commanders who ordered these attacks knew the casualties would be high and the likelihood of success was low. Therefore, they employed the wave attack only as a last resort when other types of attacks had proven unsuccessful.

The sales equivalent of the wave attack is similarly accomplished by throwing bodies at an account. A salesperson may ask the president, vice president of sales, and other senior executives from within his company to haphazardly call their counterparts at the customer's company. The salesperson may ask his technical support team (system engineers, consultants, and analysts) to establish relationships with key contacts to find out information and influence opinions and criteria. Done at the right time in the sales cycle, the wave attack is an appropriate strategy.

However, attempting the wave attack late in the sales cycle is usually a waste of time. Selection team members don't like it when vendors go over their heads and call their boss or their boss's boss. Senior executives don't like it when you usurp the selection process they defined and the evaluation team they created. Worse, an ill-timed wave attack can be a fatal career move for a salesperson as it allows the senior leaders within the salesperson's company to be eyewitnesses to his failings and shortcomings.

Bombardment   Strategic bombing is the precision bombing of high-value military targets (such as command-and-control centers) and industrial targets (such as factories and railroads). The bombardments may occur from high, medium, and low altitudes. This tactic undermines a nation's ability to win wars.

In the sales vernacular, "bombardment" refers to the tactic of sending a constant stream of technical information, business justification material, and company marketing propaganda to personnel within the account you are trying to win.

The material sent to the senior executives is quite different from the information sent to midlevel managers and low-level personnel. Senior executives should receive short, high-level summary information, such as press articles or one-page reviews. Midlevel managers should be sent more detailed case studies from other successful customers and analysts' white papers. Low-level, hands-on product evaluators should receive data sheets, user manuals, and detailed implementation guides. In chapter 6 we'll discuss in detail strategies to penetrate the C-level executive suite.

Bombardment is an excellent "beachhead tactic" to use when you are trying to develop some recognition and credibility with particular individuals before you contact them personally. As opposed to the wave attack, where many colleagues are involved, bombardment is executed solely by the salesperson, so it's far more efficient and far less risky.

Retreat Tactics

It takes a lot of discipline to walk away from an account that has involved a heavy investment of time, energy, and emotions. Knowing how to retreat from an account where you have little chance of winning is just as important as knowing when to stop working on the deal. Each of the three different types of retreat tactics is used to accomplish a different purpose.

Scorched Earth   A scorched-earth sales tactic involves using any means necessary to stop the deal from happening. At this point you are not trying to win the deal anymore; you are only trying to prevent the other vendors from winning. This is an extreme measure of last resort. Examples include calling the customer's senior management and explaining that the selection process was biased because decision makers had improper relationships with the winning vendor, complaining to interested outside parties (regulatory boards, media outlets, financial investors, and the general public) about misconduct during the selection process, seeking legal action to stop the purchase, and offering to provide your product at a greatly reduced price or even for free.

Parthian Shot Ancient Parthian horse archers employed an interesting tactic to harass their enemies. They would start to retreat from the enemy at full gallop, then stop and turn sharply to fire their arrows. The term "parting shot" refers to this tactic.

In sales, a Parthian shot is a sharp, telling remark or critical communication made by a retreating salesperson to strike a blow at the senior executives' confidence in the decision they made. Examples include warnings about failed customer installations, critical memorandums sent to executives about the selection team members' competence, or predictions about the future failure of the project.

AWOL "Absent without leave" is a military term for soldiers who are away from their posts or military duties without permission. In sales, it quite often makes sense for salespeople who suspect they are losing to go AWOL and disappear. Doing so forces an interested customer to pursue the salesperson. For example, when a lower-level employee asks for information, the salesperson will not provide it until he gets a face-to-face meeting with the senior executives. Doing nothing sometimes frustrates the members of the selection team who are working against the salesperson as it forces them to spend additional time dealing with this disruptive person. Other times, it is exactly what they would like to have happen. They want the salesperson and his solution to quietly disappear.

Should We Pursue the Deal?

The most important goal is to occupy the fortress at the end of the sales cycle. However, many times the salesperson who wins has occupied that position from the beginning even before the formal selection process began. Therefore, we must ask ourselves, "Should we pursue the deal?"

As a general rule, it is best to be the first salesperson in an account. The chance to understand a customer's environment first, establish executive relationships, and set the criteria for the selection process is an obvious advantage. If you are the first salesperson in the account, the only obstacle that can prevent you from successfully completing your strategy is the customer.

However, it's not always possible to find a customer first, and sometimes arriving first doesn't even matter. What matters is the strength of your position versus that of the competition. You can define your strength compared to your competitor's in one of three ways: you have the advantage, you are equal, or you are outclassed. And the three basic types of strength are relationship (the personal relationships you have built in the account), product (the technical merits of your product and the associated perception of your company in the marketplace), and personnel (the quality and quantity of people who are at your disposal to work on the account).

Defining your account strength can be tricky for two reasons. First, your marketing department's job is to pump out volumes of propaganda proclaiming that every aspect of the company and its product is superior to that of the competition. Therefore, your product's true strength can be ascertained only with direct customer feedback gained in past sales cycles.

The second reason is a little more complex. While salespeople will say they are directly responsible for winning a deal, the natural tendency is to blame losses on something other than themselves. In essence, the true strength of your competitive position directly correlates to the percentage of deals you win.

The only way to accurately gauge how you stack up personally against the enemy is in head-to-head confrontations. Therefore, you must make it a point to know which salesperson from the competition is working on the account. It's not enough to know you are competing against XYZ Company. You want to know you are competing against John Smith, the local salesperson from XYZ Company. This information is relatively easy to find out, but most salespeople don't even ask. You can ask the customer the question outright or soften it by saying "I've run into John Smith of XYZ Company occasionally" and waiting for a response.

The decision on whether or not to pursue an account can be a difficult one. One deciding factor is who has set the tempo in the account—you or another competitor. This is particularly important when your product has a long sales cycle that requires a large investment of your time and your company's resources. Basing the decision on an honest assessment of competitive strength is critical. For example, you should pursue accounts where you have established personal relationships. If you enjoy product and personnel advantages, you should almost always pursue an account, even if you are late into the deal. If you have product and personnel disadvantages, you must be first into the account to win. If you are on equal footing with the competition, you must be on time at the start of the evaluation process in order to build a relationship advantage. Figure 4.6 illustrates the tempo rules (when you should arrive in accounts) when your products and personnel are at an advantage, equal to, or at a disadvantage to your competitor's.

Obviously, many combinations are possible. The decision to work on an account or walk away from it shouldn't be made solely by the salesperson; it's always wise to get outsiders' opinions. The best people to help you make this call are your sales manager and the other members of your team who would work on the account with you. Not only is the personnel attribute a comparison of you against the salesperson you are competing directly against, but it also involves the availability, quality, and commitment of your team members (technical presales support, consultants, and management) to win the account. Therefore, it makes sense to get their buy-in before you move forward on any account.

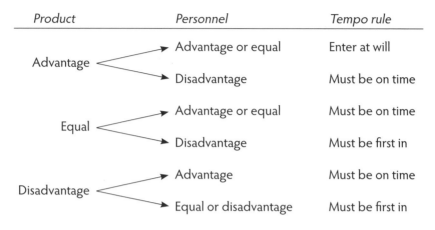

Product	Personnel	Tempo rule
Advantage	Advantage or equal	Enter at will
	Disadvantage	Must be on time
Equal	Advantage or equal	Must be on time
	Disadvantage	Must be first in
Disadvantage	Advantage	Must be on time
	Equal or disadvantage	Must be first in

Figure 4.6 When to pursue the deal

Once you're engaged in the deal, setting the tempo takes on a new meaning. While a good defense may keep you in the deal, the only way to win is to be on the offense. However, the other competitors also want to control the tempo of the deal and execute their offensive plans. Meanwhile, the customer wants to dictate the steps that will be taken during the selection process and keep control of the various vendors so they don't run slipshod through the company.

Setting the tempo is the first step in winning the war. Never forget, the only two appropriate positions to be in at the end of the deal are first place, as the winner, or last place, as the first loser. Every place in between is the result of a judgment error.

The sales cycle has a natural evolution. The first step for customers is to gather information from each vendor. As they gather more information, one vendor begins to look better than the others, its product sounds like it will work better, and the customers feel this vendor will be a better partner. Naturally, that vendor will enjoy an advantage throughout the remainder of the sales cycle.

However, customers have a dilemma. They still want to collect information from the other vendors to be 100 percent certain they are selecting the right vendor. Or they may want to complete the evaluation process to show others within or outside their organization (management, colleagues, consultants, or government agencies) that their evaluation was thorough and fair. As a result, they offer the other vendors the customer placebo.

The customer placebo is present in literally every sales cycle. One vendor is in a unique position of receiving information from the customer that the other vendors don't receive. As this favored vendor and the customer spend more time together, a higher level of rapport is developed. While this is happening, the customer is presenting misleading information to the other vendors about their position in the deal, pretending to be more interested in the products than he actually is. Conversely, he may not share critical information or access to company executives as he does with the leading vendor. Unfortunately, the other vendors continue to spend additional resources and their time and effort on the account when they have virtually no chance of winning.

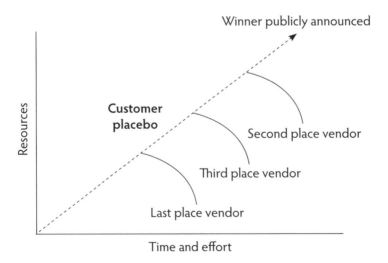

Figure 4.7 The customer placebo

Timing plays an important role in every account. You must get inside the fortress first so you can take advantage of this strategic position. This is the only place where you have continual contact with C-level executives. If you aren't in the fortress, you must embark on a mission to remove the competitor who occupies it as soon as possible because customers make up their minds very early in the sales cycle.

Conclusion

This entire chapter was structured with metaphors—analogies about war, personal stories, anecdotes, figures, graphs, and comments from C-level executives. Metaphors are more than simple anecdotes or interesting fairy tales. Their purpose is to tell, teach, and enlighten listeners or readers with the ultimate goal of changing their behavior. Metaphors facilitate the learning process by enabling people to understand new concepts in terms they already know, and they quickly communicate complex ideas.

Metaphors are also a special persuasion technique that can be used to help people bring about change. They can be used to influence beliefs, opinions, and attitudes. The primary metaphor of the chapter was the comparison of waging a sales campaign to warfare. In this regard, your most important goal is to penetrate the fortress where the C-level executives reside.

More importantly, metaphors are language structures with multiple layers of personal interpretation. They connect logical and psychological meaning together. While on the surface they provide logical stories that the conscious mind follows, their deeper layers can evoke memories, provide insights on how to handle life's problems, and impart suggestions that percolate in the subconscious mind.

One of the main responsibilities of the subconscious mind is protection. Much like a guardian angel, it's on the lookout for perilous situations and possible circumstances that might endanger the person physically and mentally. To perform this task, it assumes a third-person observation role and acts as a separate entity even though it resides deep inside the individual. Metaphors provide both a content-level message for the conscious mind and an invisible suggestion for the subconscious mind.

Metaphors are one of the most powerful persuasion tools at your disposal. The stories you tell executive decision makers about customers who are using your product, your company's future plans, and why you chose to work at your company are powerful metaphors. Even the way you dress, present yourself, and represent your product provides important symbolism to the customer. In reality, you are a walking, talking metaphor.

> It was a great presentation they gave. Their people knew the industry and told story after story about their customers. They knew our hot spots inside and out.
>
> CHIEF ADMINISTRATIVE OFFICER

5

Consider

ORGANIZATIONAL BUYING PSYCHOLOGY AND VALUE

> They were completely unwilling to think outside the box with us. We consider ourselves unique, so we like the people we work with to treat us differently. I don't know whether it was because the salesperson was so bad or the fact that their company is so rigid that they wouldn't even entertain it. After I told them we weren't moving forward with them, I almost got this autoresponse "We're sorry to hear that; keep us in mind; blah, blah, blah." I thought, "Don't you want to know why, you idiot?"
>
> CHIEF FINANCIAL OFFICER

October 18, 2012, at 4:36 p.m. eastern standard time will be a very special moment for planet Earth. That's the moment its population is estimated to reach 7 billion people.[1] But though billions of people are living in the world, you are unique. No one else has your fingerprints, and the retinal patterns of your eyes are one of a kind. No one looks exactly like you or shares your specific combination of facial features, body shape, and distinguishing physical marks. No one else has your precise disposition, philosophy about life, and sense of humor. Not one person thinks exactly like you do because no one on the planet has exactly the same life experiences and set of memories.

The customers you communicate with every day are equally unique. They have different backgrounds, attitudes, and levels of intelligence. They have diverse career goals and different life aspirations. They are an extraordinary amalgamation of individual thoughts, dreams, needs, wants, and desires. The next customer you have to call upon is like no other customer you've ever met.

Customers work in one-of-a-kind companies that are conglomerations of diverse groups of people who have different goals for their careers and various levels of power in the departments they work within and the company as a whole. Moreover, wherever there are groups of people, there will be differences in thinking and conflicting goals. As a result, politics and group psychology impact every decision that is made.

In this chapter we'll explore the buying psychology of organizations and how it is influenced by the C-level executive in charge. We'll also talk about three of the most important people involved in every sales cycle: the coach, the bully with the juice, and the emperor. These are people who help you and who will ultimately make and approve the decision.

Organizational Buying Types

If you are involved in selling an enterprise solution, you already know the importance of understanding the inner workings of the various departments within a company. Your product might be purchased by the information technology department and used by accounting and manufacturing. It might be selected by accounting and used by marketing, research and development, and other functional areas of the organization. Or it could be selected by sales and bought by the purchasing department. Almost every purchase decision requires multiple departments to become involved. Therefore, it's critical to map out the interrelationships of the departments within an organization, and most importantly, the power of the C-level executive who heads the department involved in the selection process. (I use Mindjet's MindManager mapping software [www.mindjet.com] to visualize these interrelationships.)

As a consultant, I have performed win-loss sales analysis studies for a variety of companies in many different industries. To complete these studies, I conducted blind surveys of the senior executives, departmental managers, and low-level evaluators who had selected or rejected the product from the company for which I was performing the study.

While the purpose of these studies was to improve the sales force's effectiveness, interesting patterns of organization behavior became apparent. These patterns supersede the standard hierarchical organization chart that salespeople have grown accustomed to studying.

Four models can be used to define the departmental interrelationships that influence a company's buying behavior: departments—and the executives who lead them—are either consolidators, consulters, responders, or bureaucrats. However, before we analyze each type of department, we must first define some company roles.

Liaisons serve as intermediaries between departments. There are business liaisons, whose official function is to ensure a department is working well and satisfies the needs of the other departments within the organization. Business liaisons are the intermediaries that translate business needs between departments. In larger companies, common business liaison titles are "business analyst," "project manager," "facilitator," and "technical consultant." In smaller companies, the role of liaison usually is filled by departmental managers.

In one sense, every department within a company is a customer of every other department. And every department has very sophisticated users of the services of other departments. For example, the sales department has sales operations staff members who depend upon information from the finance department. The manufacturing department has technical personnel who use information from research and development.

The employees who fill the positions described above are called "power users." To accomplish their departmental roles, power users are required to have an intimate knowledge of their department as well as other departments. Or they must use the systems, information, equipment, or resources from another department to complete their jobs. Typical power users might have titles that include "specialist," "technician," "support," "administrator," or "coordinator."

Roles in a company can be divided into three basic categories: product, management, and executive. The product category includes those individuals who work hands on with your product. These people use vendors' products to create new products for their companies. For example, a telephone operator creates communication (a product) by using telephone equipment provided by vendors. A security officer safeguards assets (a product) by using surveillance equipment from vendors. People within the product category have titles that explain exactly what they do, such as "computer programmer," "buyer," "mechanic," and "receptionist."

Individuals in the management category provide direction to one of the various departments of an organization. These departments are organized around functional areas of the company (finance, sales, marketing, manufacturing, and so on). Typically, people in this category may have "director," "manager," "supervisor," or "leader" in their titles.

In larger companies, the executive category is composed of people who have the word "president" or "chief" or "vice president" in their titles, such as the vice president of finance, chief customer care officer, and chief technology officer. In smaller companies, the executive level may also include individuals with "director" in their titles.

The four departmental types (consolidators, consulters, responders, and bureaucrats) have different orientations toward the operation of their departments. Most importantly, they buy products in different ways and for completely different purposes. It is important to understand that any department can be any type of buyer. For example, the finance department may be a consolidator at one company and a consulter at the next. Sometimes, the type of department may be associated with a specific business goal. For example, the finance department may be a consolidator when driving a project to complete Sarbanes-Oxley compliance and a responder when asked to assemble information for a sales department–driven project.

Consolidators

Consolidators are departments that have C-level executives who seek to increase their power, authority, or control within their organization. To grow their sphere of influence, they launch grand initiatives, major company-wide projects that affect the operations of other departments.

The planning and creation of a grand initiative are at the direction of the department's executive leadership. This type of project does not percolate up from lower-level personnel through the chain of command; it is driven down from the top and out to the rest of the company.

Figure 5.1 illustrates a consolidator's flow of power. In this example, the vice president of the information technology department has decided to drive an initiative to move all applications and programs off the company's aging mainframe computers onto new, less-expensive computer systems. After making this executive decision, he mandates that his direct managers fulfill his wishes. These direct reports assemble teams to plan the project and evaluate the vendors. The business liaisons who report back to the information technology department gather information from the various departments, schedule vendor demonstrations with departmental power users, and serve as intermediaries between the various departments during project implementation.

Notice that the boxes representing manufacturing and engineering are smaller than the information technology box and that the business liaisons box is larger than the power users boxes. This indicates who is more dominant and has superior power. The sizes of the boxes are different in the illustrations of the other types of departmental buyers.

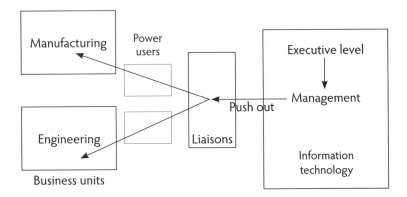

Figure 5.1 Consolidator buyer model

The underlying motivation behind grand initiatives like this one is always power, whether it's to gain more, consolidate it, or decrease that of other leaders and their departments within the organization. In the example above, the information technology department is exercising its power over manufacturing and engineering. Sometimes a grand initiative is an executive-level coup, an internal revolution intended to change the way the company operates. Many times, it is a well-orchestrated conspiracy in the guise of a logical business project. Other times, it is an act of revenge against an intercompany archenemy.

Consolidators are typically a salesperson's dream because they have a propensity to make things happen. "Big-bang consolidators" tend to buy all the equipment and services they need to complete a grand initiative all at once. "Cautious consolidators," on the other hand, purchase the products and services they need piecemeal, taking one small step at a time in order to prove their project's success.

> The decision was made in a vacuum at the highest levels of our organization. The CEO had previous experience with both vendors. He said one had worked very well for him. He said that's what we need here and we're going forward with it.
>
> CHIEF FINANCIAL OFFICER

Consulters

Consulters are departments with C-level executives who have the characteristics and attributes of a consultant to their organization. They seek to understand the problems of other departments and offer recommendations on how those problems can be solved using their services.

They proactively share their proprietary knowledge and departmental expertise or offer unsolicited advice to other departments in an attempt to show how they can improve efficiency. Therefore, they are continually polling the other departments, seeking opportunities to promote their services, and pushing out their ideas, philosophies, and opinions. Liaisons are vitally important to consulters because they are gatherers and disseminators of information. As a result, liaisons have more power and influence with consulters than they do with consolidators.

Consulters are more prevalent in massive multibillion-dollar companies than in smaller organizations. The C-level executives are less powerful than their counterparts in the consolidator model, so they have to achieve their desired outcomes through finesse rather than brute force. Since consulters are constantly seeking customers for their services, the power users are more likely to be within the consulter's department than in another business unit.

Figure 5.2 shows the information flow of a consulter department. In this example, the information technology department liaisons are constantly polling the business units for their needs and pushing out information they believe is beneficial.

For example, a liaison may seek out and meet with the vice president of sales, who expresses his dissatisfaction with the timeliness of the sales forecasting system. The liaison takes this information back to his department, and it traverses up the chain of command to where a decision is made to investigate new sales forecasting solutions. Conversely, a liaison may hear about an exciting new technology from the chief technology officer. The liaison schedules a meeting with the

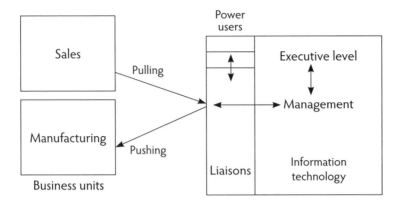

Figure 5.2 Consulter buyer model

technology vendor to learn more information. He then sets meetings with his constituents (power users of his department's services) in manufacturing to explain how the new technology may improve their operations.

Like a consultant hired on an hourly basis, consulters seek to continually validate their benefits and justify their existence to their customers. Selling to consulters differs from selling to consolidators because consulters enjoy the company of other consultants.

> We quite often find ourselves in the position of being the functional champion proactively showing solutions to the business that can help. We try to introduce new things to the business. We're always saying "Hey, could this help you?" We want their people to see something so we can get some champions behind it.
>
> VICE PRESIDENT OF INFORMATION TECHNOLOGY

Responders

Responders are weak departments with C-level executives who operate under the direction of other departments. Whereas consolidators seek to gain power and consulters seek to proliferate their services, responders are just trying to survive. Many times, responders are literally under attack from other departments that are unable to meet their objectives because of the responders' ineffectiveness. In some cases, the other departments have been disappointed by the responders' past blunders. As a result, responders tend to be treated disrespectfully and suffer from a lack of departmental esteem.

Figure 5.3 illustrates the power flow of a responder, in this case a marketing department. Once again, the sizes of the boxes reflect the departments' dominance and control. The power users can be very powerful in the responder model. In this example, the marketing department is the whipping boy of sales, constantly enduring that department's criticisms. Important power users within the sales organization complain to management that their needs aren't being met. In turn, senior executives dictate their needs to midlevel managers, who relay the message to marketing liaisons. In this instance, the liaisons' main goal is to run interference on behalf of their department, sorting out the most important requests while trying to maintain a semblance of departmental decorum. For issues of extreme

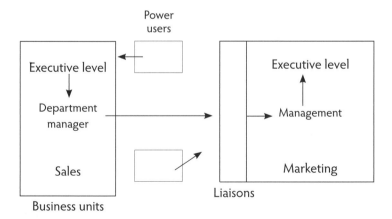

Figure 5.3 Responder buyer model

importance and urgency, senior executives of a business unit will call their counterparts in marketing directly and tell them to get something done. The power is clearly on the business unit side.

When selling to a responder, you must sell to the business unit as well as the responder, whereas with consulters and consolidators, your main sales effort should be directed inside their departments. For example, let's assume the sales department is complaining about lead generation (as always) and your company provides outbound telemarketing services. You need to make both the business unit (sales department) and the responder (marketing department) aware of your services.

> At the end of the day, a project will or won't get approved depending upon who is pushing it.
>
> PRESIDENT

Bureaucrats

The final category of departmental buyer is bureaucrats with C-level executives whose most important priority is to maintain the status quo through rules, regulations, and delaying tactics. The features of a bureaucrat department are secretiveness, a response system that reflexively rebuffs demands made upon the department, and administrative centralization around the senior leader, the archbureaucrat.

The structured environment, similar to a military command-and-control environment, stamps out innovative thinking within lower levels of the department and hinders the free flow of information from other departments. Instead, the bureaucratic monarchy considers other departments outsiders and issues edicts that must be complied with for fear of consequences.

Figure 5.4 illustrates the shield that bureaucratic buyers erect around their department. In this example, the purchasing department dictates to the manufacturing department what products it will use. Meanwhile, the engineering department's recommendation is

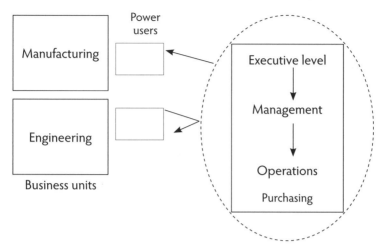

Figure 5.4 Bureaucrat buyer model

rejected, even though it is in the best interest of the company. One point to note is the lack of liaisons; the bureaucrat buyer is inwardly focused and less concerned about sensing the needs of other departments.

Every enterprise-wide sale involves consolidators, consulters, responders, and bureaucrats. You must determine a project's well-spring to know to whom and how to sell your solution. For example, at one company, every employee had to undergo ergonomics training on the proper way to use computers. Based on just this information, you might assume that the driver behind this company-wide initiative was the human resources department and that the vice president of human resources was a consolidator. However, human resources was actually a consulter, working on this project at the direction of the CFO (the real consolidator). He instigated this project so that the company would qualify for reduced insurance premium rates.

> If I don't believe the business case, then I reserve the right to exercise my veto. Even though another executive wants to do it, I have to believe the business case or I will resist it. It's not like I have an ax

to grind with R&D, marketing, or sales, but I have to remain independent and wear my corporate hat. I also have the duty to say no
when the level of change represents an unacceptable level of risk.

VICE PRESIDENT OF FINANCE

Here's an exercise that will help you understand where you win
and why you lose. Write down the company names of your last five
major wins and note whether the account was a consolidator, consulter, responder, or bureaucrat organizational buying type. Then
grade the access and relationships you had developed with the C-level
executives at the account from A (excellent) to F (none). Then write
down the same information for five major losses or no-decision deals.
Most often, you will find the losses were with completely different
organizational buying types than the wins. For example, if most of
your wins were with consolidators, most of your losses were probably with another type, such as consulters or responders. You will also
quickly realize that the grades you give to your losses are way below
those you gave your wins.

Successfully selling to the C level requires that you understand
the organizational power of the executive you are trying to close. His
power will determine whether or not he is a consolidator, consulter,
responder, or bureaucrat. Also, executive power has a pattern. When
a C-level executive joins a new company, he is a consolidator who is
on a mission to establish authority by laying out his agenda of change
and the projects that are necessary to implement that change (which
involves making purchases). This is one of the major reasons why you
should keep track of executives on the move in your industry and be
the first to call on them.

Conversely, an executive who has been at a company for many
years has an entirely different motivation for becoming a consolidator. He wants to leave his mark on the organization. He wants to
leave a lasting legacy with the employees, with the company, and even
within the industry.

Over time, a consolidator C-level executive will lose power. The projects and initiatives he championed will have less-than-spectacular results and fail to live up to their hype. As a result, he has to change his style and demeanor within the organization to accomplish his goals and therefore becomes a consulter. As he continues to lose organizational power he becomes a responder. Finally, in an effort to get some power back he becomes a bureaucrat C-level executive, as figure 5.5 illustrates.

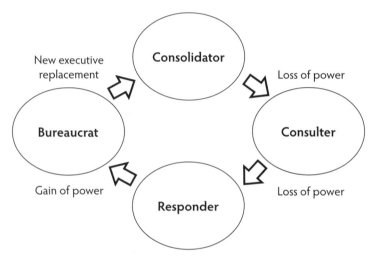

Figure 5.5 The evolution of C-level executive power

Finally, the executive team tires of working with the difficult bureaucrat and the members make a decision to change the departmental leader. They hire a new C-level executive who has a vision, a plan, and the power to change the department. The new executive is a consolidator, and the whole process repeats itself.

Types of Product Value

Because executive leaders of consolidator, consulter, responder, and bureaucrat departments have different levels of power and motivations, they have different perceptions of a product's true value. The perceived value of a product depends on the psychological, political, operational, and strategic value it provides the executive decision makers.

Psychological Value

Customers spend far more time living with their decisions than they do making the decisions. In fact, the decision to start a project or buy a particular product is usually made before the official decision-making process even begins. At the root of every decision is one of four psychological values. People buy products they believe will help them fulfill deep-seated psychological needs: satisfying the ego, being accepted as part of a group, avoiding pain, and ensuring survival. All the other outward appearances of a customer's decision-making process—the analysis, return-on-investment calculations, and other internal studies—are the means to achieving an overriding psychological goal. Therefore, the psychological value is the most important value when it comes to purchasing decisions.

Selling requires capturing the hearts and minds of customers based upon a strategy that takes into account the emotions of the decision maker as well as the logical reasons to buy. Customers aren't completely logical decision makers in the real world. The final decision-making process is a blend of human nature and logical rationalization. At the foundation of all sales is a relationship between people. The interaction between these people, the intangible part of the sales process, is ultimately responsible for the decision being made. Logic and reason play secondary roles.

Customers do not establish vendor relationships based upon the best business judgment; rather, they judge vendors based upon who establishes the best business relationships. A CIO I interviewed said it best: "We made it clear that we weren't buying a brochure or data sheet. For that matter, we weren't even buying a product. We were buying a long-term relationship with another company and, equally important, the team of people from that company whom we would have to work with on a day-in, day-out basis."

The grand strategy of selling your product is based upon the indirect strategy of selling to human nature. Figure 5.6 illustrates the three components of selling to human nature: customers' psychological needs and customers' opinions of you and your competitors.

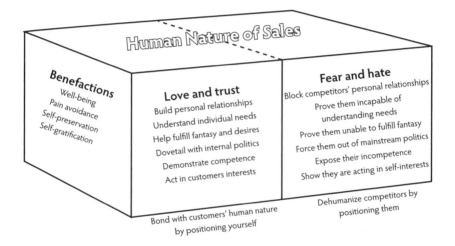

Figure 5.6 The human nature of sales

On the left-hand side of the block are benefactions, the customers' psychological needs. The term "benefaction" refers to the psychological benefits that determine a person's actions. Customers purchase products that increase their happiness, esteem, power, or wealth. They rationalize these psychological decisions with logic and facts. For example, a vice president of a manufacturing company may explain that he wants to buy a new conveyor system because it will save a million dollars a year when, in reality, he is making the purchase to show the CEO that he is a prudent fiscally conservative businessman. The desire to impress the CEO (the benefit) drives the conveyor system purchase (the action).

Four core psychological drives determine selection behavior. These four benefactions are well-being, pain avoidance, self-preservation, and self-gratification.

Physical well-being, the will to survive, is one of our strongest desires. It weighs heavily in the minds of both customers and competitors. Making customers feel their jobs are safe in your hands is a top priority. Ideally, you would like them to believe (whether it is true or not) that the competitive solutions are actually threats to their livelihood. Maneuvering the competitors into a life-threatening position in an account such that they are forced to make a direct attack on you will bolster your claims. It's also important to note that customers are equally concerned with maintaining their mental and emotional well-being.

When something is hurting you badly, the desire to eliminate the source of pain can be all-consuming. Pain is one of the best purchase motivators because customers are forced to act quickly and decisively to eliminate it. Similarly, a salesperson who is being harangued by his boss about a longstanding account that won't close is experiencing pain. You must exploit both of these pains, often by controlling the tempo of the sales cycle. Sometimes it makes sense to speed up the sales cycle, and at other times it is better to slow it down. For example, quickly assembling a "SWAT team" of personnel and showing how you can solve a customer's distressing situation will lock out the competition. Conversely, slowing down the sales cycle can cause a frustrated opponent to make a rash mistake.

We naturally seek the approval of others. Self-preservation, the desire to be recognized for our unique talents while still belonging to a group, applies to customers and salespeople alike. Customers purchase items that they believe will enhance their stature and protect their group position. They not only want to be respected by their peers, but also want to become group leaders. Naturally, salespeople want to be pack leaders too.

Everyone has a selfish ego, and self-gratification is our desire to put our own needs before everyone else's. Customers will go to great lengths to purchase something that makes them feel better about themselves and superior to others. Egos drive the business world. Unfortunately, most salespeople are taught to sell solutions based upon customer pain when, in fact, ego and self-preservation are the real motivators behind large enterprise sales.

The list below reveals the true reasons why customers buy your product. It's not your product's performance, ease of use, or efficiency that customers are in love with. It's you. Therefore, your priorities should be to earn their love and trust by understanding their personal needs, desires, and fantasies. You must know if they are just trying to hold onto a job, prop up their importance, or bring about a long-awaited promotion. Once you understand these desires, you become part of the customers' political landscape, aligned with the decision-making process. Consider these customer statements:

- I have big career ambitions.
- I want to be powerful.
- I'm risk averse.
- I want to leave a legacy.
- I want my team to be happy.
- I'm naturally skeptical of vendors.
- I like to be part of a group.
- I want the security of a marketable skill.
- I want that promotion.
- I want to keep my job.
- I'm worried about the competition.
- I am tired of working hard.
- I like new challenges.

- I want to please others.
- I want to be important.
- I want to make a difference.
- I like you!

Your grand strategy is to dehumanize the enemy by differentiating yourself personally. In other words, you want customers to view you as the only person who can address their personal needs, solve their business problems, and help them achieve their career hopes and life's desires. You want them to sincerely believe that you are the only person who is truly acting in their best interests.

People connect with others very quickly, and first impressions can have a long-term impact. Customers tend to make snap judgments early in the sales cycle based upon whom they like and respect. By demonstrating your competence, you expose your competitors' incompetence. Knowing the details of how your product works and being able to answer customers' questions about your company are obviously vital parts of sales. However, the real questions to answer honestly are, "Compared to the salespeople I am competing with, how well do I know my solution?" and "Is my industry expertise an advantage, or is my weakness a disadvantage?" If the answer to either of these questions is not known, your fear of being outpositioned and blocked from the account by your competitors may come true.

Those who are feared are hated. You want customers to realize that your competitors are riskier than you, uncaring, deceitful, and unable to fulfill the customers' fantasies. However, you need to understand what fantasies are. Most people think that fantasies have to be really big, like "One day I will be on the cover of *Time* magazine." In fact, fantasies can be very small. Some people think of fantasies only in a sexual context, when in reality most fantasies are quite mundane. Fantasies are just unfulfilled wishes. For example, you might wish to finish this book quickly. Until it's fulfilled, this wish is one of your many fantasies. You also might want to make $500,000 next year. That's a bigger, longer-term fantasy.

C-level executive fantasies can be big or small, specific or general. For example, the CEO might wish to leave work on time today in order to be home for an important family dinner. The vice president of North American sales might want to become the vice president of worldwide sales. The CFO might want to become the president and chairman of the board someday. Each of these fantasies has a different scope and duration.

Before a sales call starts, silently remind yourself that one of your objectives is to determine the fantasies of all the participants. Try to theorize what their short- and long-term fantasies are. Go ahead and make a deep psychological diagnosis about what is driving each person's fantasy. A person who wants a promotion to vice president to gain more power is quite different from someone who is seeking the promotion for personal validation or a bigger paycheck.

Remember, customers have many different types of fantasies and quite often they need help from vendors to fulfill them. Therefore, ignoring customers' fantasies is a big mistake. You must tap into them before your competitors do. However, customers will not usually broadcast their fantasies aloud. It's up to you to figure them out and convince the customers that only through your solution can their fantasies be realized.

When you have built relationships, demonstrated competence, and proved that you can fulfill fantasies, you will naturally dovetail with the internal politics of the decision-making process. Most importantly, using the indirect strategy of selling to the human nature of customers forces your competitors to use the direct strategy and sell based upon the products themselves. Because the indirect strategy is stronger, you put your competitors in a position of weakness.

Regardless of the complexity of your product or the sophistication of your customers, the final decision maker is always human nature. To validate this statement, all you have to do is think back to the deals you have lost when your product and price were best. You came in second place because you had third-rate C-level executive relationships.

Political Value

The second most important value, political value, involves organizational power. Many people think that power is dependent upon title and that the way work gets done in organizations is through hierarchical authority. However, this is not usually the case. Power is the ability to influence the environment for your own benefit. It is often used to get your way when diplomacy, consensus building, and negotiation fail. For example, while I have parental authority over my children, they have their own types of powers and associated strategies to get their way. Sometimes they will band together and recruit their mother to support their cause in order to override my authority. Companies operate in much the same way.

Your product provides customers the opportunity to achieve political power. It may enable consolidators to increase their authority, help consulters become indispensable to the company, allow responders to satisfy an internal powerbroker, or enable bureaucrats to maintain authority. Interdepartmental coordination always involves the use of power. Your product can make someone more powerful, or for those seeking to become more influential, it can provide much-needed visibility that enables them to be in contact with the company's powerbrokers.

Operational Value

The third most important value is operational value. People's success in an organization is dependent upon the success of their department's operations. Therefore, every department has inherent pressure to accomplish projects that successfully add operational value. The ways that operational value is determined are quite diverse. An ambitious consolidator might consider your product's operational value the ability to successfully complete the department's project. For a consulter, operational value might be that your product enables the department to proliferate its services throughout the company. Responders prize satisfying internal customers in other departments, and operational value to bureaucrats might be found in products that enable them to resist change. For example, a bureaucrat IT department might add a new Internet interface to its existing mainframe rather than replace the entire system.

Strategic Value

Strategic value, the fourth value, is based upon the appearance of rationality and impartiality. However, customers do not seek information that will help them make an objective strategic decision; they amass information that helps them justify their preconceived ideas of strategic value. In other words, your product's strategic value comprises the reasons and arguments evaluators give to senior management and others in the company as to why the product should be purchased, regardless of whether the reasons are real or imagined. The seven types of strategic value enable customers to

- Gain a competitive advantage (increase market share, enter new markets, defeat competition)
- Increase revenues
- Decrease costs
- Increase productivity and efficiency
- Improve customer satisfaction
- Improve quality
- Standardize operations (increase ease of business)

Consolidators will say that a purchase provides a competitive advantage or will enable them to increase revenues. Consulters might argue that a purchase will save money in the long run. Responders will show how customer satisfaction will be improved, and bureaucrats will detail improvements in operational efficiency.

Figure 5.7 summarizes how consolidators, consulters, responders, and bureaucrats view each of the four different types of value.

	Consolidaters	Consulters	Responders	Bureaucrats
Psychological value	Self-gratification Fulfill desire to achieve	Physical well-being Satisfy will to survive	Self-preservation Gain approval of others	Pain avoidance Avoid painful change
Political value	Consolidate power	Become indispensable	Draft off the powerful	Maintain authority
Operational value	Enable the grand initiative	Proliferate service offerings through organization	Reactively accommodate internal customers	Do as little as possible
Strategic value	Gain competitive advantage Increase revenues	Improve quality Decrease costs	Improve customer satisfaction Improve productivity and efficiency	Standardize operations Maintain ease of business

Figure 5.7 Different types of value based on type of buyer

The Bully with the Juice and the Emperor

Another interesting characterization of the people who are involved in the product selection process is displayed in figure 5.8, which represents four different characteristics that a person can be measured against.

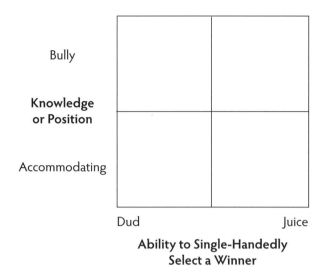

Figure 5.8 Characteristics of evaluators

The left axis is a person's insistence that things be done his way. This is called being a "bully." A bully will get his way at any and all costs. Being called a bully is not necessarily a negative term, nor does it mean that the person is physically intimidating. It is simply the description of people who will tenaciously fight for their cause. Also, people are more likely to be bullies when they have an elevated status within the evaluation team. The status could be the result of their domain expertise or their title and the authority it commands.

At the other end of the spectrum are people who are accommodating. They are apathetic to whatever solution is purchased. The degree to which people are bullies or accommodating depends on the effect the purchase decision has on their span of control, position in the company, or ability to perform their jobs.

On the horizontal axis is the concept of "juice" and the "dud." Simply put, juice is charisma. But even this definition is too simple. Some people are natural-born leaders. They have an aura that can motivate and instill confidence. That's juice. Juice is fairly hard to describe, but you know it when you see it.

Having juice does not mean that these people act like superheroes, nor are they always necessarily the highest-ranking people involved in an evaluation. Instead, they are the ones who always seem to be on the winning side. Only one member of the customer's evaluation team has the juice. Single-handedly, he imparts his own will on the selection process by single-handedly selecting the vendor and pushing the purchase through the procurement process. He can either finalize the purchase terms or instruct the procurement team on the terms that are considered acceptable. With large enterprise purchases, the bully with the juice is almost always a C-level executive.

> If you don't have strong business sponsorship at the right level, you are dead in the water.
>
> VICE PRESIDENT OF ADMINISTRATION

Duds are named after the ineffective fireworks they represent. Sometimes the fuse of a firework will burn down, but nothing will happen. Some fireworks may be very big but produce disappointing results. Duds talk big but take little action. "Accommodating duds" are people who do not take an active role in the sales process. Even worse are "dud bullies" who try to pretend they have juice but don't. For the salesperson, the realization of this situation may not come until too late.

For all the people involved in the sales selection process, you need to calculate their amount of juice and their propensity to be bullies. For example, John, Jim, Karl, and Rich are plotted by a salesperson who sells large-scale computer data storage equipment (figure 5.9). John is the senior purchasing agent. Jim is a network administrator. Karl is the director of information technology, and Rich is the CIO. They are going to make a $350,000 purchase.

As shown in figure 5.9, John is a dud bully, Jim is an accommodating dud, Rich has the juice, and Karl is accommodating to him.

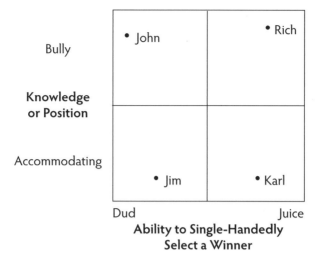

Figure 5.9 Plotting individual assessments

Even though Jim and Karl might conduct the vendor evaluations, their decision can be overridden by Rich. While they might have a vested interest in ensuring that their favorite vendor wins, you can assume their recommendation will match Rich's preference. His will may be imposed on the evaluation process through brute force or by finesse. Either way, his preference is "bullied" into the decision.

However, Rich, the CIO who has juice, probably doesn't care which toner cartridges are purchased for the company's laser printers. He will be accommodating and support the decision of the people who make that decision. Someone else has the juice for the procurement of toner cartridges. Many people have juice (charisma and authority), but only one person has the juice to single-handedly select the vendor.

Now let's assume Rich is making a $3.5 million software purchase. Once again, he is the bully with the juice and the evaluation team's recommendation matches the vendor he wants. However, he can't make a purchase of this magnitude by himself. It must be blessed by the "emperor."

In ancient Rome, the emperor would decide whether or not a beaten gladiator would live by gesturing with a thumb up or thumb down. Today, the life or death of enterprise purchases is decided in much the same way by a company president, CEO, chairman, or board of directors who have no personal attachments or vested interests in the purchase. Either this individual or the collective group will decide whether the funds should actually be spent. They will give a thumb up or down to release the funds to make the purchase, even though an exhausting evaluation of many months or even years may have been conducted by lower-level personnel.

Therefore, it is imperative that you truly understand the decision-making process and that you have an internal source of knowledgeable, reliable information to help you understand who the bully with the juice is and whether or not an emperor must ultimately approve the decision. You need someone to coach you through the sales cycle.

The Coach

Heavy Hitter salespeople know they need a constant, accurate source of information revealing the internal machinations of the customer's selection process. For many years, the term "coach" has been used by all types of salespeople, selling every conceivable product, to define the person who provides this inside information. Coaches are individuals who provide accurate information about the sales cycle and competition to you.

Think about all the relationships you have in your life—deep close relationships with friends you have known most of your life, casual relationships with colleagues and coworkers, and new relationships with customers. Regardless of how they were formed, all relationships share similar underlying characteristics. In order to find and recruit a coach, it is first necessary to understand the nature of friendships.

A big difference exists between a friend and an acquaintance. An acquaintance is someone with whom you have a cordial relationship. While the relationship is friendly, the unspoken understanding is that neither person will demand significant time of the other to maintain the relationship. Conversely, a friend is someone who unselfishly invests time to maintain the relationship and derives enjoyment from doing so. An acquaintance is someone you know slightly, a well-wisher with whom you may have pleasant lunches and other social get-togethers. A friend is a trusted sympathizer and, more importantly, an active helper. A friend is someone whom you can call at midnight to help fix your flat tire.

Salespeople sometimes believe they have a coach when in reality they don't. Heavy Hitters know they have a coach when the person not only provides them with accurate information but also helps them by fighting for their cause. A true coach will represent and promote a salesperson's solution to his colleagues and, even better to senior executive leadership. Figure 5.10 shows the five different types of coaches and their respective value to a salesperson.

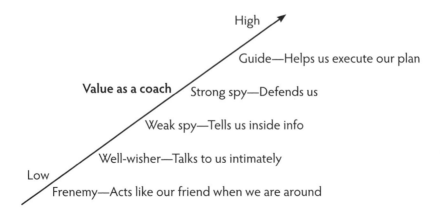

Figure 5.10 Different types of coaches

A frenemy is someone who befriends you so that you think he is a supporter. In reality, the frenemy is only acting the part and is truly an enemy who is against you. Frenemies are extremely dangerous because they lull you into a false sense of security that you are winning when they are really coordinating a plan to defeat you.

A well-wisher talks to you on an intimate, friendly basis. He provides information that you consider proprietary. However, the well-wisher is an extremely amiable person and is providing the same information to all the salespeople competing for the business.

Several specific conditions must exist in order for a friendly evaluator to be considered a valuable coach. First, coaches must have a personal reason for wanting you or your company to win. Second, coaches need to specifically say they want you to win. Ideally, they are willing to fight for your cause. Finally, the information coaches provide must be accurate.

Coaches can be either weak or strong spies. Weak spies are observers who provide you information about the internal machinations of the selection process. They report the thoughts of the various selection team members and the movements of other vendors. Strong spies are not only observers but disseminators of information as well. Strong spies have a deeper, more personal connection to you than weak spies do. They're more akin to confidants than acquaintances. In fact, they are trusted friends who will courageously defend you and your solution when you are not around to do so yourself.

Guides are your best friends. Not only are they confidants who provide all the inside details about the internal politics of decision making, but they also help you plan and execute your strategy to win the business. Guides are usually seasoned employees. They've worked at the company for quite some time and understand how to get things done. They have the business acumen and the experience to provide adept advice on how to win the deal and get the contract signed. Most importantly, after helping devise the wining game plan they play an integral part in executing it.

While in chapter 6 we'll discuss tactics to penetrate the C-level executive suite in new accounts where you don't have a coach, the most effective method of meeting senior executives is to have mid- and lower-level personnel introduce you to them. Finding a coach and developing him into a guide who cares about you so much that he strategizes with you about how to meet his boss's boss's boss is the most supreme example of the indirect strategy.

The ideal coach is the person with the highest authority or influence involved in the selection process. When this person becomes the coach, you will enjoy a unique advantage. For example, let's assume Rich, the CIO who is making the $350,000 purchase of storage technology, is your coach. Since he is the bully with the juice, you win! The next best scenario is when your coach can influence the bully with the juice.

However, the coach could be anybody inside the customer's company or even outside the company, such as a consultant working on the project. All of these advisors share a common characteristic. They have a selfish reason for wanting you or your company to win. This reason may range from the simple fact that they like you to the complicated nature of internal politics, where your solution helps them gain power, prestige, or authority.

Quite often, ordinary salespeople mistake someone for a coach when in fact the person isn't a loyal compatriot. You should always have a certain level of paranoia about your coach. Is he secretly coaching the competition? Is he acting as your eyes and ears when you are not around? Is he truthfully telling you about what the other vendors are up to and about the preferences of the various selection committee members? Is he providing privileged and proprietary information to you that the other vendors aren't receiving?

Obviously, the more coaches you have inside an account, the better the quality and quantity of information you will receive. The information you receive from these coaches can be used to determine your standing in an account and help determine your course of action.

Being at the mercy of a single person is a risky position to be in. What if your coach is wrong?

Conclusion

Knowledge is power, and this chapter was all about power. The power of the C-level executive will determine whether he is a consolidator, consulter, responder, or bureaucrat buying type. The more you know about the bully with the juice, the more power you have over your competitors.

You must secure proprietary knowledge about the accounts you are trying to close. You must have a coach to win a deal. Without one, you will never know the true nature of the organization and who has the real power.

Ideally, you want to develop your coach into a guide because the most effective method of meeting senior executives is for mid- and lower-level personnel to introduce you to them. This is also an ideal example of the indirect strategy—elegant, efficient, and effective. (In the next chapter we'll discuss how to penetrate the C-level suite when the account is brand new and you don't have a coach.)

The most important rule in all of sales is that you need a coach to win the deal. And the best coach is always the seniormost executive. Accurate information is the lifeblood of every deal, and the only way to get true information is through the use of a coach. As it is written in the book of Proverbs, "A wise man has great power, and a man of knowledge increases strength."[2]

> The initial decision was a no. The leadership committee didn't believe the contribution margin was high enough. I went back three months later and had it approved after talking with a number of their customers and building a better business case. The marketing people finally got on board and believed there would be incremental sales.
>
> VICE PRESIDENT OF CUSTOMER CARE

6

Contact

STRATEGIES TO PENETRATE THE C-LEVEL
EXECUTIVE SUITE

> I received an e-mail. I usually never bother with them. But this
> one caught my attention and I actually read the entire e-mail. I for-
> warded it to one of my managers and asked him to bring them in for
> a meeting.
>
> VICE PRESIDENT OF ENGINEERING

One of the toughest tasks in all of sales is to penetrate the C-level
executive suite. Take a moment to put yourself in the position
of the executive you are trying to contact. Your time is precious. You
are incredibly busy fulfilling your daily job duties and have a long
list of to-dos to be completed. You have superior executives (the
chairman, board of directors, and shareholders) whom you must
satisfy, employees who require attention, and unexpected fires that
need to be put out immediately. Given your frame of mind, it's easy
to understand why you wouldn't respond to a sales pitch from some
unknown salesperson.

Under these circumstances, the salesperson's job is to connect
with the busy executive and earn the right to a face-to-face meeting.
What is the best way to achieve this difficult goal? How can you win
over a complete stranger who has no interest in hearing from you?
How do you generate executive-level attention? The answers to these
questions start with understanding the nature of communication.

People communicate differently. These differences are directly related to biological factors such as intelligence, personality, and word

catalog wiring. Environmental factors, including childhood, education, and where people live also play an important role in shaping the ability to communicate. People's surroundings will also greatly impact their manner of speech. If you are in a library, for example, you will soften your voice to a whisper. However, your word selection and volume will be quite different if you are rooting for your favorite team at a football game.

The same principles hold true for the e-mails you send and phone calls you make. Personal e-mails and phone calls to friends will be more informal and natural, like free-flowing conversation. They will show your true word catalog wiring. Work-related e-mails and phone calls will be more structured, and the use of language is preplanned and regimented. Because of the internal dialogue's editing process in the business environment, much less of a person's word catalog wiring is "leaked" through the words that are written or spoken.

You have had a completely unique set of experiences in your life. And you have kept a record of your past existence by cataloging pictures, sounds, and feelings. As you make your way through your daily life, you are interacting with the outside world by repeatedly sending and receiving messages. Having the ability to send meaningful messages that are specifically targeted to C-level executives and correctly interpreted by them is necessary to achieve success. Figure 6.1 illustrates the C-level executive communication process.

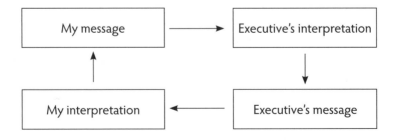

Figure 6.1 Communicating information to the C-level executive

People communicate with the purpose of achieving a specific bene-faction. As we discussed in chapter 5, benefactions are very personal prioritized psychological benefits. They are based upon pain avoidance, well-being, ego, and group leadership. For example, the goal of a sales-person is to win over the C-level executive. By doing so, he may achieve the benefaction of being the most respected salesperson in the com-pany or buying the new house he desperately wants. When he talks to customers and colleagues, he consciously and subconsciously centers all of the messages he sends around this benefaction.

When a C-level executive communicates with salespeople, he has an entirely different benefaction. He might be a consolidator with a huge ego who is driving a grand initiative, a consulter who desires to be a respected member of the executive team, a responder who is worried about keeping his job, or a paranoid bureaucrat who is trying to maintain control.

The sales cycle is nothing more than a formalized information-and-activity exchange. The customer is trying to gather as much in-formation as possible about vendors to determine if they can fulfill his benefaction and are appropriate long-term partners. Meanwhile, salespeople are trying to gather as much information as possible about the customer in order to determine if they can close the deal. Information is communicated back and forth, and each message that is sent must also be received and interpreted correctly.

However, an obstacle is inherent in this process. Since every mes-sage is subject to personal interpretation, how do you know when your message has been interpreted correctly? The most easily recognizable sign is that the executive takes the action you have suggested. In order to do so, the executive must understand what you were trying to say.

Comprehension

All communication consists of one of three types of messages—rec-reational, instructional, and frustrational. A recreational message is socially enjoyable communication. Examples include talking to a friend, listening to music, and reading a novel. This type of communication has the highest level of comprehension where the meaning, nature, and importance of the words are personally understood. At a minimum, 90 percent of the words are known and recognized.

Instructional messages are based on teaching, telling, or passing along knowledge. Instructional messages include directions, commands, advice, and even questions. When customers ask you questions, they are actually instructing you to give them the specific information they need. Instructional messages are sent during briefings, training sessions, chalk talks, and sales calls. However, they typically have a slightly lower level of comprehension than recreational communication—around 80 percent.

Frustrational messages include any type of communication that is either not understood or is considered objectionable to the recipient. Let's say you and I are having a conversation and I say that a friend of ours is a "loquacious misandrist." The level of rapport would drop if you did not know that these words meant "talkative man-hater."

Frustrational messages include offending or disagreeable messages. For example, a command given by someone who does not have greater expertise or authority over the recipient is a frustrational message. The inclination is not to follow it. Frustrational messages have the lowest level of comprehension, under 50 percent.

These three types of messages are interspersed throughout conversations, letters, and e-mails. For example, I may be talking to my wife on the phone about her day (recreational message) and she might ask me to stop by the store to pick up some groceries (instructional message). When she tells me to pick up some flipsides I become frustrated because I have no idea what they are.

In addition, comprehension requires that the message be conveyed at the recipient's communication level, not too far below or above the level of the words in his or her lexical dictionary.

Here's an exercise to determine your communication level. Gather at least ten different samples of your writing. These could be proposals, letters, reports, or e-mails. Cut and paste them into one Microsoft Word document. Under Tools click Options, then Spelling & Grammar. Check the "Show readability statistics" box. Now spell-check the entire document, and you will see your Flesch-Kincaid grade level index. (For additional step-by-step instructions, enter "Readability" in the Microsoft Word Help search.) The result is a number that corresponds to the grade level that you communicate at. For example, a score of 9.0 would indicate that the text is understandable by an average student in ninth grade.

I typically write at a Flesch-Kindcaid grade level score around 12. That is my natural communication level. It's also an appropriate communication level for my target audience. The majority of sales books that target business-to-consumer salespeople, who sell products like cars, are written at the sixth- to eighth-grade levels. Since my target market is business-to-business enterprise salespeople who typically have a university degree, a level of 12 is appropriate.

What is the communication level of the executives you sell to? If they have advanced degrees in computer science, engineering, or finance, are you communicating at their level? One way to find out is to perform Flesch-Kincaid grade level scoring on all their communications you can find on the Internet. Whether in person or via e-mail, you must make sure you are communicating at their level. If you use a level that is too low, you will not be respected and will never be in a position to establish dominance.

Successful communication and comprehension are linked together, hand in hand. Successfully reaching a C-level executive requires that your message be understood and acted upon. Most importantly, it requires a concerted and concentrated campaign that is conducted within a compelling psychological framework.

The "1, 2, 3, Rest, Repeat" Campaign

I have spent my entire career selling to C-level executives. For nearly two decades I sold enterprise software to CEOs, CFOs, CIOs, CTOs, and vice presidents of engineering. For the better part of the last decade I have sold my keynote presentations, training workshops, and consulting services exclusively to senior decision makers. In order of priority, the executives I target are the chief sales officer (vice president of sales), chief marketing officer (vice president of marketing), CEO (president and chairman), and COO (vice president of operations).

My philosophy about contacting senior executives is probably different than you think. I believe that every company will become a customer of mine because I honestly believe I can help improve every sales force. Essentially, it's just a matter of time before I connect with the executives and we work together.

My philosophy is based upon three important points. First, you must believe in what you're doing. Your efforts cannot be based upon halfhearted motivations. You must have a conviction that you, your products, and your company are the only true solution for the executive. When you have this mind-set it is impossible to consider yourself an obnoxious telemarketer or discourteous e-mail spammer. Rather, you are on an urgent mission to save the executive from making an ill-advised decision that will create a less-than-perfect workplace.

Second, your attempts to contact an executive will take time. In essence, you are running a political campaign that will take several months and in many cases over a year. While you obviously want to generate immediate interest, you need to set your own expectations so you don't get frustrated by a lack of results and stop campaigning. The campaign ends only when the executive buys your solution or specifically tells you to stop contacting him.

Third, the reason why an executive doesn't respond to your message is not that he's disinterested or too busy. Do not misinterpret a lack of response and assume he doesn't want your product. Rather, consider it your fault because you didn't send him the right message. While you didn't get the message right this time, you should also know that you will get it right over time. Therefore, you should never be bashful about contacting him again. However, you must send a different type of message or history will surely repeat itself. And in the words of Albert Einstein, "The definition of insanity is doing the same thing over and over again and expecting different results."[1]

I call the strategy to penetrate the C-level suite the "1, 2, 3 Rest, Repeat" campaign. It is based upon sending a series of three unique messages that have different structures and intentions. This is followed by a period when you go quiet and do not make any attempts whatsoever to contact the executive. Once this time frame is over, you start another campaign with a series of different messages.

> *Step 1—Send an initial credibility message.* This introductory message identifies in an interesting way who you are and what you do.
>
> *Step 2—Send a tactical offer message.* This message is centered upon a business problem or industry theme.
>
> *Step 3—Send a final message.* This message is the culmination of the campaign.
>
> *Step 4—Rest.* During this period, you do not contact the executive.
>
> *Step 5—Repeat.* After the rest period has ended, you start another campaign with a series of three entirely new messages.

Most companies and salespeople make two critical mistakes when they try to reach C-level executives. They either contact them once and stop if they don't get a response or contact them way too much. They mistakenly believe they are gaining "mindshare" by sending a newsletter or announcement every other week or once a month when the exact opposite is true. They are devaluing and diluting their message.

Your strategy to penetrate the executive level suite should not be a one-time action. Instead, it requires an ongoing campaign that can utilize all three communication vehicles at your disposal: e-mail, telephone cold calls, and letters (direct mail). Ideally, you should coordinate the order in which you send the communiqués. For example, you could send a letter in step 1, follow up with an e-mail in step 2, and cold call the executive a few days later. Here's why you will gain psychological benefits by sequencing your messages.

The customer has had many interactions with salespeople over the years. At both work and home, he receives telemarketing calls and is barraged by all types of spam and junk mail. Each of these communications is a stimulus that requires a response. Usually the response is negative (hang up on the telemarketer, throw away the junk mail, etc.).

When you send a customer an e-mail or make a cold call, you too are creating an unexpected stimulus that requires him to respond. Based upon past negative experiences, the customer's natural tendency is to automatically respond from his "hot emotional system" and immediately disregard your message. In other words, the customer acts quickly without thinking and deletes your e-mail or voice mail because of negative associations from the past.

In order to reach the customer, you want to elicit a response from his "cool cognitive system." This is his neutral and more thoughtful system for responding to stimuli. Therefore, we need our messages to stand out, to create a different psychological response, and to be respectfully sent. Typically, the time frame to accomplish the first three steps should be between sixty to ninety days. If you try to shorten the contact period, your messages will run the risk of being considered a nuisance.

The rest period should be at least twice the time it takes to execute steps 1 through 3. For example, the two sequences I typically use to reach C-level executives are e-mail, letter, e-mail and e-mail, e-mail, e-mail. I will sequence these messages on a once-a-month basis over a three-month time frame. I also use a longer rest period of nine months before I will attempt to contact the executive again.

Communication Vehicles

If selling is about speaking the language of the customer, then there are as many varieties of languages as there are customers. However, you have only three basic communication vehicles at your disposal to reach executives: cold calls, letters, and e-mail. While you can use any of these three communication vehicles during any of the steps, let's take a moment to review the pluses and minuses of each method.

Cold Calls

I recently conducted a win-loss analysis for a high-tech company that had a marvelous telemarketing team. These guys were relentless and pounded the phones day in, day out. As a result, they uncovered a lot of new opportunities for the outside sales reps in the field. These prospective customers were in different stages of evaluating vendors, ranging from midway in the sales cycle to nearly complete.

The results of the study were fascinating. The loss rate for these cold-call-driven opportunities was greater than 95 percent. In other words, only fifty out of one thousand actual opportunities the tele-marketing team uncovered were ever closed. Conversely, the win rate of the outsides sales reps and their field-driven opportunities was over 75 percent. The reason for this is that the company had product and personnel disadvantages, and the tempo rule (discussed in chapter 4) mandates that you must arrive early in the account when facing this situation. Most importantly, the combined revenue that resulted from those fifty wins generated by telemarketing was less than the costs of the telemarketing department to produce them. This is one example of how the positive impact of cold calling can be misinterpreted.

I receive a lot of cold calls from salespeople who are trying to sell me everything—sales force automation software, productivity tools, search engine optimization, online meeting solutions, marketing services, trade show events, business insurance, and the list goes on and on. Almost all the time these salespeople don't reach me and are forced to leave a voice mail.

Sometimes the funniest part of my day is listening to these voice mails. Here are a few of my observations. First, salespeople are either nervous, bored, or both. Most of the time their tempo is too fast for me to understand what they have said. I like to pay attention to how they say their phone numbers. Since the number is given at the end of a long-winded speech, it is said the fastest. Is someone really going to replay the voice mail three times to get your phone number right?

Some salespeople assume I already know exactly what they do. Just because they have been saying the same thing all day doesn't mean I understand their terminology. At times I'm tortured as they ramble on and on about something in a dreary, unexciting way. Why should they expect me to have any enthusiasm for what they're selling when they don't show any? I feel like Simon Cowell on *American Idol* with my finger poised over the Delete key. There's no way they're going to finish their audition.

But here's the really bad news. In the past ten years I have never returned a cold call from a salesperson. Not once. The C-level executives I have spoken to about this have said the same. Also, I've had salespeople cold call me for weeks or months at a time. I guess they think their persistence will win me over, but I actually hate them and will never do business with them. This is because I have to listen to their voice mails to get to my more important messages. In one sense, these salespeople are infringing on my personal time and space.

By the way, I have a very different attitude about e-mail because it is a cafeteria-type communication channel. Voice mail is a serial communication channel. I have to go through messages in order, one at a time. E-mail is different; I can pick and choose which e-mails I open and do so in whatever order I want when I want to. Therefore, it doesn't bother me when someone sends me an occasional unsolicited e-mail. I can always add the person to my Block Sender list if the frequency gets too intrusive.

Here's the most important point about cold calling. You have a one in a hundred chance of actually speaking with the C-level executive. You're going to voice mail most of the time. You must be able to leave a succinct voice mail. In no more twenty seconds you must identify who you are and why the executive should call you back. Your message must be delivered in a clear, commanding, yet approachable tone. Therefore, every time you plan on making cold calls you should rehearse leaving the voice mail. I suggest calling your own voice mail five times and practice leaving the message you plan to use. Listen to your voice mail, put yourself in the C-level executive's place, and ask yourself if you would call yourself back.

Should you cold call senior executives? Yes, cold calling does have a specific purpose during the 1, 2, 3, Rest, Repeat campaign. However, it should be used only as a follow-up device after an e-mail or letter has been sent in the preceding step. And it should be used sparingly. However, I have a totally different attitude toward cold calling lower-level and midlevel personnel: Life's short. Go for it! Phone away!

Letters

Letters sent by snail mail can be used in steps 1, 2, and 3 under one important condition: the letter and associated marketing collateral that is sent to the C-level executive must be totally unique.

The people in your marketing department believe that the product brochures they have created are something truly unique. After all, they painstakingly selected the colors, font, graphics, and words to be used. However, product differentiation is at an all-time low and you could very easily substitute the name and logo of your archrival on your marketing collateral. That's why I am not a big fan of sending executives brochures and literature packs. Whereas lower-level personnel might look through them, executives will almost always place them in the circular file (trash can).

The material and message you send should vary according to the level of personnel in the account you are trying to penetrate. Senior executives should receive short, high-level summary information, such as press articles, one-page reviews, and case studies about their competitors whom you are doing business with. Save the company brochure, white papers, data sheets, and other detailed information for the midlevel and lower-level personnel.

Think about all the different types of items you can send to a potential customer other than a standard letter of introduction. You can send interesting news clippings and serious sounding industry updates that help validate your marketing claims. You can send company tchotchkes such as T-shirts, baseball caps, and mouse pads that carry your company's name and logo. Most of the time these items are taken home and given away to family and friends, and it's great advertising when junior parades around the house wearing your company's T-shirt. Remember, whatever you send should be as unique as possible while still promoting a professional image. For example, if I cold call a vice president of sales to introduce myself, it's highly unlikely my call will be returned. However, when I send a personally inscribed copy of one of my books first, I will almost always hear back from him.

One of the most common problems with letters and e-mails is they're too long and recite an unbelievable list of reasons why a product is so wonderful. I call this the "it slices, it dices, it juliennes" syndrome. This phrase was made famous by Ron Popeil, the first infomercial personality, as he described all the incredible features of the Ronco Chop-O-Matic. A senior executive is a sophisticated buyer, and telling him how great your product is like a carnival pitchman won't earn you a meeting. Such pitches actually do more harm than good.

They're too aggressive in their sales tactics, and this is upsetting. Big organizations like us have a process you must go through. It's good they don't take an initial no for an answer, but they're kind of relentless in contacting us. Once they reach the ultimate decision maker who says "not at this time," they keep looking for different people and angles to work. But it eventually goes from "not at this time" to "I don't want to work with those guys!"

GENERAL MANAGER

E-mails

One of the first lessons every new salesperson learns is to "call high," to try to reach the most senior-level executive. Therefore, it's not surprising that senior-level executives are continually harassed by salespeople. When you try to call the CEO, president, or vice president of a company, you face a monumental challenge because the entire organization is designed to protect him from you. Most likely, you will be screened by an assistant or directed to an underling whose most important job function is to say no to you. The letters you send to executives tend to suffer the same fate. Given this reality, the preferred vehicle of communication is e-mail.

The subject line is the single most important part of the e-mail. Its sole purpose is to catch someone's attention and motivate the person to open the e-mail. I call this the "cowcatcher." Most people associate the term "cowcatcher" with the metal grill on the front of a locomotive. However, the word has an entirely different meaning in the entertainment industry: it's a show's opening moments in which the performers try to grab your attention and cause you to stop and look. The best e-mails start with a great cowcatcher. Here are some actual examples of bad subject lines e-mails I have received.

- *Subject: Increase Revenues 1000%!* This overpromising subject line means the e-mail will immediately be considered spam and deleted before it has a chance to be read.

- *Subject: Business Proposal Information.* This subject line incorrectly sets readers' expectations. They'll feel deceived when they open the e-mail and see it is from a stranger trying to sell them something.
- *Free White Paper.* A C-level executive doesn't want to waste time reading this.
- *Would you be interested in XYZ Product?* The answer is no when the question is presented this way.
- *Don't Break the Bank! Product of the year saves money and eliminates network bottlenecks.* It's just too long to bother with.

The hook is the catchy part of the e-mail. It's the first few sentences that deliver a punch and motivate you to keep reading. The cowcatcher and the hook work together synergistically. Great e-mails have an interesting cowcatcher and a provocative hook. Here's an example of a terrible e-mail exactly as I received it with my critique immediately following.

Subject: Please advise

The pressure is on to grow revenue faster. How will you adapt business to reach goals?
XXXX can help you gain a strong competitive edge.
Let me show you can use XXXX to:

- Drive better results.
- Increase customer satisfaction and loyalty
- Expand your market share.

Do you have time this week or next for a brief discussion about your business needs? Please reply with the best time for me to contact you.

Best regards,
XXX XXXXXX

This e-mail has the wrong subject line. It is titled "Please advise," which gives the reader the impression it is from someone the reader knows about a business issue the sender needs advice on. When the reader opens the e-mail and sees that it is spam, it creates a "negative receptive state" because the reader feels deceived. If this e-mail was intended for a vice president of sales, a better title would have been "Increase revenues by increasing sales calls." If intended for a CFO, "Five tips to decrease your cost of operations" could have been used. These titles set the readers' expectations and create a "positive receptive state."

The e-mail suggests the sender is a simpleton. In chapter 3 we discussed the roles of dominance and submission during communication. This submissive e-mail is written at the fifth grade Flesch-Kindcaid level. Is a senior-level executive really going to want to meet with an elementary school student? This e-mail actually demeans the recipient by inferring the reader is at the same communication level.

The e-mail is too generic to grab the reader's attention. It uses strategic terms like "grow revenue," "competitive edge," and "increase customer satisfaction" generically without any explanation. These terms are so overused in this manner by everyone in sales that they are what I call "dead words"—they have no meaningful impact. We'll talk later in the chapter about how you add meaning to your claims through operators.

Finally, the sender didn't conduct any background research so that he could craft a message that would appeal to the recipient. You can differentiate your solution using strategic value, operational value, political value, and most importantly, psychological value. The best way to tap into these values is by tailoring your message directly to the intended recipient based upon the person's role within the company. A one-size-fits-all e-mail is less effective because the vice presidents of marketing, sales, and finance face very different day-to-day challenges.

Investigative Research

Before you attempt to penetrate any new account, you need to re-search the business. Old-fashioned detective work is still vitally important today. Fortunately, the Internet makes information more readily available than ever. Study every page of information on the cus-tomer's Web site as though your life depended on it. Read the annual report, press releases, and product information, and scan all the vari-ous financial documents. From these documents you can derive your initial thoughts about your product's strategic, operational, political, and psychological value.

Another critical type of investigative research has a profound im-pact on whether or not your efforts will be successful: you must find the "right" people to contact within the account. You can find out who's who in any company in several ways. First, the company's Web site probably has an "about the company" page that may list senior executives. If the company is public, senior executives will be listed in the financial reports that can be found on its "investor relations" page. You can also search financial Web sites such as Yahoo! Finance (finance.yahoo.com) and the Securities and Exchange Commission Web site (www.sec.gov) for financial filings. However, this informa-tion is far from complete for the purpose of penetrating the account.

Ideally, you want to collect four critical pieces of information. First, knowing the date the company's fiscal year ends will help you coordinate your 1, 2, 3, Rest, Repeat campaign. Three to six months before the fiscal year ends, C-level executives will start thinking about their next year's goals along with the initiatives to accomplish them and the budget associated with each initiative. This is a crucial time to be gaining mindshare. Budgets begin to be shaped through an iterative process with the CEO, CFO, or entire executive team. They become set in stone after the budget has been approved by the board of directors, usually before ninety days into the new fiscal year.

For example, I contact sales and marketing executives at companies who have January through December fiscal years in the September-to-December time frame. I want to catch them during the new-year planning cycle.

> It's all about timing. There are certain points in the year when the strategic conversation is academic and other times it's important. You have to know when we are planning for the new year.
>
> CHIEF EXECUTIVE OFFICER

Second, you want contact information about employees at all levels of the organization (midlevel managers and lower-level project people along with all the different executive-level leaders). For example, if you were selling security software, you would like contact information for the chief information officer, chief technical officer, chief security officer, and vice president in charge of networking or infrastructure. You also want contact information for midlevel managers (director of information technology, director of security, manager of global networks) and key lower-level personal (senior firewall administrator, IT security specialist, and lead network engineer).

Third, you need each person's precise title. There's a big difference between finding out that someone is the "vice president of global manufacturing applications" versus knowing someone who goes by the more nebulous title "vice president of information technology." Knowing the more detailed title will help you send better targeted messages.

Finally, you need accurate and complete contact information. You need the correct spelling of each person's name and his or her personal usage (whether someone goes by Charles or Chuck, for example), as well as the person's mailing address, direct phone number, and, of course, the all-important e-mail address.

Where can you get this detailed level of information? You are probably familiar with the major providers of marketing data such as Hoover's and Dun & Bradstreet. However, the data they provide may not help you meet your objective for a variety of reasons. They might provide only the headquarters location address, but the executives you need to contact may work in other facilities. They might not provide a person's direct-dial phone number, only the main switchboard number. This is a huge problem because the phone system usually routes you to people who are employed to screen you out. Most importantly, these data providers usually don't have e-mail addresses.

You can turn to many different sources for finding contact information. I like to use Jigsaw (www.jigsaw.com). One of the reasons why I use Jigsaw is the way the company collects data. The traditional data providers hire telephone agents who call businesses and verify data once or twice a year. Since these operators do not have sales-related backgrounds, they talk to the first person they reach (usually the switchboard operator). Conversely, Jigsaw's marketing data is actually provided by the sales community itself, so it has deeper and more detailed contact information. For example, Jigsaw provides hard-to-find e-mail addresses.

I also like to use ZoomInfo (www.zoominfo.com) for researching key executives. ZoomInfo is unique in that its semantic search engine gathers publicly available information from the business Web—millions of company Web sites, news feeds, and other online sources—twenty-four hours a day, seven days a week, then automatically compiles it into easy-to-search-and-read profiles. It has 45 million contacts in its database at last count. One of the main reasons I use ZoomInfo is to search for interviews and writing samples of the executive I am trying to contact.

Message Structure

Because people have different motivations, they have different perceptions of a product's value. The perceived value depends on the psychological, political, operational, and strategic value it provides the evaluator.

As we discussed earlier, at the root of every decision is a desire to fulfill one of four deep-seated psychological needs: satisfying the ego, being accepted as part of a group, avoiding pain, and ensuring survival. Psychological value is the most important value in terms of motivating purchasing action. Therefore, you should understand your product's psychological value and how it applies to the person you are trying to reach.

Political value involves organizational power. Your product can make someone more powerful outright, or it can provide much-needed visibility that enables a person to be in contact with the company's powerbrokers.

People's success in an organization is dependent upon the success of their department's operations. Everyone has a resume that lists accomplishments and successful projects, so you can think of operational power as how your solution impacts a person's resume.

Finally, strategic value is the reasons evaluators give to others in the company as to why they are purchasing a product. Strategic value includes gaining a competitive advantage, increasing revenues, decreasing costs, increasing productivity, improving customer satisfaction, improving quality, and standardizing operations.

The message you send to customers should be based upon these four values. You must communicate to potential buyers that you can help them solve critical department problems and help them become experts and an internal source of knowledge, thereby making them powerful. Let's look at an example of a generic e-mail for a marketing campaign targeted at senior executives in the automobile industry.

Subject: Increase Profitability and Maintain Dealer
         Partnership Loyalty!

Dear Mr. Smith,

My name is John Johnson from XYZ Corporation. We are the leader in providing solutions that help accelerate time to market and improve customer communications. We're helping customers such as Ford, Toyota, and Honda automate their relationships with their distributors, dealers, and parts suppliers.

In a recent strategic implementation, we were able to deliver Ford a robust solution that allowed them to communicate more effectively with their worldwide dealer distribution channel, drastically increasing customer service and loyalty.

XYZ Corporation can help you

- Improve communications with critical partners
- Speed time to market and increase dealer retention
- Implement a "best practices" approach for all enterprise communications

For a free evaluation of our robust solutions, please call or e-mail me at your earliest convenience.

Best regards,

John Johnson

What follows is my version of the same e-mail. While the main message isn't changed significantly, my goal is to employ a better cowcatcher and hook and to tap into all the different types of customer value.

Subject: How Toyota Maintains Its Critical Dealer Relationships

Mark,

Q. How do Toyota, Ford, and Honda maintain near-perfect dealer relationships?

A. XYZ Corporation has helped them automate and streamline all aspects of partner communications.

For example, Toyota distributes thousands of unique messages and memorandums to its worldwide dealer distribution channel on a daily basis. Toyota has drastically reduced turnaround times while increasing customer service using XYZ's solution. As a result, they have cut costs, accelerated time to market, and improved dealer communications.

For a free dealer communication analysis or to learn how you can standardize relationships with all your important business partners, please call or e-mail me at your earliest convenience.

Thank you,

John Johnson
John.johnson@XYZcompany.com
(123) 456-7890

The most important aspect of the e-mail is not the bullet points of benefits; rather, it is the psychological impression it creates on the reader. In this regard, my goal was to invoke the Stockholm syndrome, a psychological phenomenon in which hostages develop a bond with their captors, named after an incident involving kidnapped bank employees in Stockholm. The most often-cited example is newspaper heiress Patty Hearst, who helped rob banks with the radicals who kidnapped her.

When salespeople try to penetrate a new account, they are considered enemies, akin to bank robbers, so they are met with disdain and fear. Salespeople must turn negative resisters into positive accomplices. In the above example, I was trying to make the e-mail recipient become psychologically attached to the sender. One reader (a consolidator) might envision starting a grand project like Toyota's for his own personal gain. Another (a consulter) might want more information so he could impress others with his expertise. Someone else (a responder) might have criticized his company's dealer communications in the past and thought, "If it is good enough for Toyota, it should work for us." He just wants this painful problem solved. Finally, another (a bureaucrat) might be excited about standardizing all the various communications the company must send to its partners because it would enable him to maintain his authority. The psychological storyline of the e-mail speaks to different psychological drives and buyer types.

The purpose of your investigative research is to enable you to tailor your cowcatcher and hook. For example, if the company you're contacting has recently gone public, you might title your e-mail to the CEO "How to maintain profitability after an IPO." If it made a recent acquisition, you might use "Revenue strategies from acquisitions." Such e-mails are more likely to be read and less likely to be considered spam because they are personalized around a timely event.

Another key reason for conducting research is to help you determine the different values your solution offers. Reading the CEO's letter to the stockholders in the company's annual report will help you understand the state of the business and the major initiatives planned for the new year. Reviewing the 10-K financial report will provide you with details about the business challenges the company faces. Press releases announce new programs and company crusades that are being undertaken. Meanwhile, industry analyst reports explain how the company is faring compared to the competition.

Take a moment to complete this exercise by answering the following questions:

- What is my solution's psychological value?
- What is my solution's political value?
- What is my solution's operational value?
- What is my solution's strategic value?

Only when you understand the different types of value your product offers should you begin writing your e-mail, letter, or cold-call script. Now let's look at some sample messages that can be sent during the first three steps of the 1, 2, 3, Rest, Repeat campaign. While all of the examples are e-mails, this message structure can be directly applied to letters as well.

Step 1—Credibility Message

The purpose of the first message is to establish credibility and develop some level of recognition with the C-level executive you are trying to reach. Pay particular attention to the tone of the e-mail example above. It's not too personal. Since we have never met this person, the message is intentionally more formal. However, we don't want to be overly formal with our use of language and the salutation or the recipient will discount the letter as a sales pitch. In the example below, Michael Corleone, a salesperson for Acme Advertising, is trying to reach Vincent Vega, the chief marketing officer of ABC Technology Company, a multibillion-dollar technology giant.

To: Vincent Vega, CMO@ABC Technology Company
From: Michael Corleone@Acme Advertising
Subject: Vincent, Marketing Campaign Meeting Request

Hello Vincent,

Acme Advertising has developed marketing campaigns for many leading technology companies including:

Apple	IBM	NEC
Cisco	Intel	Oracle
EMC	McAfee	SAP
Hewlett-Packard	Microsoft	Sun Microsystems

Our clients have cost-effectively improved their brand recognition while increasing new sales opportunities.

"Acme Advertising's direct response marketing campaign increased our lead generation activities nearly threefold."
Jack Sparrow, CMO, Oracle Corporation

"Acme's 'One World, One System' commercial series has improved our name recognition across all our key market segments."
James T. Davis, CMO, Hewlett-Packard Corporation

"We were thrilled to win the prestigious Zippy Award for best print advertisement in a technical magazine."
David Bowman, CMO, Intel Corporation

I'd be delighted to meet with you and share some thoughts and ideas we have for ABC Technology Company.

I look forward to hearing from you,

Michael Corleone
Michael.corleone@acme.com
(123) 456-7890

The subject line is the cowcatcher, solely intended to encourage Vincent to open the e-mail. His name is part of the subject so the inference is that the message is from a real person asking for a meeting, not from an automated spambot. As he opens the e-mail, the first thing his eyes will focus on is the list of recognizable company names. This is the hook that makes him go back and read the entire message.

Notice how this e-mail avoids making outrageous claims like "Acme is the world's leading advertising firm." Rather, it is completely factual: these are our clients, and this is what they have to say about us. Nor does the e-mail go into a detailed explanation of what Acme Advertising does.

The subject line and first sentence use the term "marketing campaign." To a CMO like Vincent, the term can mean a wide variety of things: advertising campaigns, lead-generation programs, online marketing, customer research, competitive research, brand development, and so on. Intentionally, the e-mail does not point out what it's referring to. This is an example of a broadcast-unicast messaging technique. It's intended to let the recipient derive his own personal meaning from an ambiguous term. His internal dialogue believes the message is intended solely for him.

While researching the business, Michael found out that ABC Technology's sales are down from last year. Therefore, he theorizes that the sales department is haranguing marketing about needing more qualified leads. If this is the case, Vincent might interpret the e-mail from the standpoint of lead generation, and Michael has a higher likelihood of securing a meeting. The first customer quote reinforces this interpretation. This is an example of a background suggestion.

The two types of suggestions are foreground and background. Foreground suggestions are explicit, but they deflect the source of the request from the demander. Background suggestions lead recipients to believe they are acting of their free will when in fact they have been directed to follow a message. For example, let's pretend I am a passenger in your car and I feel you are driving too fast. A command would be "Slow down!" However, it's human nature to resist commands. A foreground suggestion would be "You know the speed limit is forty-five mph and police ticket a lot of speeders here." A background suggestion would be "A speeder was in a horrible accident last week in this exact spot." While the background suggestion is more subtle in its delivery, it triggers a more profound reaction. In a sales situation, a foreground suggestion might be "*Consumer Reports* gave our product the highest rating and recommended it as the best buy." An example of a background suggestion is "One of my customers tried the other company's product and recently switched to ours."

The list of companies provided in this e-mail is extremely important. Examples of the customers that are successfully using a company's products and service are the most important metaphors a salesperson can use. The personal connection between the customer example and its relevancy to the prospect's experiences will determine to what extent the salesperson's claims are accepted. Therefore, the pertinence of the examples chosen is critical. Presenting a company that closely mirrors the prospect's business environment will make the salesperson's statements more powerful. Presenting a company that the prospect doesn't recognize will have less impact. In reality, it may actually hinder the argument because the prospect might think the product is not pervasive or popular.

At the lowest level of relevance, the example used could be a well-known organization, such as Coca-Cola or Shell Oil. Certainly, these are companies that would be known by the CMO. The level of relevance improves when the example company is known for its past innovations, such as FedEx, or is well respected for its quality and brand, such as Mercedes-Benz or Nordstrom. By providing examples of customers that have a dominant position in an unrelated business, such as Amazon or Starbucks, you also receive implicit approval since it is highly likely the prospects have successfully used the services or products of these companies personally.

Geographic proximity is a very compelling attribute of a reference. If the customer's company is based in New York, a reference to a company that is based in Los Angeles is not nearly as strong as a reference to one that is based in New York.

The ideal references are direct competitors in the company's industry. These examples provide the highest level of relevance and the most persuasive argument to use the salesperson's products. Since Vincent works for a giant high-technology company, Michael gains immense credibility by providing a list of companies in the same industry and with the same business initiatives.

Specific customer quotes were selected for this e-mail. Since Michael has never met Vincent, he really doesn't know what's on the CMO's mind. He doesn't know if he thinks his job is in jeopardy or he's next in line to become the president of the company. So Michael wants quotes that will connect to the different benefactions. The first customer quote focuses upon pain avoidance. Based upon Michael's past experience working with CMOs, he knows that lead generation is always a source of pain. The second quote can relate to multiple benefactions. Maybe Vincent feels inferior to his peers at the other companies listed in the e-mail. He might hire Acme so he can be part of the group. This is self-preservation. Or since he's worked with his current ad agency for seven straight years, he might feel it's time for a refreshing change. This is mental and emotional well-being. The third quote is based upon self-gratification. What CMO wouldn't want to win a prestigious Zippy Award and prominently display the trophy in his office?

The final sentence is an example of the imagination messaging technique, which entails directing the recipient to form mental images, concepts, situations, and sensations. Michael wants to share some thoughts and ideas his company has for Vincent. Upon reading the sentence, Vincent will probably start to wonder what these ideas are. Michael is guiding Vincent's internal dialogue to become curious.

Now, go back and take a moment to reread the e-mail titled "Please advise." While the e-mail titled "Vincent, Marketing Campaign Meeting Request" has about fifty more words, it is fifty times more impactful.

Step 2—Tactical Offer Message

Assuming the C-level executive didn't respond to your first e-mail, you send him a second, tactical offer e-mail. In the example below, Luke Skywalker, a salesperson for XYZ Technologies, is trying to secure a meeting with Norman Bates, chief information officer at Wonderful Telecommunications.

> To: Norman Bates, CIO@Wonderful Telecommunications
> From: Luke Skywalker@XYZ Technologies
> Subject: Norman, Recession Strategies for CIOs
>
> Norman,
>
> During today's tough times, IT organizations are required to maintain round-the-clock uptime with smaller budgets and fewer resources than ever. Below, you will find links to articles that address this critical issue.
>
> 7 CIO Strategies to Maintain Application Availability with Fewer Resources
>
> Garner Group Study of the Recession's Impact on Long-Term IT Planning
>
> How to Reduce Operational IT Costs by Outsourcing
>
> When and Where Outsourcing Makes Sense
>
> XYZ Technologies has helped hundreds of CIOs maximize their IT budgets through application outsourcing.
>
> *"We were surprised by the cost savings. It has been 20 percent more than we expected."* Charles Foster Kane, CIO, AT&T
>
> *"We started small by outsourcing non-mission-critical applications three years ago. Today, 70 percent of our applications are outsourced."* Forrest Gump, CIO, Johnson & Johnson

"We've achieved our primary goal of reducing costs while maintaining our service levels. Now we've freed up valuable resources to work on critical new business projects." Stanley Kowalski, CIO, General Electric

Norman, please let me know if you are interested in our complimentary outsourcing cost-savings analysis. The complimentary study takes approximately two days to complete and will provide you with a detailed savings assessment, key risk factors, and completion timelines.

Luke Skywalker
Luke.skywalker@xyz.com
(123) 456-7890

Based upon Luke's research and experience, he knows that one of the main challenges CIOs face during tough economic times is providing high levels of service with less money and fewer resources. "Norman, Recession Strategies for CIOs" is a topical cowcatcher. It's quite different from "Norman, Meeting Request." The subject line also indicates that the e-mail is not from a salesperson asking for a meeting, but from an important source of independent information that could potentially help the CIO.

Obviously, Luke wants to secure a meeting so that he can begin the cost-savings study. However, any forward progress in starting a relationship with the CIO should be considered positive. For instance, if Norman clicks on a link to one of the articles, this is a positive step.

This e-mail has three major parts. The first part is the offer. This fulfills the e-mail's requirement that it provide independent information. Four links are provided to articles that most CIOs would find relevant and interesting. Although they may have been written by XYZ Technologies, they are informational as opposed to vendor-centric promotional collateral. (It's important to note that e-mails

with attached documents are more likely to be caught by spam fil-
ters.) The articles are the e-mail's hook.

The second part is composed of customer metaphors, stories from
customers confirming the salesperson's solution or company. Since
most CIOs are extremely risk averse, all of the quotes are intended to
make Norman feel more comfortable that outsourcing is mainstream.
Included are quotes from CIOs of another telecommunications company and traditionally conservative companies General Electric and
Johnson & Johnson.

These customer quotes are also examples of the simulation messaging technique. Simulation is structuring language to provoke a
particular emotional or physical response. For example, salespeople
want the customer to simulate the benefits and feelings of owning
their product during the sales cycle. Car salespeople are experts at
using simulation. The test drive is a way to get the buyer to simulate
the fantasy of owning the car. They want the test driver to enjoy the
smoothness of the ride, experience the "new car" aroma, and feel the
power of the acceleration. They know that a person who successfully
simulates ownership during the test drive is a good prospect for a sale.

The same principle applies to the CIO. If Luke can get Norman to
envision being a happy customer while reading the e-mail, he is well
on the road to securing a meeting. Simulation exercises the senses,
engages the personality, and occupies the internal dialogue. Luke
wants Norman to ask himself, "Why aren't we outsourcing?"

The third part of the e-mail is the tactic to get the initial meeting. This is the call to action. The earlier e-mail titled "How Toyota
Maintains Its Critical Dealer Relationships" was a tactical e-mail
based upon telling customer stories and offering a free dealer communication analysis. In the above e-mail, Luke is asking Norman to
participate in a cost-savings analysis project. A tactical e-mail needs
to have a much stronger closing statement than a credibility e-mail
because you are specifically asking the executive to take action to fulfill one of his fantasies.

All sales involve selling a fantasy. The fantasy is that somehow the product you are selling is going to make the customer's life easier, make the customer more powerful, save money, or enable the customer to make more money. The feature set of your product validates the fantasy elements of your "story." The features promote the customer's fantasy. During the sales cycle, you communicate how you can turn your customer's fantasy into a reality when your product is purchased.

Step 3—Final Message

At this point, you may have attempted to contact the executive twice without success. You can either send another credibility message, a follow-up tactical offer message, or the "final" message of the campaign. In the example below, Willy Loman, a salesperson for Interstar Networks, is trying to reach John Blutarsky, the chief technology officer of Freedom Financial Investments. Through his research, Willy knows that Freedom Financial Investments is using his archrival's product, Schlomo Networks. Please note that it is more important to pay attention to the more aggressive tone and structure of the language in this example than to understand the technical terms being used.

> To: John Blutarsky, CTO@Freedom Financial Investments
> From: Willy Loman@Interstar Networks
> Subject: John, Schlomo Networks Performance Comparison
>
> John,
>
> I've sent you e-mails to explain Interstar Networks' advantage over Schlomo Networks. We offer superior performance because our architecture is based upon virtual processes. This is more efficient than Schlomo Networks' architecture, which uses a single-machine address. While the single-machine address solution redundantly broadcasts all messages, our solution

sends specific information packets to the applicable computer. This results in up to 75 percent less network traffic.

For example, ABC Company recently switched from Schlomo Networks and improved its network performance by over 60 percent. I would be delighted to set up a conference call for you to talk with John Smith, ABC's CTO.

Willy Loman
Willy Loman@Interstarnetworks.com
(123)456-7890

A good rule of thumb is to always assume the salesperson you are competing against is as friendly, professional, and knowledgeable as you are. Like yourself, he is trying to win over the C-level executive with his product knowledge, business acumen, and personal charm. To the executive, the claims you both make will sound identical. Just open your corporate sales presentation and see how many of these terms and phrases you can find.

World leader	Increase revenues	Scalable
Market leader	Reduce costs	Manageable
Best in class	Competitive advantage	Reliable
Best of breed	Greater productivity	Powerful
Cost effective	Dynamic	Easy to use
End-to-end solution	Improve customer satisfaction	Better visibility

These are dead words that have been so overused that they actually have a negative impact or no impact at all. So while you're thinking you are saying something profound to customers, they're rolling their eyes and saying to themselves, "Here we go again!" Operators are required to take these generic claims and translate them into proof points the customer understands and believes.

There's a big difference between telling a customer your solution is "fast and reliable" versus saying it is "fast and reliable, will print two hundred pages per minute, and has a 99.99 percent uptime rate." With the additional operators, you have communicated something meaningful.

The above e-mail shows several examples of how operators can be used. For example, in the e-mail to the CTO the general word "performance" is being operated on by the descriptor "architecture is based upon virtual processes." The term "more efficient than" is being operated on by the phrase "uses a single-machine address." The sales-person then details the differentiation between the two architectures, which is less traffic and faster performance.

To further validate his argument, Willy offers a specific customer example to illustrate his claims. Equally important, to have his claim accepted as the truth, he offers to introduce the prospect to the existing customer. In other words, he says, "Don't take only my word on this, talk to my customers!"

Little meaning can be derived from standard product claims unless operators are added. Here's how to incorporate operators into your messaging. Start with a high-level statement and then continue to define the statement into meaningful terms, specific benefits, and proof points.

We	help save you money
	increase your revenues
	provide better technology
	offer a more comprehensive solution
	provide better functionality or ease of use

Because of our	superior technology or functionality
	quality, people, or support
	ease of use or breakthrough paradigm

In comparison to	the way you conduct business today
	how the competitor's product operates
	how your existing process functions
As a benefit, you will	increase revenues by 30 percent
	save 25 percent
	improve your output by 3,000 units
	achieve 45 percent improvement
For example	ABC Company implemented our solution and has saved $750,000 in the first 6 months
	DEF Company increased revenues by $10 million in the first year
	XYZ Company improved production by 400 units per day
Final proof point	I would be delighted to introduce you to John Smith at ABC Company.
	If you like, I could arrange a visit to DEF Company.
	Here's the case study on XYZ Company for further reading.

For centuries, psychics, fortunetellers, and astrologers have known that a word's meaning is determined by the operators the receiver adds to the message. Look at the following examples and try to determine if any of these apply specifically to you and whether the astrological sign is yours.

- Astrological sign: Members of this sign are admired for their generosity and sensitive nature. They often make excellent

businesspeople or salespeople because of their honesty, skill, and genuine communication.
- Psychic: Someone you know is having troubles.
- Fortune cookie: You will soon receive good news from a faraway place.

What happened? When you were reading these sentences, you most likely added your own operators to gain some personal meaning. As you read about the astrological sign, did you think it was your sign? Nearly everyone wants to be admired for his or her generosity and honesty. You may have even thought of a specific person (spouse, child, or friend) or an event (giving a donation) to validate the idea that you are generous and honest.

The psychic understands that everyone knows someone who is having troubles. "Troubles" could be anything ranging from a flat tire to a life-threatening disease. The fortune cookie leaves you to interpret what "soon" means. Is it hours, days, or months? What is considered "good" news and how far is the faraway place?

So why are horoscopes and fortune cookies important to salespeople? They show that if the customer doesn't add operators, the claims are in fact unbelievable. That's why every claim you make should be backed up with operators.

Conclusion

While the origin of the written word is debated by researchers today, one of the earliest examples of written language is cuneiform, which dates back five thousand years to ancient Mesopotamia (modern-day Iraq).[2] The first writers are thought to have been businessmen who traded goods with the surrounding Egyptian and Indian civilizations.

Since those early beginnings, written language has continually evolved. Today, written language is undergoing significant change.

One thousand new words are added to the English language each month versus one thousand per year just a century ago. The impetus for many of these new words is the computer industry and the Internet.

The Internet is fundamentally changing the way people communicate. "It's the beginning of a new stage in the evolution of the written language. The Internet is fostering new kinds of creativity through language," according to David Crystal, a language historian at the University of Wales in the United Kingdom.[3] The purpose of this chapter was to help you take advantage of one of the most important communication developments of your lifetime. You must master how to use e-mail to penetrate the C-level executive suite. Your success will increasingly depend upon it in the future.

> What's wrong with salespeople is they're typically selling a product. I don't need a product unless it solves one of my business problems. The challenge is getting face time with a significant leader. Times are tight; leaders are busy. Unless you can spark the interest of a senior leader, you are not going to get their time, and you won't understand their problems.
>
> PRESIDENT

Part III

How to Convince Company Leaders to Buy

Although closing a complex enterprise account may take many months to complete, every deal has a critical moment or turning point where it is won or lost. Most often, this moment occurs in face-to-face meetings with C-level executives. We typically equate persuasion to solely satisfying the analytical mind. However, the conversations you have with C-level executives are quite complex. They consist of verbal and nonverbal messages that are sent consciously and subconsciously. In this part we address how to build rapport, present your solution, and answer difficult questions so that you convince both the rational and emotional minds of C-level decision makers to buy.

7

Calculate

PREPARING YOURSELF FOR THE
C-LEVEL SALES CALL

> We are a skeptical group, and they lost the deal during their presentation. They said they were different and much better than what we have, but they didn't provide enough proof. What they said didn't really apply to us.
>
> CHIEF FINANCIAL OFFICER

You might be surprised after getting two-thirds of the way through a book about sales psychology that you have not read anything about personality types. You haven't read that some of your customers will be feeler-thinkers, some will be extroverts, and some will have type A personalities. Well, now it's time to make an even more provocative statement than "There's no such thing as reality" (at the beginning of the book). As they relate to face-to-face sales calls, traditional personality assessments are basically unimportant. They simply don't apply.

Early in my career, I made the transition from a technical position as a computer programmer to my first job as a salesperson. My new employer sent me to several well-known sales training programs. Each of these programs taught some form of personality assessment using a variation of Carl Jung's philosophy of psychological types. Most frequently, it was the Myers-Briggs Type Indicator (MBTI). The MBTI uses four measurements to classify a personality into one of sixteen different types.[1] These measurements include your level of extroversion, how much you trust logic versus feelings, your intuitiveness, and finally, whether you make instantaneous decisions.

Armed with this newly learned information, I eagerly went about trying to apply it to my sales opportunities. However, it didn't match what I was experiencing. I quickly realized that the traditional descriptions of personality types didn't help my sales efforts. It seemed to me that the customer's personality was situational. That is, depending on the sales circumstance and whom he was surrounded by, the same person acted quite differently. For instance, a prospect might be quite reserved in a sales presentation where his boss and peers were present. Yet later when we were having lunch alone he would be quite outspoken. It seemed customers' behavior was being influenced by the complex group dynamics involved with decision making. It was obvious that personality isn't uniform across all circumstances, as the trainings I took suggested.

Personality is only a generic label for behavior. The typical descriptions of personality types have little relevance to sales calls and vendor presentation settings. When a customer is making a buying decision, there truly is no such thing as personality because every selling situation is completely unique.

Most importantly, people are influenced by other people during sales calls and presentations. I have witnessed so-called extroverts turn into introverts when someone more extroverted entered the room. I have seen rational thinkers turn into emotional feelers when someone in the meeting voiced a different opinion. The dynamics of group interactions and peer pressure subdue and override traditional personality traits.

I don't believe a personality framework exists today that can fully address the fleeting nature of customer behavior during a sales call. At best, current models provide high-level tendencies. A more sophisticated model is needed that helps salespeople anticipate behavior based on the unique roles that each person assumes during the group decision-making process.

Group Decision-Making Roles

Whenever a company makes an enterprise purchase decision that involves groups of people, self-interests, politics, and group dynamics will influence the final decision. Individuals will jockey for position to ensure their favorite vendor is selected, align themselves with more powerful coworkers for political gain, or stay out of the fray and refuse to take part in the decision.

Tension, drama, and conflict are normal parts of group dynamics because typically any decision on what to do is not unanimous. Selection team members always feel an underlying tension because they are never 100 percent certain they are picking the right solution. Drama builds as the salespeople make their arguments and provide conflicting information to refute their competitors' claims. Interpersonal conflict between group members, as evidenced by disparaging remarks and criticisms, occurs whenever there is intense competition for a highly sought-after prize.

Beyond their formal titles and their position on the organization chart, people take on specific roles when they are part of a selection committee. Some assume roles they believe will enable them to take control of the group and steer the decision toward their preference. Others adopt new behavioral roles to deal with the tension, drama, and conflict. You may not have realized it, but even your presence as a salesperson also influences how customers act.

Selection committee members, ranging from the CEO to the lowest-level evaluator, will adopt four different group decision-making roles during sales calls and sales presentations. These roles are based upon information, character, authority, and company.

- *Information Roles.* Information roles are based on the type of information people believe they should gather and the unique way in which they process and transmit information.

- *Character Roles.* Character roles are based on the way people feel they should behave when they are part of a decision-making group.
- *Authority Roles.* Authority roles are based on people's degree of command and their ability to dominate the group.
- *Company Roles.* Company roles are based on the political power people wield and their personal disposition toward their company.

While it makes sense to determine the role of every person during sales calls, it is crucial to understand the roles of the C-level executives. Ideally, you want to anticipate their behavior beforehand so you can use the right demeanor, create the right messages, and then deliver those messages in the way that they will be best received and understood.

In addition, you probably aren't going to attend C-level sales calls alone. You might bring along your sales manager, vice president of sales, product marketing manager, professional services director, and even your CEO. Therefore, you need a common terminology to describe the C-level executive to others. Understanding these roles will help you communicate your sales call strategy to colleagues and prepare them for the type of executive they are going to meet.

Figure 7.1 summarizes the four different categories of roles that prospects adopt during sales calls and presentations.

Now we'll introduce each of these roles and explain how they specifically apply to C-level executives during sales calls and presentations.

Information Roles

Everyone involved in the selection process has the responsibility to assess vendor information for accuracy and provide an opinion as to which solution is best. However, evaluators assume this duty with different levels of due diligence, ranging from focusing on minutiae to

Information Roles	Character Roles	Authority Roles	Company Roles
Anal analytical	Class clown	Bureaucrat	Hired gun
Gullible	Dreamer	Dictator	Fifth columnist
Intellectual	Hothead	Empty suit	Vigilante
Sergeant Schultz	Maven	Old pro	Intern
Summary seeker	People pleaser	Proctor	Politician
	Schadenfreuder	Pundit	Pollyanna
	Straight shooter	Soldier	Revolutionary

Figure 7.1 The four group decision-making roles

being big-picture oriented. Here are the most common information roles that evaluators assume.

Anal Analytical　　Anal analyticals are full of doubt and have the highest levels of skepticism. They verify every statement made by a salesperson, and they want to validate every piece of information. Therefore, anal analyticals immerse themselves in features, functions, and specifications. They take their role as information gatherer very seriously and do not want to be embarrassed by missed details.

C-level executives with advanced degrees in the sciences (computers, mathematics, engineering, etc.) are more likely to be anal analyticals. When you visit the executive management page on a prospect's Web site and see that the executive has a master's degree and doctorate in chemical engineering, there's a good chance you're going to meet an anal analytical. This should not be a surprise since he's had years of systematic education followed by a business career that was heavily focused on scientific methods and data analysis.

When meeting with a C-level anal analytical, do not go on the call without someone on your side who has commensurate technical or industry knowledge. You have only one chance to make a great first impression, and being unable to satisfy the executive's analytical mind will be the death knell of the meeting.

However, the overriding objective is not to let technology talk or deep discussions about minutiae dominate the entire meeting. Rather, you must keep the meeting on track and drive the agenda to reach your desired outcome for the call. Finally, never let your own technical team hijack the meeting and take control. They should know in advance that they are there under your direction.

Gullible   "There's a sucker born every minute" is a quote that is often credited to P. T. Barnum, the famous showman and cofounder of the Barnum & Bailey Circus.[2] There's a little bit of P. T. Barnum in every salesperson because there are always gullible customers who unquestioningly accept salespeople's information at face value.

Some C-level executives are not well versed in working with salespeople or buying products. It might be early in their career and they might be new to the senior management role or the company. Gullibles don't know what questions to ask or how to make a major procurement within their own company. If this is the case, you must adopt a different familial role with them than when working with an anal analytical. You need to mentor them through the process like a father explaining to his adult son how to fill out his tax forms or an older brother explaining to his younger sibling the criteria that should be used when selecting a college.

While gullibles are rare, they have the propensity to be found in certain departments. For example, the vice president of human resources, chief talent officer, or chief learning officer are wired quite differently than the CFO, CEO, and CIO. Usually, they're not as adept at dealing with salespeople. Since they don't wield much organizational power, they often don't know how to make enterprise purchases happen. Therefore, if the salesperson considers the senior-most leader in the deal to be a gullible, there is a higher likelihood that no purchase will ever be made.

Intellectual When it comes to details, an intellectual is the opposite of an anal analytical. Intellectuals are more interested in the theoretical and philosophical aspects of products. Intellectuals approach the gathering of information in a cerebral, professorial way. They are open to learning and seek personal enlightenment. For example, an anal analytical might want a side-by-side checklist comparison of a product's features, whereas an intellectual would be more interested in the product's underlying architecture and why it was made in the first place.

Be forewarned about intellectuals. You're going to think a meeting with them went great because the topic of conversation was at the 30,000-foot level. Usually, meetings with intellectuals end on a positive note and with everyone involved feeling good. That's the style of intellectuals. They're not typically going to confront you and devalue your solution in person. For them, every meeting is a learning experience.

Later, intellectuals will let their department members sift through the details. You should anticipate that this team will find technical objections and a variety of other reasons why your solution won't work for them. Therefore, you must continually be selling at all levels of the organization if you suspect the C-level executive is an intellectual. Solely executing a top-down sales strategy will most likely fail.

Sergeant Schultz Sergeant Schultz customers will conduct a low level of due diligence and a cursory verification of the information that is presented to them. The moniker is based upon the character from the classic television series *Hogan's Heroes*. In the series, whenever Sergeant Schultz was asked a question, he always responded, "I know nothing. I see nothing!" A Sergeant Schultz doesn't know, doesn't care, or will mistakenly ignore important information. In addition, he will deny that he knows anything when asked tough questions by salespeople.

Yes, there are C-level Sergeant Schultzes. They are typically found in very large companies with immense bureaucracies where one department has no clue what another is doing.

While Sergeant Schultzes are rare, you might run into one in the federal, state, and local government accounts or monolithic industries such as automobile and insurance.

The single most important question to ask yourself when you meet a Sergeant Schultz is, "Does this senior-level decision maker have the wherewithal to make a purchase?" Nine times out of ten the answer will be no.

Summary Seeker   A summary seeker is a curious person who is more concerned with the big picture than small details. Summary seekers quickly grasp complex subjects and tend to make snap decisions about the relevance of information. They are typically more trusting than anal analyticals but less patient than intellectuals. Heavy Hitter salespeople love to sell to summary seekers.

It's not surprising that the majority of C-level executives are summary seekers because they are extremely busy. The nature of running a department or company means they have to manage down to employees, out to customers, and up to even more important executives and the board. Therefore, they don't have the time or mental bandwidth to process tons of detailed information. That's why important facts, risk assessments, value judgments, and the rewards of moving forward with the purchase should be summarized and presented to them in a succinct manner that is easily understood.

Here's a general breakdown of the informational roles for C-level executives. Remember, these are general guidelines of what to expect, and the percentages vary greatly by industry. For example, there are more anal analyticals in the semiconductor business because of the technical nature of designing and manufacturing computer chips. There are far more summary seekers in the advertising industry, and this makes sense because people tend to make quick decisions on ads based upon first impressions. Over time, your goal should be to develop the specific breakdown for C-level executives you call on for the industry you're in.

Summary seeker	40 percent
Anal analytical	30 percent
Intellectual	20 percent
Sergeant Schultz	5 percent
Gullible	5 percent

Character Roles

Just as people change their behavior whenever they are in groups, evaluators adopt new character traits depending upon their colleagues on the selection committee. This also applies to C-level executives. They will behave quite differently in front of fellow employees than when they are alone. Here are the most common character roles that evaluators assume.

Class Clown   Class clown customers thrive on being the center of attention and always seem to have a smart remark or joke handy. While a psychiatrist might say the class clown's disruptions are driven by thoughts of inadequacy, this character role serves an important selection process function: the class clown's silliness releases the evaluation team's pent-up stress.

Be careful when you meet with C-level executives who are class clowns. Since they are so friendly and jovial, it is easy to be lulled into a false sense of security and take their word at face value. Moreover, when C-level executives become class clowns, they are attempting to remove themselves from the stressful position of being the final selector and dissociate themselves from the decision.

I once worked with a CIO who was also a part-time actor and member of the Screen Actors Guild. He was hilarious, and every meeting revolved around his antics. In hindsight, I see I spent far too much time on the account. When a smaller-than-expected purchase was finally made, it was nearly nine months after the CIO said it was initially going to happen. The opportunity cost was too great, and I would have been better off spending my time elsewhere.

Dreamer   Whether they have a momentary daydream about a vacation to a tropical destination or a fantasy about marriage that has been fostered since childhood, people love to dream about the future. Some dreamers are fixated on one goal, while others long for just about everything. During the selection process, dreamers tend to fall in love quickly with a particular salesperson or the solution they believe will help them realize their fantasy soonest. However, they are impulsive buyers who suffer from immense mood swings, which can cause them to second-guess their initial selection and frequently change their minds.

As opposed to the class clown, dreamers are salespeople's dreams come true. Their main motivation is usually based upon satisfying their ego, and that's a powerful purchase driver. In a perfect world you want your dreamer to also be a powerful consolidator—someone who can make the grand initiative happen because he is the bully with the juice. However, you should be extremely skeptical of consulter buyer types who are dreamers because they will talk the big talk but in reality are duds.

Hothead   Based upon a survey of 9,282 adults, the National Institute of Mental Health estimates that 5 to 7 percent of the population suffers from intermittent explosive disorder, which is characterized by raging outbursts that are way out of proportion to the situation.[3] While these destructive temper tantrums are most commonly associated with road rage, customers have fits of rage as well. If these figures are correct, one out of every twenty customers you encounter is a hothead.

You definitely know when you meet with a C-level hothead. Sometimes hotheads explode during the sales call and publicly berate their own employees and colleagues. Worse is when they are combative and condescending to you. Hotheads don't like to meet with salespeople, so they verbally abuse them in front of their staffs!

The best way to handle this intentional act of humiliation is to maintain your composure as best you can and not take the attack personally. Remember, you are dealing with a person who suffers from a mental disorder. Many company founders happen to be hotheads. They are used to barking orders and getting their way through domination.

Maven   The goal of maven customers is to use the selection process to demonstrate their knowledge and intelligence to others. They're smart and they know it. Quite often, mavens are fascinated by electronic gadgets and own the latest technologies. They adorn their bodies with these precious objects in an expression of prowess.

They typically won't listen to the opinions of others or accept personal criticism because they already know exactly what's best. Therefore, you won't win arguments with mavens. Selling to them requires an indirect psychological sales strategy as they will not be swayed by any vendor's logic or reason. Mavens march to their own drumbeat.

Rather, you must sell to a maven's ego. At every opportunity elicit his feedback, not so much for its own merits, but so your maven can hear himself talk about your solution. Bring the specialists within your company to your meeting—technical gurus, product managers, and various members of the executive staff. If you treat the maven with the respect he deserves, you'll find out he isn't such a tough person to sell to after all.

People Pleaser   Some evaluators feel compelled to befriend every-body, including all the salespeople from the various companies who are calling on the account. People pleasers dislike confrontation and feel very uncomfortable knowing that someone is at odds with them. Therefore, the information they provide must always be dis-counted because it is being given for the sole purpose of pleasing the questioner and may not be the actual truth. People pleasers will be amenable to any decision because they always go along with the group.

Personally, I cannot stand C-level people pleasers. I want to know where I stand in an account. I want to know the answer to the most important question in all of sales: "Will I win the deal?" When think-ing of C-level people pleasers I am reminded of the climax of the movie *A Few Good Men*, where Jack Nicholson's character exclaims, "You can't handle the truth!" Well, I *can* handle the truth. Just tell it to me as soon as possible so I don't waste my precious time. I don't want prospective customers to tell me what they think I want to hear. I want the truth, and so should you.

Schadenfreuder   Some people take delight in the failure and misfor-tune of others. This delight is called "schadenfreude." While a hot-head wears his emotions on his sleeve and might explode in rage, a schadenfreuder plots quietly behind the scenes against you. While a hothead is searching for the best solution and actually plans on buy-ing something, quite often the schadenfreuder never intended to buy from you in the first place. It is all a game to him and he delights in tormenting salespeople. The most extreme schadenfreuders are mis-anthropes—they hate people.

C-level schadenfreuders are truly evil, and you will have psycho-logical scars at the end of your encounter to prove it. Sometimes they present just enough optimistic information to keep a salesperson engaged when they really have no intention of buying his product. They'll entice the salesperson with claims of big purchases that are just off in the horizon. I remember attending a meeting with one of my salespeople who called on a schadenfreuder CTO. At one point the CTO asked the junior salesperson how he was going to spend all the commission he was going to make off the sale. It was a sadistic trick and I wanted to punch him in the nose. You must have the self-respect to walk away from the schadenfreuder's account.

Straight Shooter Straight shooters have a strong sense of honor and integrity. They are not alarmists but usually even-keeled evaluators who will listen to what each salesperson has to say. Heavy Hitters love selling to straight shooters. Straight shooters are sincerely interested in finding the best solution for the people who will implement and use it. They work together with their colleagues toward a common goal and vision. They are open-minded, they listen to others' opinions, and they take pride that they are part of the team.

The best way to sell to a C-level straight shooter is to become one yourself. While an aggressive, high-energy strategy might be appropriate in certain sales situations, mirroring the straight shooter's behavior is an equally effective strategy. Every communication with him should be structured and well documented. Don't fudge on the truth; give definitive truthful answers to his questions. Consciously slow down your speech, breathing, and mannerisms from your normal hyperactive pace.

The straight shooter's orientation is long-term, and you will probably not be able to accelerate the selection process. The evaluation process will be well thought out and lengthy. The winner will be the last vendor standing, the one who exhibited the attributes necessary to satisfy the straight shooter. In essence, the sales cycle is a miniature dry run of the long-term relationship.

Here's a general breakdown of the character roles for C-level executives. Again, these are guidelines; your goal is to develop a specific breakdown for your industry and the products you sell.

Maven	30 percent
Straight shooter	30 percent
Dreamer	15 percent
Hothead	13 percent
Schadenfreuder	5 percent
People pleaser	5 percent
Class clown	2 percent

Authority Roles

People's authority does not always correlate to how long they have worked for their company or have been employed in their profession. In reality, selection committee members adopt authority roles in order to influence their colleagues and the decision outcome. Here are the most common authority roles that evaluators assume.

Bureaucrat   Bureaucrats are focused on selection processes and procedures. However, they will use the selection processes for their selfish gain or to exercise their political power. Many bureaucrats are consumed with maintaining the status quo. Most frequently, the best way to prevent change is to stop the purchase process entirely, so that is what bureaucrat customers often try to do.

A sales call with a C-level bureaucrat can be extremely frustrating for two reasons. First, the meeting with the bureaucrat is typically arranged by an underling (midlevel or low-level person) who enthusiastically supports you and your solution. Because he has been championing your cause internally, you are optimistic about your chances of winning the business. However, when you finally meet the C-level bureaucrat you quickly realize that a purchase will never happen or that the C-level bureaucrat has other ideas about whom the company should do business with. After months of time and effort, all the hopes you had to win the account are gone. This is why you must meet with C-level decision makers early in the sales cycle.

The second reason has to do with how the bureaucrat behaves during the meeting. He will use a variety of psychological coping mechanisms (consciously used defense mechanisms) to dominate you. We'll talk more about coping mechanisms later in this chapter.

Dictator   Dictator customers are focused on decreeing the company's direction. Whereas a class clown uses humor to keep himself in the spotlight, dictators use unrelenting power to maintain their prominence. These domineering taskmasters are usually interested only in immediate results, what your solution has to offer here and now.

Even if an evaluation team has been assembled under the guise of making an impartial selection, the C-level dictator rules its members through oppression, intimidation, or fear. Most C-level dictators are narcissists (preoccupied admirers of themselves). However, they are typically very polished executives. They don't necessarily broadcast their power or goose-step around the office like a fascist ruler, but they rule their obedient masses with the same ruthlessness. When you shake the hand of a C-level dictator, you are always shaking the hand of the bully with the juice.

Empty Suit   Empty suit customers protect themselves by hiding behind inflated job titles that are not justified by their experience, knowledge, or ability to lead. While empty suits may be charming and gregarious individuals, they have misconceptions about their own strengths and how the organization views them.

A C-level executive who is an empty suit will typically make a great impression on the first sales call. However, each subsequent meeting becomes more frustrating. Because C-level empty suits are mainly preoccupied with keeping their jobs, they are extremely hesitant to move a purchase forward or to ruffle the feathers of others within the organization.

Old Pro   Old pro customers are case-hardened evaluators who have years of experience working with vendors. They are experts at managing the selection process, they know what to expect from the vendors, and they command respect.

You don't exaggerate to a C-level old pro because he'll call you on it every time. Even though the C-level old pro's demeanor may be gruff and cantankerous, deep inside is an individual who seeks friendships. Heavy Hitters love to sell to old pros. The key is finding an intersecting activity you have in common and selling yourself to them by establishing a trusting familial relationship.

Proctor   In the academic world, proctors oversee the administration of tests to ensure that none of the students cheat. The business world has proctors whose sole purpose, so it seems, is to ensure that the selection process is followed to the letter.

Whereas a C-level bureaucrat is motivated to stop the purchase decision, a C-level proctor seems more concerned about following the rules of the selection process than the actual selection itself. For example, a vice president of purchasing who is a C-level proctor will punish vendors who violate the selection process. This obviously creates a challenge because your goal is to implement the indirect strategy and change the selection process. Therefore, you must either be in the account first and attempt to set the rules with the proctor or develop another C-level executive, an old pro for instance, into your coach so that he can override the proctor.

Pundit   Every group has a pundit—a person who feels compelled to continually parade his or her opinions. On selection committees, these constant critics are the equivalent of a backseat driver. They assail other committee members, find fault with the direction they are taking, and attack vendors with a barrage of criticism.

C-level pundits will authoritatively pass judgment on you and your solution in your presence to throw you off track. They'll say things like "That will never work for us" or "Your competition is better." These assaults are C-level pundits' self-defense mechanism for avoiding a relationship with you (because they favor another competitor) or dissociating themselves from their decision-making responsibilities. Never forget, one of a customer's most prized possessions is his or her opinion.

Soldier   The word "soldier" originated from the French term *soudoior,* a man who fought for pay.[4] Corporate soldiers are paid to perform their jobs without question. Soldier customers have the lowest level of power and will dutifully follow orders passed down the chain of command. The soldier's mantra is "Ours is not to question why, ours is but to do or die."

When the CEO tells the CFO what company to do business with, the CFO becomes a soldier C-level executive who has just received his marching orders. This is why you should always sell at the highest possible level in every account.

Here's a general breakdown of the authority roles for C-level executives.

Old pro	30 percent
Dictator	25 percent
Bureaucrat	15 percent
Proctor	10 percent
Pundit	10 percent
Empty suit	5 percent
Soldier	5 percent

Company Roles
People's titles tell only part of the story about their role within a company. In the business world, selection committee members take on additional company roles beyond their position on the organization

chart. These roles show their true political power and their personal disposition toward their company. Here are the most common company roles that evaluators assume.

Hired Gun   Hired guns are corporate expatriates. They are not emotionally invested in their jobs or completely committed to the company they work for. They tend to select products they believe will help them get their next job. The motto of a hired gun is "There is no such thing as a bad product if it helps you get your next job."

C-level hired guns are market-share sensitive. They like to do business with gorillas, the dominant players in the market. Therefore, if you sell for a chimp-sized company, you are in an extremely dangerous position when the bully with the juice is a hired gun.

Fifth Columnist   Fifth columnists are rebels who are dissatisfied with their personal predicament inside the company. The term "fifth column" originated during the Spanish Civil War and refers to a group of people who clandestinely plan to undermine a larger group. In the business world, fifth columnists feel cheated by their company in some way. They might believe they are not receiving the recognition and respect they deserve.

Frequently, C-level fifth columnists are out to prove themselves greater than another company executive or to prove that their department is the best in the company. They'll purchase products not only to further their cause but to undermine the success, power, and authority of others inside the company. During the sales cycle, they will frequently identify with and relate to a salesperson more than to their own coworkers. Contrary to meeting with every other type of C-level executive, it is actually best to meet with a C-level fifth columnist alone so that he will share his secret plans with you.

Vigilante   Company vigilantes are extremely pessimistic people who want to protect their company from the claims of vendors. Usually they are eternal naysayers, out to prove that none of the vendors' proposed solutions will work for their company. Vigilantes see their right to voice their opinion as a sacred trust. They take the decision-making process very seriously and vote for the product they believe adds the most value to the company's day-to-day operations and long-term strategy.

C-level vigilantes are skeptical and do not trust salespeople. They'll make every vendor respond to immense RFPs and complete laborious spreadsheets. Each product feature and operation has to be fully documented to prove it exists. They'll require meticulous hands-on evaluations of each product and painstakingly documented findings. They won't buy until they are completely satisfied, and when they meet with salespeople, they are cross-examiners as opposed to collaborators like C-level fifth columnists.

Intern   Interns either will delegate their evaluation responsibilities to others or are the junior members of the selection team so they can't contribute to the selection process. They may be new to the company or profession or lack experience in selecting products.

Sometimes, an executive is classified as a C-level intern because he doesn't care to be involved with the procurement process. The project is not important enough to warrant his time and attention. Since the C-level intern doesn't have industry domain expertise or technical aptitude, the bulk of the evaluation work falls on the shoulders of midlevel managers who are experienced with company operations or low-level personnel who have deep technical knowledge. These people become the bullies with the juice in the account while the C-level intern is the emperor. C-level interns typically become involved very late in the sales cycle, after the preliminary recommendation had been made for their review.

Politician   Politicians in a company are smooth schemers who opportunistically maneuver to hold onto or gain power within the organization. They speak with carefully selected words and try to display a professional demeanor at all times. They would agree with French essayist Paul Valery, who wrote, "Politics is the art of preventing people from taking part in affairs which directly concern them."[5]

It's not surprising that the C-level politician is the most prevalent company role because it requires political acumen to make it to the top. C-level politicians are the influential statesmen of companies. They are experienced in dealing with company issues, know how to make things happen, and get their way in the process. They're more reserved than vigilantes and more polished than interns. They hold their cards close to their chest and won't broadcast their intentions until the salesperson has proven that it is in their political interest to do so.

Pollyanna   Pollyannas believe the company they work for is the best, whether it is or not. Usually, they absolutely love their jobs and find good in everyone and everything. Typically, these overly optimistic customers are hard workers and may have spent their entire careers at a single company.

C-level Pollyannas have a tendency to ignore ugly facts and underestimate the complexity of the solutions they purchase. As opposed to vigilantes, they are genuinely excited about the upcoming purchase, and Heavy Hitters are grateful for their naiveté. Obviously, it makes sense for salespeople to mirror their excitement and enthusiasm.

Revolutionary   Revolutionaries are out to create upheaval in their organization. They are agents of change who seek to remake the company's culture, its mind-set, or the way it does business.

As opposed to fifth columnists, C-level revolutionaries have sincere motives and want the company to succeed. For example, they might be trying to change a technology-driven company to a customer-focused one, to reinvigorate company morale, or to enter new markets. They seek solutions that will help them accomplish their revolution. Whenever a new executive joins a company, he becomes a C-level revolutionary who seeks to consolidate his power by creating grand initiatives. That's why you should always keep track of executives on the move and be the first salesperson to meet with them in their new job.

Here's a general breakdown of the company roles for C-level executives.

Politician	35 percent
Vigilante	20 percent
Revolutionary	15 percent
Intern	10 percent
Hired gun	10 percent
Fifth columnist	5 percent
Pollyanna	5 percent

During sales calls and the selection process as a whole, the role each team member adopts will depend on the roles other members of the decision process occupy. For example, there typically can be only one dictator, maven, and class clown at a time. Selection team members have to assume other roles once these roles are taken. Conversely, a team can have multiple pundits, schadenfreuders, and anal analyticals. People assuming these roles actually encourage other selection team members to join them.

The roles people take on during the sales cycle determine how you will communicate with them. Most interestingly, these roles can vary from purchase to purchase. For example, a CIO who has a vested interest in the Internet provider his company uses to run its business might be an anal analytical during the selection process. Conversely, he's a Sergeant Schultz when it comes to the purchase of toner cartridges because he doesn't care.

Perhaps the most important aspect of customer role-playing to remember is that customers do not play the same role with each vendor. For example, a C-level evaluator might present himself as a schadenfreuder and vigilante to you while being a straight shooter and politician with your competitor. Under these circumstances, you will not win this deal. Therefore, you must evaluate not only how selection team members are relating to you but, equally important, theorize how they are relating to your competitors.

C-Level Executive Coping Mechanisms

Like salespeople, senior executives experience stress during the selling process. They enter the sales cycle with preconceived ideas about each vendor's product and capabilities. Even before the first sales call, they have formed preferences and biases regarding the vendors. This alone causes stress because they will probably have to meet with salespeople they already know they won't buy from.

We naturally assume that executives will react in one of two ways to our pitch: they'll like it or they won't. However, customer behavior is far more complex. Customers use sophisticated coping mechanisms when facing the stressful situation of selecting between salespeople and their solutions. Coping mechanisms are psychological and behavioral strategies people use to manage stress and threatening situations.

The coping mechanism a C-level executive uses depends greatly on the group decision-making roles he assumes. Here's a list of the common buyer coping mechanisms you can expect to encounter on sales calls with C-level executives along with the roles they're most frequently associated with:

- *Attack.* Some executives categorize all salespeople as unethical evildoers and therefore attack you as being part of the group. Do not take this attack personally. These buyers are not excited about making a purchase decision. Generalizing all salespeople into a single group helps them handle the ordeal of buying.

Applicable roles: anal analytical, hothead, schadenfreueder, dicta-tor, pundit, vigilante

- *Avoidance.* Certain executives will seek to avoid the people and sit-uations that cause distress. They'll keep the conversation solely at the surface level and won't answer tough questions. Confronting executives who use this coping mechanism causes them to avoid stressful people and situations all the more.

  Applicable roles: intellectual, sergeant schultz, class clown, people pleaser, empty suit, intern, pollyanna

- *Business-level conversation.* Some executives instinctively try to keep the conversation at a business level with the nonfavored salespeople. They do this to protect themselves because they don't want to let anyone down. This is one of the most prevalent coping mechanisms buyers use to deal with salespeople.

  Applicable roles: gullible, intellectual, maven, bureaucrat, proctor, vigilante, politician

- *Compensation.* Executives sometime make up for a weakness in one area by overemphasizing another. For example, a business-oriented senior executive who can't follow the technical conver-sation of subordinates with a salesperson may blurt out, "I'm in charge of the selection."

  Applicable roles: gullible, hothead, dictator, empty suit, proctor, vigilante, revolutionary

- *Intellectualization.* Some executives will avoid showing any emo-tion and focus instead on facts and logic. However, even the most analytical and unemotional customers have a sentimental favor-ite that they want to win.

  Applicable roles: anal analytical, intellectual, summary seeker, maven, schadenfreuder, straight shooter, bureaucrat, proctor, sol-dier, vigilante, politician

- *Passive aggressiveness.* Some executives project a friendly superficial presence but are secretly plotting against you. This is one of the worst predicaments for any salesperson to be in.

  Applicable roles: summary seeker, dreamer, people pleaser, empty suit, hired gun, politician, pollyanna

- *Rationalization.* Certain executives use logical reasons in an illogical way to publicly validate their emotional favorite. For example, they'll say they can't use your product because it doesn't support international monetary conversions, even though they don't conduct any international business.

  Applicable roles: gullible, sergeant schultz, class clown, maven, schadenfreuder, hothead, pundit, empty suit, proctor, hired gun, fifth columnist

- *Reaction formation.* Some executives take a polar opposite position to everything you say. They simply don't want to buy from you.

  Applicable roles: hothead, schadenfrueder, bureaucrat, dictator, pundit, hired gun, fifth columnist, vigilante, revolutionary

- *Trivialization.* Some executives trivialize a favored vendor's major deficiency while maximizing the minor shortcomings of the other vendors. This is another sure sign that they are against you.

  Applicable roles: anal analytical, maven, intellectual, straight shooter, soldier, intern, pollyanna

Finally, sometimes what customers say about you really applies to them. They'll say your price is too high when, in reality, they couldn't have afforded it in the first place. They will say your solution is technically inferior when they don't have the wherewithal to implement it. In other words, the most significant and prevalent customer coping mechanism is lying.

If I gave you car keys and placed you in a parking lot with a hundred different cars, you would know what to do with the keys based upon your knowledge of how cars work. You would be able to open the car door, start the car, and drive it away, even though you may have never driven or seen this type of car before. You have developed a pattern of behavior based upon your cumulative experiences of driving and being in cars.

Similarly, the C-level executive has developed a pattern of behavior for dealing with salespeople after hundreds of interactions. Since it is usually based upon negative experiences, the first goal of every sales call should be to perform a pattern interruption. You want to dissociate yourself from all the other salespeople and their previous negative sales calls. One way to accomplish this is by using reverse psychology and doing something completely different or totally unexpected. We'll talk more about how to use pattern interruptions in chapter 9.

You also want to perform a pattern interruption when the C-level executive resorts to his favorite coping mechanism during your sales call. When a hothead attacks you by saying "Your price is too high!" you might say "I could rationalize all the reasons why we charge what we do, but those would be 'rational lies.' Tell me how can we find the middle ground to make this business happen."

Questions to Ask Your Coach

The best sales calls take into account the human nature of customers. The psychological theory of holistic interactionism centers on the notion that behavior is not based solely on personality but ultimately influenced by a person's situational interaction with the environment. (For example, a gregarious extrovert is quiet and reserved while in a library.)

The holistic view of personal behavior acknowledges the interaction between people (their thoughts, emotions, and personalities) and the world that surrounds them at the same time. The situational nature of this theory helps explain why some executives don't want to disappoint salespeople during the sales call so they tell the salespeople what they want to hear. Meanwhile, other executives seek to avoid face-to-face confrontations so they keep their objections to themselves.

A successful sales call depends on your understanding the complete environment and the interactions between the audience members. The optimum way to conduct a sales call is through holistic interactionism, a person-centered approach that combines concrete thought processes (facts, features, and functions) with abstract thought processes (politics, environment, feelings, and benefactions). It's not enough to explain how well known your company is and how your product works. The goal must be to get executives to envision using the product so they drop their biases against you and your company and rally together around your cause.

The process of holistic interactionism starts with an investigation before the call to ascertain what the meeting environment will be like. Will you be interrogated Spanish Inquisition style or attend a Woodstock-like love fest? While it is easy to find out who is attending and what their official titles are, understanding the internal machinations of the customer's decision process requires a coach. Only a coach can tell you who is for, against, or ambivalent to your solution. Only a coach can prepare you for the various objections that will be raised during the presentation, objections that could you throw you off track. Involving your coach in the creation of the presentation topics, finding out what points to cover and what to avoid, is critical. Previewing the presentation with your coach is ideal.

Let's assume Mitch is our coach during this selection process. He's been providing us with accurate, proprietary information about the decision-making process and has actually told us he wants us to win. He is guiding us through the sales process and has arranged the meeting with his boss, Nancy, and his boss's boss, Bob, the C-level executive. Mitch is a great source of information about the group decision-making roles we can expect from Bob during our upcoming meeting, and we want to ask him questions that will help us prepare for them in advance, such as the following:

What is Bob's background?
How long has he been with the company?
What's it like to work for him?
Is he a down-to-earth person?
Is he outgoing with a sense of humor, or is he more serious and sullen?
Is he an optimist or a pessimist?
Is he big picture or detailed oriented?
What kind of work hours does he keep?
What are his personal hobbies?
What projects has he promoted and were they successful?
Is he well liked by the other company leaders?
How does he typically treat salespeople?
What are his perceptions about my company and me?
What should I watch out for?

These are just a few of the many questions you could ask your coach to understand the C-level executive's conscientiousness, gregariousness, and clout within the company. In the next chapter we will review the five steps to conducting a successful C-level sales call.

Conclusion

According to a poll conducted by the Pew Research Center, 46 percent of those polled favored the introduction of private Social Security accounts, while 38 percent opposed the new idea to secure Social Security's tenuous future.[6] Furthermore, 50 percent of college-educated responders were in favor while only 35 percent of those who had less than a high school education approved of the idea.

The top reason people opposed the idea was fear—they were uncomfortable with the uncertainty and potential risk. A study from psychologists at Swarthmore College and Stanford University shed light on the root of apprehension.[7] In a word association exercise to define what the word "choice" means, students of college-educated parents used words like "freedom," "action," and "control," whereas students of high-school-educated parents said "fear," "doubt," and "difficulty." The researchers' conclusion was that people do not uniformly welcome more choices into their lives. Furthermore, the sophistication level of people's environment drastically influences how they interpret information and make decisions.

Over the course of your career you will have to win over the hearts, minds, and souls of a wide variety of C-level executives in extremely diverse environments. Some executives seek power, want to take action, and desire to take control while others are filled with skepticism, doubt, and a fear of difficulty. We are trying to sell all of them one complete package, even though we talk about our company, products, features, benefits, and even ourselves individually. Ultimately, we are selling them something much larger—the idea that we can help change their lives for the better and enable them to be a part of something greater than themselves. We know we can make them happy.

> I think they did a much better job at listening to what we wanted to do. I credit our rep for his tremendous follow-up. Anytime we had a question, he attacked it. He would get their people on the phone within a day to answer how we could do something. He listened to what we were trying to do and he knew his resources. The other guy had more of a canned pitch: "Let us show you a demo," and the demo was supposed to do all the talking. They didn't take the interest to say "Exactly what are you trying to do and who do you want to be? Now let me tell you how my system can make you that."
>
> CHIEF INFORMATION OFFICER

8

Converse

> Almost all salespeople I meet with don't know how to be strategic. Once we set a direction, how do you help us get there? I am skeptical of asking for help from salespeople because the answers they come up with naturally revolve around their product. They should take a long-term approach, not force-fitting the products they have to sell today. Tell us what's best for us based upon your other customers. Your approach should be about the value you provide to me.
>
> CHIEF INFORMATION OFFICER

Sales is a process, the process of building a relationship and turning a skeptic into a believer and making a stranger your friend. Language and the words you say are the tools you use to achieve these results.

A question I'm often asked is, "What should I say to persuade the CEO, CFO, or CIO to buy?" Unfortunately, I don't know of any magic words. This is because no two CEOs, CFOs, or CIOs are exactly alike. Each is a unique individual who works in a one-of-a-kind company environment with its own set of business challenges and opportunities.

However, I usually give a two-part answer to this question, and the first part might surprise you. A critical aspect of the C-level sales call is not necessarily what you have planned to say on your call or in your presentation. Rather, it is how you handle the tough questions the executive asks you. Your question-handling ability during and after your presentation is what separates you from the pack.

The second part is that you need a methodology to determine the unique attributes of the executive you are going to be meeting with. You need to create a model of his behavior. Only after you build your model of the C-level executive can you effectively talk to him and anticipate his questions. Without a model, you're just doing a canned presentation and reciting your standard company pitch.

Here's a story that illustrates this point. A former client who was a vice president of sales asked me to review his resume that he hoped would land him the perfect job. Nothing was wrong with his resume: it was a detailed account of his background.

I asked him to describe in very specific terms whom he envisioned reading his resume. After several minutes of discussion, he finally came to the conclusion that they would be CEOs of private Silicon Valley application software companies with revenues between $15 and $100 million. Most likely, they were in their late thirties or early forties and one of the founders of the company. Once we had a more precise model of the target C-level executive, we were easily able to craft a compelling message centered on his past experience leading two sales organizations through successful public offerings. This is what the target CEOs would want to hear about, yet he didn't emphasize it in his initial resume. Remember, you can't effectively message to someone whom you don't personally identify with.

All senior salespeople are aware of their product's features, benefits, and specifications. Their company has identified a process to educate customers about their products and has established procedures to determine customers' business qualifications and technical requirements.

However, the intangible influence of human nature during the sales process is ultimately responsible for the decision being made. Since most salespeople find the human element of selling to be more complex, unpredictable, and difficult to manage, they don't fully take advantage of customer behavior or they misinterpret and ignore it. They don't know how to build the most important part of the model, nor do they know how to describe it to their teammates who will work with them on the account. Ideally, we want to build a model of human nature of the C-level executive to predict and influence his behavior.

The C-Level Executive Model

The purpose of the first seven chapters of this book has been to help you build a complete model of the C-level executive you must win over, to make you think about him as an individual with personal needs and desires who is leading an organization that is part of a complex political environment. Let's take a moment to review the C-Level executive model.

Attribute	Behavior
Organizational buying type	Consolidator, consulter, responder, bureaucrat
Sales cycle type	Renewal, persuasion, creation
Customer decision-making role	Informational role, character role, authority role, company role
Stress	Informational stress, peer pressure stress, corporate citizenship stress
Motivation	Psychological value, political value, operational value, strategic value
Language	C-level language, business operations language, technical specification language, intersecting activity language, physical language, internal dialogue language, word catalog language

Figure 8.1 The C-level executive model

The impetus for every enterprise purchase is power, and the executive is either a powerful consolidator, a weaker consulter, a debilitated responder, or a bureaucrat protecting himself with rules and regulations. The executive is involved with purchases that are quite diverse. He's renewing vendor relationships, considering new vendors, and comparing vendors head to head against each other.

His behavior during the decision-making process is complex and based upon group roles. He will process information and behave in a certain way. He has a unique ability to influence the group and exert his will on the evaluation team.

The executive is under tremendous stress and constantly trying to discern whether or not the information he is receiving is accurate. He has to please peers, subordinates, customers, and the executives above him. He's always balancing what's best for the company with what's best for himself.

He thinks of vendors in terms of value and whether they can help him accomplish his strategy, improve his operations, make him more powerful, and help him feel better about himself and his personal situation.

Finally, language is at the foundation of the model. The C-level executive transmits and receives information via his word catalog wiring, he's always talking to himself via his internal dialogue, and his body is continually emanating information. You have intersecting activities in common you can talk about, and you both use the technical language that is part of your industry. The executive speaks about the process of his business operations and his strategies. If he trusts you enough, he'll speak the confidential C-level language and share his personal plans and motivations.

Applying the C-Level Executive Model

For the purposes of applying group decision-making roles, let's pretend we are part of the sales team working on the Acme account, a Fortune 1000 company that is making a million-dollar purchase of state-of-the-art business software to replace its existing antiquated mainframe software. The Acme decision-making team is composed of Bob Adams, chief information officer; Nancy Smith, director of information technology; Mitch Jackson, project leader; and Mortimer Jones, vice president of purchasing. They are evaluating different enterprise software solutions.

Since the initiative to replace the mainframe software was championed by Bob, we surmise he is a consolidator buyer type. Therefore, we must sell at the C-level to Bob. This is also a persuasion sales cycle type because it has a well-defined selection process and has issued an RFP, and we know we are competing against our two archrivals. We know there is a 30 percent chance the team already has a favored vendor who will win the deal. Therefore, we need to determine if biases exist and build relationships at all levels as soon as possible in order to develop a coach.

Next, we make our assessment of the customer decision-making roles of the Acme evaluators (figure 8.2).

	Information Role	Character Role	Authority Role	Company Role
Bob Adams CIO	Summary seeker	Straight shooter	Old pro	Politician
Nancy Smith IT Director	Intellectual	Maven	Soldier	Pollyanna
Mitch Jackson Project Leader	Anal analytical	Maven	Pundit	Hired gun
Mortimer Jones VP of Purchasing	Anal analytical	Hothead	Bureaucrat	Vigilante

Figure 8.2 Acme's decision-making roles

Bob's a seasoned executive with the business skills and political acumen to lead the organization. Nancy has worked for Bob for seven years and is a maven who understands the details of the daily operations of the department. She's an optimistic soldier who marches to Bob's orders. Mitch is an accomplished technical expert. He's a cocky pundit who has little loyalty to the company. Mortimer is a hard-to-get-along-with numbers guy.

We theorize and prioritize the kinds of stress each person is under. Bob is mainly under corporate citizenship stress. He's worried about cutting costs during tough economic times. Nancy is under pressure from Bob. Bob has mandated that she cut her budget by 30 percent this year. She's worried about how Bob perceives her. Mitch is an anal analytical who wants to understand every technical detail, so he makes sure they are selecting the product with the best functionality. He suffers from informational stress. Mortimer is consumed with corporate citizenship stress. He's an anal analytical who wants all aspects of the business relationship documented in the contract. He believes he is the company's fiscal watchdog.

All of the evaluators have different motivations based upon their company roles. As a result, their perceptions of our solution's strategic, operational, political, and psychological value will be different. Here are the different values we provide Bob:

- Our strategic value is that we are the most cost-effective solution the team is considering.
- Our operational value has many aspects: we automate a number of functions that employees currently do by hand, our system is faster so they will be able to process orders faster, and the software has more functionality so user satisfaction will increase.
- From a political standpoint, our state-of-the-art graphical user interface will help improve the image of the IT department within the company.
- From a psychological standpoint, Bob's been worried about the old system for years, ever fearful that it will crash at critical times of the month and year. Our system will bring him much-needed peace of mind.

We will have to speak a variety of different languages with each decision maker. We'll talk visually to Bob, kinesthetically to Nancy, and auditorily to Mitch and Mortimer. We'll talk about technical specifications with Mitch and provide higher business operations level information to Bob. We'll even mirror the way Bob speaks—his tone, tempo, speaking patterns—to ensure our sales call is successful.

In order to establish personal relationships, we want to talk about the intersecting activities we share with the evaluators. We collect personal information about the evaluators through research, casual conversations, and quick examinations of the pictures, objects, and mementos in their offices. Bob's biography on the company Web site says he is an avid golfer, Nancy has three children (all girls), Mitch likes sailing, and Mortimer wears a wedding ring, so he must be married.

Once you have completed and applied the C-level executive model, you are ready to conduct your sales call.

> They nailed it. They knew our hot spots and understood our business inside and out.
>
> CHIEF EXECUTIVE OFFICER

The Five Steps to a Successful C-Level Sales Call

The most important events during the entire sales cycle are the face-to-face meetings with C-level executives. Here are five steps to completing a successful executive sales call:

Step 1—Determine your goal and personal outcome
Step 2—Ask questions to discover reality
Step 3—Match your selling style to the group decision-making roles
Step 4—Align value to your solution
Step 5—Get to the confidential C-level language

Let's discuss each of these steps in detail.

Step 1—Determine Your Goal and Personal Outcome

The first step is to determine your goal and outcome for the meeting. The ultimate goal for the C-level meeting is simple: you want the executive to expose his internal dialogue to you. You want him to honestly explain what he is trying to accomplish and why he is doing it from a business and, more importantly, personal standpoint. You want him to tell you about his personal needs and career desires along with how he plans to fulfill them. You want him to speak the confidential C-level language with you.

You are not there to sell anything. Your goal is to become a trusted advisor by asking questions and intently listening to the answers so that you can apply your expertise to solve the executive's business problems or complete his initiatives. The conversational theme starts with establishing a personal connection, followed by problem investigation and a discussion of possible solutions. Ideally, the conversation flows into an off-the-record talk about the politics of his organization and his ulterior motives. Accomplishing this requires you to speak the progression of languages represented in figure 8.3.

I know you might be worried that this big meeting may be your only chance to meet with the executive; therefore you feel you *must* explain to him how wonderful your company and products are. Well, if you go into this meeting with the intention of selling something, you'll be proven right: it will be the last time you get on his busy calendar. Never forget, although you are excited about the meeting, the C-level executive isn't that excited about your products and not all that interested in your marketing pitch. He's heard them and seen them before, and they all sound the same. You will be granted continual access if you can demonstrate how you can help solve his business problems and help him achieve his personal ambitions.

Unfortunately, the majority of executive conversations never reach the confidential C-level language. The discussion gets stuck at the technical specification language or the business operations language. Usually, this is because the salesperson is too busy talking about

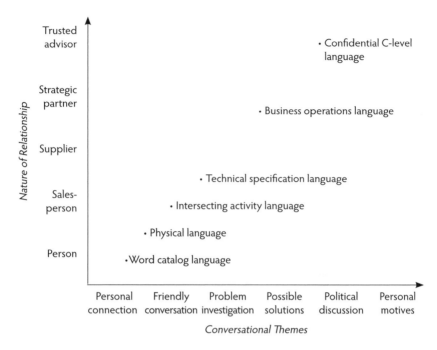

Figure 8.3 Ideal progression of languages during a
C-level sales call

his products and what they do instead of what the executive wants to change. At other times, this is by design because the executive doesn't trust and believe in the salesperson enough to speak frankly and share his thoughts with him.

Moreover, too many C-level meetings end without any definitive results. These first meetings are short and the time passes quickly. All too soon, the meeting is over and you leave without any significant new developments or agreed-upon action items. Therefore, it is important to identify a specific personal outcome of the meeting beforehand so you can judge whether you have achieved your goal.

Professional athletes understand personal outcomes. Sprinters will visualize an entire race and see themselves on the winner's stand receiving the gold medal. College basketball coaches will ask their team to mentally rehearse cutting down the net after they win the national championship.

Athletes describe their field of vision narrowing while they are focused on their personal outcome. A professional baseball player will see the stitches on a ninety-mile-per-hour fastball. Golfers that are surrounded by members of the gallery won't hear or see them while they focus on the next putt.

Your personal outcome may be to have the C-level executive tell you at the end of the meeting "It sounds great. Send me your contract!" In this example, you create a mental picture of the person and hear those words being said as he shakes your hand. You can measure the success of the call based upon what actually happens and how closely that matches this visualization.

The tactical objectives for the executive-level meeting can be quite diverse. The objective could be to *gather* information and find out how you are perceived versus the competition or other details about the selection process. It could be to *impart* information about your products or make a special pricing offer. It could be to *create* relationships or *influence* opinions. It could be to *negotiate* terms and conditions.

Whatever the tactical objectives for your meeting may be, you should define the words the executive must say to know that they have been achieved. You want to hear the executive say something definitive like "You are our preferred solution" or "Yes, we have a deal," not "We are still evaluating options" or "We'll consider that." Only when you hear the C-level executive say the words that validate your meeting's outcome have you actually achieved it.

Step 2—Ask Questions to Discover Reality

The most important part of the executive sales call is the beginning of the meeting when you have the opportunity to ask questions. This is your "discovery" part of the sales call, and the executive's answers help you determine his word catalog wiring and find intersecting activities in common. The questions you ask also provide the opportunity to demonstrate your command of the technical specification language used in your industry and show the executive that you understand how his company runs by speaking the business operations language. Successful discovery is the first step toward building a foundation of trust and respect that leads to the executive speaking the confidential C-level language.

In chapter 1, we discussed how everyone operates in his or her own individual reality. While you may have had twenty meetings with low-level and midlevel personnel, the goal of asking the C-level executive questions is triangulation. Triangulation is the process of checking multiple data points of information about an account with various decision makers to ensure it is accurate and true. In order to identify true reality, these data points should always include information from C-level executives.

The six types of questions to ask executives are based upon "what," "how," "why," "when," "who," and "would." "What" questions include "What are you trying to accomplish?" and "What business problem are you trying to solve?" "How" questions include "How will you make a decision?" and "How will you implement the solution?" "Why" questions include "Why is the company evaluating new suppliers?" and "Why is this particular person on the evaluation team?" "When" questions include "When will a decision be made?" and "When is the project to be completed?" "Who" questions include "Who will perform the evaluation?" and "Who will sign the contract?" "Would" questions include "Would you like to meet with our CEO?" and "Would it make sense for me to start meeting with your contract team?" Most salespeople are well versed at asking who, when, and how questions but don't spend enough time asking what, why, and would questions.

Suppose we sell enterprise software to banks and we have our first meeting with the CFO of Acme Bank, one of the world's largest banks. We are competing against Archrival Software. We assemble our sales team and make a list of all the possible questions we can ask the CFO. Here are some of the questions we could ask:[1]

> What worries you most about today's financial environment, and how do you think this affects your company?
> What is your most pressing business problem?
> What would you say the top five most significant challenges are?
> What has prevented you from addressing these business challenges in the past?
> Why do you believe this project will address all of these problems?
> What is the biggest area of opportunity?
> What can you tell us about your vision to be the premier provider of financial services?
> What goals will you fulfill if this project succeeds?
> What is your vision for this project?
> What metrics does your CEO tend to be most interested in?
> What are your plans to deal with the recession?
> What do you fear might happen at ACME Bank given the current economic conditions?
> What's the impact of your recent merger on your business and systems?
> If we could wave a magic wand and make a problem go away, what problem would you choose and why?
> What are the consequences of keeping the same software?
> What customer service issues do you think need to be addressed ASAP?
> What time frame did you have in mind for a solution to be implemented?
> What are your impressions of the various companies in our space?
> What workarounds have you had to come up with to handle the limitations of your current solution?

What would happen if the project was delayed for a year?

What are the selection criteria you will use to judge the companies you are evaluating?

What is the toughest part of your job?

From what you have seen so far, do you think we have the ability to address your issues?

What company has impressed you most during the evaluation?

What are the three most important qualities you look for in a business partner?

What's your budget?

Why are you looking for new software?

Why wasn't this project started a year ago?

Why are these problems getting attention now?

Why is your budget $10 million for this project?

Why are you in charge of this decision, as opposed to the CIO or COO?

Can you tell us why you think Archrival Software's solution is a better (or worse) fit than ours?

How much time do we have today?

How long have you worked at Acme? Where were you before?

How do you think the new software will impact you in the short term and in the long run?

How did this project originate?

How familiar are you with us and the solutions that we offer?

How far along are you with the evaluation process?

How do projects get prioritized, and where is this project in the priority?

How would you say that current technology limitations are affecting your daily operations?

How did you hear about our company? We just want to make sure we send a bottle of Dom Perignon to the right person!

How long do you think it will take from selection to contract approval and signing?

How do we stack up against the competition?

When will the evaluation be complete?

When can we meet again?

When will the contract approval process start, and how long would it take to get the project approved?

When can we show you a demonstration?

Who prioritizes projects like this, and how are they prioritized?

Who else are you looking at right now?

Whose solution looks the best to you?

Who will be part of the evaluation team? Why have they been selected?

With whom should we work in each step of the evaluation process?

Who in the organization will be adversely impacted when the current solution is replaced?

Who will have input into this decision?

With whom will we work from your legal and procurement departments?

Who has worked with Archrival Software before?

Have you personally met with all the vendors yet?

I see John Smith from Archrival Software periodically. Is he your account rep?

Are you aware that Big World Bank is now moving to our solution because of our superior service and track record?

Would you like to meet the CFO of Big World Bank next week?

I have an RFP template based on another project that was very similar to yours. Would you like to see it?

Would you like to meet with our president next Thursday when he is in town?

We usually partner very closely with our customer executives and have regular advisory council meetings. Would you like to attend one?

Would you like to make site visits to other financial institutions that are using our solution?

What is the most important thing that I could do to help you make a decision in our favor?

If we were able to do X, would you do Y?

Would you like to attend the Super Bowl with me next weekend?

What are the most important questions on this list? It depends. Aside from qualification questions, the best questions to ask are called "leading questions." These questions are planned in advance so that the executive's answer guides the discussion to your product's unique strategic and operational value. For example, you could ask, "What metrics does your CEO tend to be most interested in?" in order to provide the opportunity to explain the unique metrics your executive dashboard provides.

Take a moment to complete the following exercise. Write down five leading questions you could ask a C-level executive.

1. _____

2. _____

3. _____

4. _____

5. _____

Even though we may have asked the same questions many times of low-level and midlevel personnel, we need to ascertain reality according to the C-level executive in charge. The C-level executive's perception of the pain, problem, and future plans may be vastly different than the reality that has been presented to us by his staff.

Obviously, you won't be able to ask a hundred questions during your brief C-level meeting. Therefore, you must prioritize your list to ensure it includes your top ten most important qualification and leading questions.

Step 3—Match Your Selling Style to the Group Decision-Making Roles

How do you communicate with a C-level executive you have never met before? How do you best present your story, and what demeanor should you use to convince him to speak in confidence with you? In chapter 7 we identified the different C-level group decision-making roles. These roles help us understand evaluators' dispositions and motivations and the granularity of the information you should present.

Identifying the information roles helps you understand whether to present a high-level summary to a summary seeker or be prepared to dive into the details with an anal analytical. If the latter is the case, you know that you must bring along your colleagues who have a commensurate industry background and technical expertise.

Knowing the character roles informs you how to act in their presence. You adopt a "tell it like it is" demeanor with a straight shooter, carefully select your words with a hothead, and foster the fantasies of dreamers.

The authority roles provide insight into the decision-making process. Is the executive a dictator who will bully the selection committee? Is he a proctor who is more concerned about the rules of the selection rather than the selection itself? Is he an empty suit who lacks the wherewithal to make any decision at all?

Identifying company roles helps you understand how each executive perceives himself within the organization. Is he dissatisfied with his company, is he new to the company, or does he want to change the company solely for his own benefit?

Why should you understand the different customer decision-making roles? Because they will help you strategize, plan, and execute your C-level sales call. Figure 8.4 summarizes the purpose of determining each role category.

Information role	Helps determine how you will present information and who should attend the C-level sales call
Character role	Prepares your colleagues for the unique group dynamics of the C-level meeting
Authority role	Provides insight into the C-level executive's decision-making process
Company role	Explains the executive's ulterior motives, how he perceives himself, and his power within the company

Figure 8.4 Purpose of determining customer decision-making roles

Some group decision-making combinations are dangerous and unpredictable. Be extremely cautious when meeting executives who are hothead dictators, schadenfreuder bureaucrats, pundit fifth columnists, and proctor vigilantes. One bad move during sales calls with these executives and the account is lost. Conversely, Sergeant Schultz class clowns, gullible people pleasers, empty suit pollyannas, and soldier interns are extremely bad combinations for another reason. The likelihood that these executives can make a major purchase happen is infinitesimal.

Your goal is to mirror the executives' group decision-making roles. "Mirroring" is a psychological term for the conscious act of changing your behavior to match your surroundings. In part I of the book we discussed how to build rapport by mirroring the tone, tempo, and speaking patterns of Auditories, Visuals, and Kinesthetics. Now you have to adapt your selling style to match the unique combination of executive group decision-making roles.

Your selling style is influenced by a complex combination of your instinctive drives. You naturally use these instincts to exert your will upon customers. Seven basic instincts determine your selling style and your actions at any particular moment: dominance, hyperactivity, pride, greed, transparency, curiosity, and empathy. Let's discuss each of these instincts and apply them to the various group decision-making roles.

Dominance—the drive to take command of a situation—is instrumental to a salesperson's success. Some salespeople have such a strong dominance instinct that they think of customers as naturally inferior people. Conversely, a salesperson with a weak dominance instinct is more apt to operate under the direction of customers. Usually, you should seek the equilibrium point between dominance and submission. It's the point where the customer respects your conviction and is not offended by your persistence.

However, certain group decision-making roles require you to have low dominance, where you are submissive, or high dominance, where you must take control. For example, you will most likely sabotage your sales call if you try to establish dominance over a maven or hothead. Conversely, you must establish dominance over a dreamer to create a tangible action item from the meeting, and you need to push back against the unreasonable demands of a bureaucrat.

Use high dominance: gullible, Sergeant Schultz, class clown, dreamer, people pleaser, bureaucrat, and intern.

Use low dominance: anal analytical, hothead, maven, straight shooter, dictator, old pro, revolutionary, and politician.

You can think of the instinct of hyperactivity as your sales metabolism, the pace at which you conduct yourself during the call. Some salespeople can't stop moving. They're always talking and nervous or uncomfortable when the conversation stops. Other salespeople are more deliberate in their moves, and they take longer to complete their sentences. Whether one pace is better than the other depends upon the person you are meeting with.

Use high hyperactivity: gullible, summary seeker, dreamer, empty suit, and intern.

Use low hyperactivity: anal analytical, intellectual, maven, straight shooter, bureaucrat, and proctor.

You may not have initially thought of pride as an instinct, but it is one. Pride is the measure of self-importance and your opinion of your own worth. Pride is also the midway point between arrogance and humility. A straight shooter expects humility. A schadenfreuder doesn't expect prideful resistance; he wants to intimidate you. In general, arrogance is a very bad attribute during a sales call. However, some meetings actually require self-importance and pretentiousness.

Use high pride: gullible, schadenfreuder, pundit, hired gun, and fifth columnist.

Use low pride: hothead, maven, straight shooter, old pro, soldier, and politician.

We normally associate greed with a miserly scrooge or a corrupt character. While this may be society's definition, in sales, "greed" takes on an entirely different meaning during C-level sales calls. You have probably worked with many different types of salespeople, and you may have noticed that some gravitated toward working on only big deals, while others nickel-and-dime their way to their quotas. The greed instinct is actually a key influencer in the way salespeople work on a deal.

Should a salesperson try to make the deal as big as possible and include all the potential options and services? Or should he keep the deal small and more affordable so that it elicits the least amount of organizational scrutiny? Obviously, you want to propose a big deal to a gullible, while the proposal to a vigilante should be the bare-bones minimum.

> *Use high greed:* gullible, intellectual, dreamer, dictator, hired gun, pollyanna, and revolutionary.

> *Use low greed:* hothead, people pleaser, straight shooter, old pro, pundit, soldier, and vigilante.

Transparency is the ability to be exactly who you are and the propensity to be perfectly frank about it. In other words, what people see is what you are. Some salespeople are completely transparent. They are very comfortable with themselves, let others see exactly who they are, and tell it like it is. On the other hand, other salespeople tend to display less personality and shield themselves behind a more formal demeanor. They play the role of the salesperson.

We normally don't associate confrontation with sales calls. After all, we're trying to build relationships. However, transparent salespeople aren't afraid to be frank with their customers. They will confront the empty suit and question the intern. Meanwhile, passive salespeople distance themselves from any confrontation. They are more likely to yield to the opinions of others and play it safe.

> *Use high transparency:* Sergeant Schultz, summary seeker, class clown, straight shooter, old pro, and soldier.

> *Use low transparency:* anal analytical, hothead, people pleaser, dictator, and politician.

Like people in general, salespeople have different levels of curiosity. Some salespeople have a healthy curiosity and a strong need to know every detail, probably because they have to satisfy their insatiable desire to know the truth: "Will I win the deal?" Others are more likely to take a customer's words at face value. They won't question the customer outright but will make their own subjective judgment about the truthfulness of the information later.

Use high curiosity: all customer decision-making roles. Always exercise high curiosity with the executive until you sense your questions are breaking your rapport!

When we watch someone else perform an action, mirror neurons in our minds fire off and respond as if we were doing it ourselves. Mirror neurons help explain why laughter is contagious, why we grimace in pain for people we don't even know, and why we feel like crying when we see others cry. However, not everyone has the same amount or strength of mirror neurons. Therefore, we must put ourselves in the "mental shoes" of the executive we are meeting with to truly understand his plight. However, remember that there are some executives who will interpret your empathy as a sign of weakness and inferiority.

Use high empathy: dreamer, people pleaser, pundit, soldier, hired gun, fifth columnist, and revolutionary.

Use low empathy: anal analytical, hothead, maven, dictator, bureaucrat, proctor, and politician.

Now that we have defined each of the seven instincts, let's do an exercise and apply the instincts to the next C-level executive you will be meeting with. On a scale of 1 to 5, low to high, circle the number that best represents the strength of each of the instincts you should use when you meet with that executive:

	Low				*High*
Dominance	1	2	3	4	5
Hyperactivity	1	2	3	4	5
Pride	1	2	3	4	5
Greed	1	2	3	4	5

	Low			High	
Transparency	1	2	3	4	5
Curiosity	1	2	3	4	5
Empathy	1	2	3	4	5

Although you can achieve success with any combination of the seven instincts, the most successful Heavy Hitters are chameleons who know they must dominate one executive and be submissive to another. Sometimes they follow orders and other times they question authority. While they are comfortable being exactly who they are, they can take on any role required to win business.

Another important trait plays a key role in determining your sales success. Your mind's ability to store information is very sophisticated. Modeling is the ability to link like experiences and similar data into predictable patterns. Salespeople continually learn through the ongoing accumulation and consolidation of information from sales calls and interactions with executives. From this knowledge base, salespeople can predict what will happen and what they should do in light of what they have done in the past. The ability to combine attributes from different sales calls into themes and models of behavior forms your intuition. The strength of your intuition determines your ability to predict the future.

> We didn't hit it off. There just wasn't any real connection. It was awkward, and I guess I just didn't like him.
>
> VICE PRESIDENT OF SALES

Step 4—Align Value to Your Solution

An important mantra to always keep in the back of your mind when meeting a C-level executive is this: the purpose of the C-level sales call is to talk about *his* problems, not *your* products. A successful sales call is not based upon how much product propaganda you impart but how much information you collect about his problems.

The conversation will be conducted using the technical specification language and the business operations language. It will typically take place in two phases. The first phase is the salesperson's discovery of the problem: understand the executive's specific problems, their cause, the goals that will be realized when the problems are solved, the possible options and vendors being considered to solve the problems, and the employees who will assist him in solving them.

The second phase is the executive's discovery of the salesperson's solution. Once the problem is understood, the salesperson then defines how he might solve the problem by explaining how he has helped companies in similar situations. He accomplishes this by providing real-world examples that equate his solution to the four different types of product value. While these examples straightforwardly explain the strategic and operational values, the political and psychological values are suggestions that are inferred by the executive when listening to the stories. Finally, the salesperson will describe the unique features and functions by which his solution achieves the strategic and operational values.

Here's an example to help you understand and apply this concept. Let's assume you work for a software company that provides workforce productivity software—the Laborsaver 2000—and you are meeting with the COO of a large food processing company. The sales call starts with your asking questions to discover the COO's problem. In this case, the CEO (consolidator) has mandated that all departments cut their budgets by 20 percent. The COO (responder) will comply with this request by cutting raw material, labor, and shipping costs. He determines that half of the cost savings will have to come from reduced labor costs. However, he dreads laying off people and wants to avoid across-the-board pay cuts and employee reassignments. He would rather drive the labor cost savings through less-intrusive methods that don't hurt employee morale.

After you conduct your discovery, you frame your solution based upon examples about how other large food processor customers,

Dole Food Company and Kraft Foods, have reduced labor costs 10 percent through more efficient and more accurate scheduling of skilled employees against actual demand. As we discussed in chapter 6, the metaphors to be used are important and should be chosen with care. These stories show the COO how he can accomplish his reduction goals and provide him strategic value (he can tell the CEO he's cut labor costs 10 percent) and operational value by improving his department's efficiency. Politically, he has satisfied the powerbroker CEO, and psychologically, he has gained the approval of his employees for preserving their livelihoods.

As the conversation progresses, the executive wants more details about how the solution works and is implemented. You then describe the relevant features and functions of the Laborsaver 2000 software that specifically explain how the strategic and operational values are achieved. The structure of the sales call is represented in figure 8.5.

One major mistake salespeople make during C-level sales calls is to talk too much about topics that aren't important. Your solution has a laundry list of benefits and many interesting features and functions. However, the only ones that merit mentioning are the ones that lead to the specific business benefit of achieving the executive's goal. Don't waste the precious minutes you have with the executive on nonessential topics.

> As I look at our business, I see our people have been here a really long time. In other words, we have our own version of the truth, and what we know is what we know. We don't have a lot of insight into best practices from other companies. We wanted their sales team to tell us if there was a better way of doing processes and being more efficient. We would like them to come to us with recommendations and game-changing advances.
>
> VICE PRESIDENT OF MANUFACTURING

Problem	Cause	Goal	Possible options	Applicable solution	Strategic and operational value	Political and psychological value	Product
I have to reduce department costs that consist of raw materials, labor, and shipping	Sales are down and the CEO mandates 20% budget cuts	Realize a 10% labor cost savings with minimal impact on my employees' lives	1. More efficient workforce 2. Employee reassignment 3. Pay decreases 4. Layoffs	Improved workforce planning and labor budgeting	A 10% labor reduction at Dole and Kraft	Satisfy CEO while maintaining department morale	Laborsaver 2000 features and functions that create the labor cost savings benefits

Executive converses in business operations language

Salesperson discovery: asking questions

Salesperson converses in business operations language

Executive discovery: asking questions

Figure 8.5 C-level sales call structure

Step 5—Get to the Confidential C-Level Language

In the preceding example about the sales call with the COO, the conversation may have never reached the confidential C-level language, but the call still could have been deemed successful. The executive thought your solution would solve his problem and you felt great about your performance. Everyone left the meeting excited about the prospects of doing business together, with you being the most excited of all.

However, the sales call had four major problems. First, the CEO is the consolidator and the emperor, while the COO is the responder and the bully with the juice. The CEO will ultimately approve the method the COO uses to reduce costs. Even though the COO may decide to go with the Laborsaver 2000, the CEO might not want to spend the time or money implementing it. He wants layoffs instead. So even though you met with the highest-ranking departmental C-level executive, you might not have a deal here after all.

Second, one of your competitors might use the indirect strategy and outflank you and reach the CEO first. When the COO presents his recommendation about the manner he intends to cut costs and the vendor he intends to use, he'll be overruled. The third problem is that the COO has several meetings with other competitors scheduled in the days ahead and could easily change his mind.

The biggest problem with the sales call with the COO was that the confidential C-level language wasn't spoken. The confidential C-level language is a personal language the executive uses to explain what he wants to do and why. The language is based on accomplishing future objectives to increase or retain power. The sales call conversation stayed at the business operations level and never approached confidentially, where the COO's true motivations would be revealed. An example of the confidential C-level language would be if he had said, "Our CEO is a real mean SOB and he told me that it would be my hide if I didn't cut costs 20 percent."

Furthermore, the COO did not enlist you to help him execute his strategy of avoiding layoffs. The COO could have confided to you,

"This will be a tough sell to my CEO. Is there any way we could arrange a meeting between him and the CEO of Kraft to talk about how they are saving money during these difficult times?" So even though plenty of enthusiasm was exhibited by both sides, real trust wasn't established.

How do you establish the level of trust necessary to get to the confidential C-level language? The answer isn't simple. You know you must understand your products, the industry, and the operations of the executive's business. We have discussed how you should speak the different C-level languages and understand the attributes of the executive's group decision-making role. But three additional factors greatly determine your ability to establish executive-level trust. They are your question-handling ability, the congruence of your communication, and your impact on the executive's conscious and subconscious minds. Let's examine congruence and your question handling now. We'll discuss how to influence the executive's conscious and subconscious minds in the next chapter.

> Your people will tell you what you want to hear. It's a little bit like being the emperor who wore no clothes. What I need out of a partner is not just someone who will do what I tell them to do. I need someone who knows as much or more about the marketplace, who can shape my thinking and requests so that they can provide the most value.
>
> PRESIDENT

Handling Tough Questions

Answering questions from C-level executives enables you to tell your point of view about the industry, display your business operations expertise, and demonstrate your sales acumen. However, many times salespeople are too eager to give an answer to a question that wasn't even asked. That's why the first step in answering a question is to always clarify the question and make sure you understand what the executive is asking.

When an executive asks you a question, you will provide either an instantaneous answer from your short-term memory or a calculated answer that involves your long-term memory. The instantaneous answer is available immediately since it involves the recall of a logical fact or the recollection of a flashbulb episode. Logical facts include details committed to rote memory, such as product specifications, features, and performance details. Flashbulb episodes are emotional, physical, or cerebral experiences that were so overpowering that they are permanently imprinted in short-term memory. For example, when someone says "9/11" you might immediately think of the twin towers of the World Trade Center. Both logical facts and flashbulb episodes reside in your short-term memory, which is accessed faster than long-term memory.

Meanwhile, the calculated answer is akin to solving a mathematical equation in your mind by searching for and selecting the right answer or creating an appropriate answer based upon a set of rules learned from prior experiences residing in your long-term memory.

Three types of calculated answers are constructed in long-term memory. The first type uses a key attribute to search previous experiences. For example, recalling previous meetings with COOs will help you answer a question asked by a COO.

The second type, pattern recognition, requires a more complex calculation involving multiple attributes. Let's say you were asked by a skeptical, detail-oriented anal analytical vigilante COO how your product is different from your major competitor's. The creation of your answer is based on previous encounters with this particular circumstance. Pattern recognition can be thought of as trying to find the what, when, where response—*what* you should do *when* you are in this circumstance *where* you need to respond to a question or execute a sales-related action.

Finally, sometimes you are presented with situations you have never encountered before and you will have to use your imagination to create an answer. Making a best-guess answer requires a pattern recognition search to find closely resembling experiences plus additional hypothetical reasoning to create a new model. Obviously, this process takes the most time. In fact, psychological testing has proved it takes 30 percent longer to imagine something than to recall the truth.[2]

The C-level executive expects you to respond to his question within a certain time frame. When you are face to face, this time is measured in seconds and there is a penalty for delay. If the expected length of time is exceeded, the C-level executive will perceive that you don't command the facts or worse yet, that your answer is untruthful. When this occurs, it is difficult to establish that you are his equal because you have lost the executive's trust. As a result, the executive will not speak the confidential C-level language with you. Figure 8.6 illustrates the impact of selection pressure during the C-level sales call.

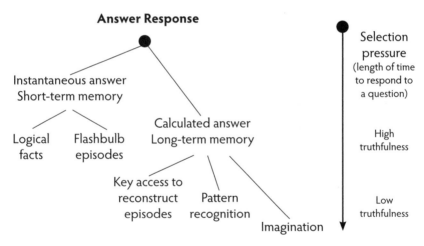

Figure 8.6 Question handling and selection pressure

The main point of this discussion is that you need to anticipate the questions the executive will ask and have answers prepared and internalized in advance. In other words, you need to create a list of all the toughest questions he could ask and then verbally rehearse your answers so they are smoothly and quickly delivered. The answers should not be more than thirty seconds long and should succinctly answer, not evade or redirect, the question. Referring to the example earlier in the chapter where we sell enterprise software to banks and are meeting with the CFO of Acme Bank, here are some of the tough questions we should be prepared for:

Why should we do business with you?

What makes you different?

Why haven't I heard of you before?

Why are you so expensive?

How does your pricing structure compare to the competition's?

Why aren't you a publicly traded company (or why is your stock so low)?

How do you plan to be successful when your competition is twice your size?

Your ROI is way too high. Are you sure it's right?

What are three companies that are exactly like us and using your solution?

Whom can I talk to at these companies?

Why should we select you when you are the smallest player we are evaluating?

Who is your unhappiest customer and why?

Why did ABC Bank switch from your solution to Archrival Software Company's?

Can you describe how you support worldwide customers like us?

What happens when there is a catastrophic system failure?

We do all of our business using *our* contracts. Is this a problem?

You claim your technology is a big differentiator. If so, then why do your competitors run some of the world's biggest banks?

Who will be assigned to our account?

What's the biggest deficiency in your solution?

What does your product road map look like, and why is it better than Archrival Software Company's?

May I see your financial statements for the past three years?
Why is your market share smaller than Archrival Software
    Company's?
Can you tell me a little bit about yourself?

The selection pressure on salespeople forces them to produce an answer promptly. Quite often, when salespeople lie to a customer, it is more likely because of the pressure to produce an instantaneous answer, rather than a conscious decision to mislead. In any case, the executive will determine if your statements are true or false depending upon your congruence. Congruence can be thought of as "truth in communication," while incongruence suggests a person is not telling the entire truth. Be forewarned, the customer will always spot lies. Whether he calls you on it publicly depends upon group decision-making roles and whether he is a vigilante or a people pleaser.

When you have a private moment immediately following every C-level sales call, write down all the questions that you can remember being asked. This will help you build your personal knowledge base of your own C-level experiences. Obviously, taking insightful notes during sales calls will help you recall the meeting. However, during the next sales call, you won't have time to search through your notes to find the "right" answer to an executive's question. You must make information available instantaneously by committing it to memory.

Here are six principles to help improve your sales call memory:

1. *Sensory information.* During the sales call, consciously gather as much information as possible from your sight, hearing, and touch senses. A vivid event is more likely to be memorized than a dull one.
2. *Association.* Thoughts and experiences are more readily recalled when they are linked to a specific association. A very simple association would be the success or failure of the call.

3. *Specifics and details.* The persistence of a memory is directly related to the precision of details that are input at the time of the experience.

4. *Unique events.* Many sales calls are free-flowing events that lack a strict organization of facts. Therefore, it is easier to remember any unusual and unique aspects of a sales call that stand out from the ordinary and mundane.

5. *First and last.* Most salespeople are quick to remember how a sales call began (the big opening) and how it ended (the grand finale). This is a natural characteristic of memory, whereby we tend to remember the information that is presented first and last more than the details in between. This particularly applies to longer sales calls, more than an hour. One way to help remember all of the in-between information is to mentally break the sales call into smaller segments (or chunks) either by time, presenter, or topic of discussion.

6. *The good, the bad, and the ugly.* Be forewarned, your brain has been trained to block out unpleasant images. However, it is critical that all information during a sales call, both good and bad, be stored.

Memory plays a fundamental role in determining the strength of your sales intuition. Never forget that how something is remembered will determine how much is remembered.

Congruence

How people speak is also a good indicator of congruence, the truthfulness of their communication. When people aren't telling the truth, their tempo speeds up or slows down, their volume gets louder or softer, and their tone is higher or lower than normal. For example, Visuals may slow down their speaking, Kinesthetics may speak faster, and Auditories may change their tone. In addition, people's choice of words will change when they are not telling the truth. People telling the truth will talk in a straightforward manner using ordinary terms. When creating misrepresentations, their word selection is more careful, and they tend to use more sophisticated words. They also speak with precision and are mindful not to repeat the same word twice, unlike in natural conversation.

Congruence is at the heart of persuasion. How can you improve your congruence? First, you should know your product inside out. This alone will build your credibility. I am constantly amazed at how little average salespeople know about the products they sell. You can't believe in what you don't understand. You need to understand your company: its history, what makes it unique, how it compares to others, and its future direction. You need to understand the customers you sell to and the problems they face, and you need to understand yourself. Why would someone buy from you? What are your strengths and weaknesses?

Congruence is attained when thoughts and languages are aligned to communicate the same conscious and subconscious message. Do you have congruence? Here's a short exercise to test your congruence. Take a moment to answer the following questions:

- Do you honestly believe customers are better off when they choose your product over your competition's?
- Do you think your company is the best in your industry?
- Do you truly believe in yourself and that you are in the right profession?

What were your answers? Do you exude conviction about your product, your company, and your profession? If not, why would you expect someone else to believe in you?

Conclusion

Researchers at the University of Wisconsin have made an amazing discovery about how the use of language changes behavior. People who speak two languages unconsciously change their personality when they switch languages. From their study, the researchers found evidence of "frame shifting," the change in a person's self-perception and underlying behavior depending upon the language the person used. For example, test subjects were more assertive when they spoke Spanish versus English.[3]

The concept of frame shifting is extremely relevant to salespeople. Think about it for a moment. Your job is to build rapport with a wide variety of people across different companies. You have to communicate with lower-level operations people, midlevel managers, and most importantly, C-level executives. In order to do so, you need to change your demeanor and speak different languages depending upon the person you are meeting with. You wouldn't think of talking to and treating a CFO as you would a shop floor foreman. Intuitively, you already know you must frame shift your behavior and language to match the customer's in order to build rapport.

Finally, the words you say to yourself are the most important words you use all day. Do you continually question yourself or give yourself positive reinforcements throughout the day? Do you tell yourself "It's just a job," or are you excited about what you do for a living? Your internal mantra, whether good or bad, will be conveyed to customers. Is it negative and hurtful or reaffirming and helpful? In the end, nothing else really matters.

> We consider ourselves an extremely ethical company, maybe to a fault. We find our industry is not endowed with that attribute. Of all the companies we have dealt with, the one thing I have felt about their sales team is that they have maintained an ethical standard far above most players. If you form a partnership based upon trust, you don't have to keep one eye open in the night to make sure your wallet isn't being picked.
>
> VICE PRESIDENT OF FINANCE

9

Close

THE CONSCIOUS AND SUBCONSCIOUS
C-LEVEL SELL

> It was an emotional decision. In fact, at the very end when we were making the decision there were days that I really felt the evaluation team was emotionally spent. It was hard on them because we had developed very good relationships with the sales representatives of both firms. I am sure the other solution would have worked for us. If I had to tell you the main reason why we didn't go with them, I am not sure I can. I know that I hurt the gentleman who was selling for them, and that disturbs me greatly. Relationships and people's self worth are very important to me. He truly felt for very good reasons that we were going with him.
>
> CHIEF EXECUTIVE OFFICER

Unconscious competent—that's a term I have heard used a lot by the one thousand top salespeople I have interviewed to describe themselves. While these Heavy Hitter salespeople knew what they did and knew how they did it, they found it very difficult to explain to others exactly what has made them a success.

However, I think I know the answer. They have mastered the psychology of sales. They understand that the most important aspect of selling is people, not products. They know the roles intellect and emotions play during customer decision making. They verbally connect with customers and develop friendships with these strangers by building credibility and trust. Most importantly, they intuitively know that the battle between salespeople for the customer's heart, mind, and soul is fought with words.

In this regard, the salesperson's most important competitive weapon is his mouth, and the winner is the salesperson who uses words that reduce the customer's doubt and ease his fears. That's why it is critical that salespeople master sales linguistics, the study of how the customer's mind uses and interprets language. The goal of this final chapter of the book is to help you employ sales linguistics techniques to convince the C-level executive's rational conscious and skeptical subconscious minds to buy.

Who Are You?

While neuroscientists have named the parts of the brain and know their overall functions, the three-pound pale gray organ that has a texture similar to that of pâté remains a mystery. Even today's scientists using all of their sophisticated equipment cannot explain the origins of faith, hope, and love.

Most of the recent advances in understanding the inner workings of the mind have come from brain scans and neuroimaging techniques such as PET (positron emission tomography) and FMRI (functional magnetic resonance imaging), which make it possible to observe human brains at work. They reveal changes in activity of the various brain regions depending on physiological activities. For example, while a person is seeing, hearing, smelling, tasting, or touching something, certain areas of the brain light up on the scan.

Be aware that no one truly knows how the mind works, but somewhere deep inside you is you. You are surrounded by your conscious, or "controllable," and subconscious, or "uncontrollable," minds. Your internal dialogue surrounds your subconscious and conscious minds. It is very dominating. It's always on, always engaged, and always talking to you. It drives the language you speak to others as well as your actions. The conscious mind, subconscious mind, and internal dialogue impact your external communication in terms of the words actually spoken, voluntary (planned) body movements in conjunction with the spoken words, and involuntary (unplanned) body movements. Figure 9.1 represents the interaction between external communication and the mind.

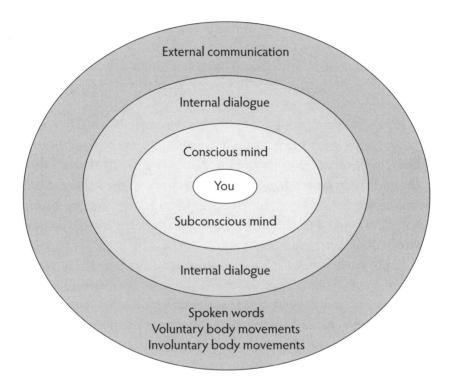

Figure 9.1 External communication and the mind

The conscious mind is obsessed with achieving benefactions (pain avoidance, well-being, self-preservation, and self-gratification). When you're in pain, your conscious mind is fixated on removing it. Meanwhile, your subconscious mind is constantly sensing and filtering data that is necessary to achieving other important long-term benefactions. For example, one of the reasons you're devoting time to reading this book is because you want to achieve success and satisfy your ego.

The subconscious mind retains information that the conscious mind doesn't. It simply isn't efficient to store everything in your conscious mind. Remember the last time you misplaced an important item (your keys, wallet, glasses)? At first, you employed a conscious strategy to find it. You may have thought about where you had recently been and gone back to those locations. If you didn't find the item, hours, days, or weeks may have gone by. Then suddenly, without specifically thinking about it, you knew exactly where it was. Your subconscious mind found it.

Here's another example of how the subconscious mind works. Over the last few years I met many different authors of business books. Almost all of us like to write first thing in the morning—usually very early, at three or four. I theorize that this is because the subconscious mind is busy while we sleep, creating, aggregating, and organizing ideas. Now before I go to bed, I mentally review what I would like my subconscious mind to solve.

In the same way, when your prospective customers say "Let me sleep on it," they are actually saying "Let me see if my subconscious mind has any objections since it has some additional information that I don't have right now." During the C-level sales call, your words and actions can have an immense effect on the conscious and subconscious minds. Let's review the best techniques to use when making presentations to C-level executives.

Customer Metaphors and the Subconscious Mind

Heavy Hitters understand that customer success stories (a specific type of sales metaphor) play a very important role in influencing executives to buy. The power of customer success metaphors lies in their individual interpretation. Remember, while the conscious mind is listening to the content of the surface-level story, the subconscious mind is deciphering its own message. On the surface, explaining how a customer is successfully using a product is a story the conscious mind will follow logically. Underneath this story, another message can be sent to the customer's subconscious mind that it is in his personal interest to select your product.

The average person will hear only seven and a half minutes of a one-hour presentation and remember only half of the words he or she hears.[1] In essence, we don't listen to and we reject far more words than we actually hear. However, the subconscious mind acts as a reservoir for this overflow of information. Therefore, a metaphor's structure is critical.

An effective method of structuring customer success stories is by breaking them into four parts: history and situation, options, evaluation process, and decision reason and results. Below, you will find an example of each part and ideally what message should be sent to the conscious mind and the connection to the subconscious.

Part 1 describes the history and situation.

- *Conscious message.* Describe the business problem or condition the customer was trying to solve or improve and the situation that created it.
- *Subconscious connection.* Specifically identify the people involved in the selection process, including their names, titles, and backgrounds. These are people the customer can identify with.
- *Example.* "I would like to take a moment to tell you about one of our most difficult customers, ABC Company. Their requirements were so complex that they were unsure whether any off-the-shelf product would work for them. Frankly, we had never seen a business that processed so many transactions. Their CIO, Bob Smith, was also one of the most meticulous and demanding customers I have ever met."

Part 2 presents the options.

- *Conscious message.* Describe the different products or methods that could have solved the problem or improved the customer's situation.
- *Subconscious connection.* Explain the impact of these circumstances in terms of the decision maker's job, career, or emotional state of being.
- *Example.* "Bob decided to bring in the top two products, ours and XYZ's, for intensive evaluations, even though he honestly believed that neither product would handle their requirements."

Part 3 delineates the evaluation process.

- *Conscious message.* Outline the process the customer undertook to determine the best solution.
- *Subconscious connection.* Describe the personality, preferences, and motivations of the evaluation team members.
- *Example.* "Bob tested every aspect of the solutions: installation, ease of use, performance, and technical support. One month into the pilot test, Bob stopped testing XYZ's product because it just wouldn't scale. He spent another two months verifying every feature of our product. He wanted to make sure everything worked precisely as advertised."

Part 4 describes the decision reason and results.

- *Conscious message.* Describe the final selection and its impact on the decision makers or company.
- *Subconscious connection.* Translate the outcome into personal terms.
- *Example.* "When Bob was completely sure of his decision, he finally purchased our solution. Today, Bob is one of our happiest customers and their project has been a complete success. I would be delighted to introduce you to him."

When salespeople meet with a customer, they know they must establish trust and demonstrate competence in order to reduce the personal angst of the customer during the selection process. Customer success stories are valuable tools for proving that the salesperson and his company are the authority on solving the customer's problem. An authority is someone who has the ability to gain the trust and willing obedience of others. This is one of the most important reasons why you should always include customer metaphors on your sales calls and include them in your presentations.

Structuring the C-Level Presentation

After evaluating hundreds of corporate sales presentations, I can honestly say that they all are basically the same. You could take slides from one company's presentation and insert them in another's and no one would notice. They are all fact-based infomercials with no discerning differences.

It's not enough to say that to stand out you have to be different. Rather, you need a more sophisticated, indirect approach that differentiates your solution in the minds of customers. You can't *tell* customers you're unique, different, and one of a kind. You must *demonstrate* it to them, starting with the psychology of the corporate presentation.

Traditional corporate sales presentations are typically organized into six sections: my company, my products, how they work, their benefits, our customers, and a call to action. Your C-level presentation should be divided into four sections. It should start with a pattern interruption, move on to customer metaphors, be followed by explanations, and close with suggestions. This way of presenting is distinctly different from the presentations of your competitors. Let's examine each section of the presentation in detail.

Section 1—The Pattern Interruption

Put yourself in the position of the C-level executive for a moment. You've sat through hundreds of sales presentations through the years. Because these presentations have been based upon marketing propaganda, one of your primary objectives is to delineate fact from fiction. Therefore, you are skeptical.

You've also met hundreds of salespeople during these presentations and have found most of them to be friendly, courteous, and professional. Each of them also wants to build a personal relationship with you. You can't let this happen. You aren't going to build friendships with everyone when you know only one person will be around for the long term. It's not practical or comfortable to do this. Therefore, you are reserved and on guard and you keep your distance.

Since you're actually the salesperson, the first goal of your presentation should be to perform a pattern interruption to break the executive's mode of thinking and stand out from the competition. The pattern interruption starts the process of building rapport, engages the audience, and provokes open-mindedness. Your pattern interruption will consist of an attention-grabbing cowcatcher and your unique hook. (Refer back to chapter 6 for a detailed explanation.)

A great cowcatcher engages the mind, appeals to the imagination, and helps the presenter gain credibility. For example, I worked at a company whose core technology was originally developed by the California Institute of Technology and funded by a grant from NASA. Explaining the origins of the company—not with one simple slide with a few bullet points but using highlights of the project and its results set against the black backdrop of outer space with its millions of stars—was a great cowcatcher. We differentiated ourselves and gained instant credibility.

Another company I worked for was the top-rated NASDAQ stock for a period of five years. In fact, during one two-year time frame, $32,000 worth of this company's stock grew to be worth $1,000,000. I always opened my presentations with a chart of the stock price and some facts about the stock's appreciation. The customers would be more than intrigued; they were downright fascinated and eager to learn more. Many would buy my company's stock that very day!

Unfortunately, the first few slides of most corporate presentations have little panache. The obligatory introduction states some facts about the company's financial position, how long it has been in business, and its office locations. (The worst actually show pictures of the company's buildings as if this were something astounding.)

Section 2—Customer Metaphors

One of the biggest problems that most salespeople have on sales calls is that they are too eager to tell the customer about their products. The same is true for a corporate presentation, and when this happens, the presentation does not build a storyline that piques interest. Instead of launching into slides about the product line and technical aspects of the products, the second section of the corporate presentation should focus on customers.

Following the cowcatcher, you need a hook. Now that the listeners' interest is piqued, you need to hook them on why they should use your product. Your best hook is to tell them stories about your customers. Most corporate presentations include an obligatory slide that shows twenty or so logos of the major companies that use the salesperson's products. That's not what I am referring to here.

The second section should include six to eight slides of how specific customers are using the products, the operational results that have been improved, and the financial impact on the bottom line. In addition, it should include a quote from a customer whose name and title the audience can identify with psychologically. For example, include a quote from a customer's CFO when presenting to a financial department. Finally, this section should have some eye-catching graphics that tie the whole story together. These could be pictures of your product at work, the person who provided the quote, or an example of the end result.

As we discussed before, the pertinence of the customer examples is very important. Presenting examples from companies that closely mirror the prospect's business objectives will make the statements more powerful. Presenting examples from companies that the prospects don't recognize will have less impact.

> The sales team didn't prove it would be cost effective, and it was hard for them to prove they would create incremental sales. They need to get some real-life examples, customer case studies that spell it out. They tried to explain it, but it wasn't believable.
>
> CHIEF FINANCIAL OFFICER

Section 3—Explanations

The third section of the presentation is based upon an intellectual appeal to the executive's conscious mind. Here the goal is to continue to build credibility by methodically explaining background information and facts behind the customer metaphor slides.

For example, let's say you are selling manufacturing shop floor equipment and one of your customer metaphor slides is about how General Electric saved $20 million in the first year of using your product. In this section you would drill down through critical features of your product that streamlined operations. You could explain in detail how the features that enabled the savings to occur work technically and how they compare to other methods of accomplishing the same tasks.

The explanations section is typically the largest of the presentation. As a rule of thumb, use two slides of information for every customer metaphor slide. However, keep in mind that iPods, television, and the Internet have changed people's attention spans and the way they want information presented to them. The best presentations deliver information in small chunks. No single slide should take more than two minutes to cover. If it lasts longer than that, you may lose the audience's attention. Therefore, if a slide takes four minutes to explain, split it into two slides to keep the presentation moving.

Since most salespeople are well versed in the logic of selling, it doesn't make sense to reiterate here what you already know. Instead, let's emphasize some steps you can take to make an intellectual appeal more compelling.

- Provide independent confirmation of your facts wherever possible.
- Provide quotes from authorities (customers, analysts, and the press).
- Quantify beneficial claims with specific numbers.
- Use real-world examples, which are more powerful than hypothetical statements.
- Arrange your arguments from strongest to weakest.
- Keep it simple. Remember Occam's razor: the simpler explanation is always preferred.
- Be prepared for contradictory facts from other vendors and have factual responses ready.
- Quantify results from adverse consequences (for example, loss of revenue due to equipment downtime).
- Present the extremes and worst case scenarios to make the other options to solve the problem look worse than they really are.
- Use alliterations—repetition of the same letter or sound of adjacent words—so that concepts are more easily remembered (for example, "durability, dependability, and adaptability").
- Use the rule of three: whenever you make a claim, support it with three different facts.
- Create your own euphemisms that reflect the importance of your product or a particular feature. For example, a rubber band could be called a "multipurpose business instrument."
- Understand that it is all right to draw big conclusions from small statistics. Sometimes the biggest points can be made from the smallest samples.

- Brighten up the facts with interesting graphics that represent them pictorially.
- Become a storyteller, not a human dictionary. Use metaphors to explain concepts. Instead of saying "A poll showed customers prefer us three to one," say "Harris Poll surveyed four thousand buyers from across the country and found that three thousand, or 75 percent, thought our solution was far superior."

Logical arguments alone, no matter how well you present them, will not change skeptics into believers. Finessing customers to change their opinions requires an emotional appeal to their human nature.

> Their ROI model was way off, and the general perception within our company is that their sole concern is for them, not us. Frankly, it is to the point where our people don't even want to deal with them. They present recommendations as if they are in our best interest but are really solely in theirs.
>
> VICE PRESIDENT OF BUSINESS DEVELOPMENT

Section 4—Suggestions

The typical close to a corporate presentation is a one-slide summary of the major topics that were covered. The salesperson basically says "I hope we passed the audition." A better way to end a presentation is with a very specific action item that is based upon the goal you wanted the presentation to accomplish.

For example, if the goal of the presentation was to make the customer's short list, an appropriate close would be to explain the seven reasons why you believe you should be on the short list. If you are further along in the sales cycle and your goal was to close the deal, walking the customer through the implementation process or explaining your pricing methodology is an appropriate close.

These action items should be worded in the form of foreground and background suggestions. Examples of foreground suggestions include "I spoke to my contacts at General Electric yesterday and told them I was presenting to you today. They extended an invitation to come to their operation for a site visit" and "All of the analyst firms strongly encourage that customers benchmark all the products they are considering."

Background suggestions are indirect. Showing your pricing model is a background suggestion to negotiate price. If earlier in your presentation you described how the customers at General Electric made their decision, what products they evaluated, and why they selected your solution, walking the customer through their implementation process is a background suggestion to make the customer think about implementation. Another example of a background suggestion is "The regional vice president for Archrival Software just joined our company because he was tried of dealing with continual product support problems." While this background suggestion is more subtle in its delivery, it triggers a more profound emotional reaction as the customers will want you to tell them why.

Two very important slides that should be included in your presentation are called the "strategy slide" and the "money slide." The strategy slide clearly defines the business problem that needs to be solved (or the opportunity that can be created), the cause of the problem (or reason for the opportunity), the goal realized when the problem is solved (or when the opportunity is realized), and all the possible options that could be utilized to solve the problem or achieve the opportunity. The strategy slide is based upon defining the first four boxes of figure 8.5: problem, cause, goal, and possible options.

The strategy slide is not vendor specific. Rather, it presents the customer's situation from an unbiased third-party point of view. You know you have created the perfect strategy slide when the C-level executive asks for a copy of it so that he can post it on his office wall.

Conversely, the money slide shows how your specific solution solves the problem from the strategic, operational, and most importantly, financial perspectives. This slide summarizes the strategic value of your solution including all costs, ROI, and pay-back assumptions. It also shows the operational value of your solution that results from its unique features and functions. This slide summarizes why the executive should select your solution over all the others.

The strategy slide and the money slide can be used at the very beginning of your presentation as the pattern interruption. Or they can be placed at the end and incorporated into a background or foreground suggestion. In reality, your entire presentation boils down to these two slides. Do you understand the executive's problem and have you developed the credibility to recommend a solution? Have you demonstrated that you can solve the problem better than the competition?

Let's finish the discussion about presentations by talking about the look and feel of your slides. Did you know the color of your car says a lot about you? Studies have shown that upbeat people drive dark blue and silver cars, people with a sunny dispositions like yellow, aggressive people prefer red, and people drawn to power and elegance choose black. What colors are used in your corporate presentation? I like to use two basic color schemes in my slides. Red signifies change, aids memorization, and subconsciously tells people to slow down and pay attention—like a stop sign. Blue encourages creativity, and people associate it with explorative feelings and a sense of wonder—like the sky.

How well your presentation is received will vary depending on whether it was created by a Visual, Auditory, or Kinesthetic and who is in the audience. Slide after slide after slide of bullet points will torment Visuals. A sterile look and feel turns off Kinesthetics. Don't show Auditories too many graphs and pictures because they need something to read. When you take into account word catalogs, you will connect much better with the subconscious mind.

The Subconscious Decision Maker

To further understand the impact of the subconscious mind on decision making, let's study Bob, a college-educated professional with a doctorate in computer science. Successful in his career, he has become a C-level executive of a Fortune 500 company. Bob is a smart businessman who possesses sound business practices and the acumen to get to the top of the corporate ladder.

Let's say Bob is facing two very important decisions. The first decision involves making a multimillion-dollar purchase to upgrade some equipment of the division he runs. The second decision involves proposing marriage to Maggie, his girlfriend of nine months. Bob approaches each of these decisions in a very different way.

For the business decision, he first conducts an in-depth study of the inefficiencies of his current infrastructure. Next, he presents his findings with an internal rate-of-return study for replacing the old equipment with state-of-the-art machinery to the senior management team of the parent company. Then he performs a detailed analysis of the various equipment vendors and makes a final selection.

Getting married is one of life's most important decisions. Bob has fallen in love with Maggie. He feels good being with her, thinks about her often, and looks forward to their time together. She has the qualities he admires, and when compared to girlfriends of the past, she is the best. Bob decides he will ask her to marry him.

However, as he moves forward in his decision-making process, an unexpected change in Bob's thought process occurs. The subconscious mind, the self-regulating system designed to prevent us from making unwise choices, is on vigilant watch. It drives Bob to perform a "gut-check" of the rational, logical information regarding the equipment purchase. Beyond the facts and figures, does the decision feel right? He second-guesses himself and asks whether the move will help or hurt his career.

Conversely, the emotional high associated with the idea of marriage is tempered by reality. He now evaluates Maggie's little habits that he once thought were cute with a more rational eye. He studies other aspects of their relationship with equal intensity. Figure 9.2 illustrates the changing nature of the decision-making process.

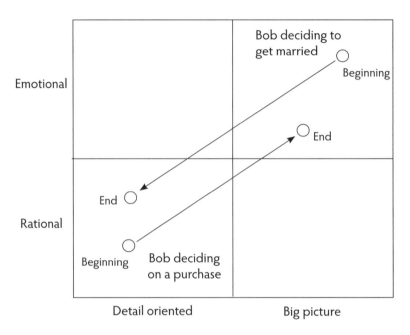

Figure 9.2 The changing nature of decision making

We've all worked on accounts where, after studying every aspect of your and your competitor's product, customers went into analysis paralysis. They had so much information that they couldn't make a decision. On the opposite end of the spectrum are customers who change their minds on a moment-by-moment basis. You might be winning one moment and losing the next. Overwhelmed with information, the conscious mind vacillates from one extreme to the other.

At this point, the subconscious mind takes an active role in decision making. One of its main responsibilities is protection. Much like a guardian angel, it's on the lookout for perilous situations and possible circumstances that might endanger the person physically and mentally. To perform this task, it assumes a third-person observation role and acts as a separate entity, even though it resides deep inside the individual. It guides an executive decision maker from the emotional to the logical and vice versa. Therefore, you need to use different types of words at different times that correspond to logic and emotions.

> I wasn't completely sure their solution would work, and my job hung on the success of the project. I took a leap of faith and believed what they had told me.
>
> CHIEF INFORMATION OFFICER

Elevator Pitch: Your Words Are Your Weapons

How many of the exercises have you finished of the sixteen you have been asked to complete so far? Even senior salespeople find the next exercise to be very challenging. What makes this exercise difficult is that you already think you can do it easily. The exercise requires you to time yourself because it must be completed in no more than forty-five seconds. Ideally, you want to be in a private place where you can say your answer aloud.

I would like you to pretend that you are in an elevator at one of your industry's trade shows. You are heading down to the lobby when the doors open on the thirtieth floor. You instantly recognize the executive who walks in and quickly glance at his name badge to confirm he is the CEO of the most important account you would like to start working with. You have never met him before nor have you been able to generate any interest from his organization. You have forty-five seconds to introduce yourself, explain what your company does in a way the CEO would find interesting and applicable, and motivate him to take the action you suggest. Ready, go!

So, how did you do? You are to be commended for completing this exercise. Even the most successful salespeople find this pressure-packed exercise difficult. At sales meetings, I will ask salespeople to perform this exercise with me in front of their peers. Many times they become flustered or quit halfway through and they ask me if they can start over again. My answer is always no because you only have one chance to make a great first impression. Here are the six most common mistakes salespeople make:

1. *They use truisms.* They believe their company's own marketing pitch, which makes claims that are not considered entirely true by the listener. As a result, they instantly lose credibility.
2. *They describe themselves using buzzwords.* They'll repeat industry buzzwords or, worse yet, use technical buzzwords that are known only within their company.
3. *They use fillers.* They make too much small talk or ask frivolous questions that reduce their stature and make them even more submissive to the executive.
4. *They demean themselves or the listener.* They make statements that relegate them as mere salespeople, not business problem solvers. Salespeople unintentionally demean the listener by asking impertinent questions or assuming the listener knows exactly what they are talking about.
5. *They present an unreasonable close.* They don't take into account that they are talking to a senior company leader and use a close that is unrealistic or demands too much of the executive.
6. *They are incongruent.* Their tone, pitch, and tempo of speech don't match. They speak too fast and their quivering tone broadcasts that they're nervous and submissive.

Here's an example of a poor elevator pitch. Luke Skywalker, a salesperson for XYZ Technologies, is attending a trade show and happens to be in the elevator with Norman Bates, chief information officer at Wonderful Telecommunications.

Hello, Norman. How are you today [filler]? Do you have a moment to talk [filler]? My name is Luke Skywalker and I work for [demeans salesperson] XYZ Technologies. Have you heard of XYZ Technologies [demeans listener]? Well, we are the leading provider [truism] of business transformational outsourcing [industry buzzword]. We have a unique extended-hybrid implementation methodology [technical buzzword]. Do you have time for me to buy you a cup of coffee and hear more about it [unreasonable close]?

Your words are your most important weapons. If you understand how listeners process language, you can help them manage the process of deciphering meaning. This ensures that your message will be successfully received and the action you suggest will be followed. A successful elevator pitch will incorporate the following linguistic structures:

- *Softeners.* A softener eases listeners into the next thought or is used to set expectations. When you say "I'm sorry to bother you," you are using the preapologizing softener technique.
- *Facts.* A fact is the undisputed truth. Facts are recognized instantaneously.
- *Logic.* Logic is inferred by the listener to be true. Two main types of logic are used in sales situations: linear and geometric. The formula for linear logic is A plus B equals C, meaning when A and B are true statements, then the C statement or idea is also true. For example, "Our solution is 10 percent faster" and "we are 25 percent cheaper"; therefore, "we are the better solution." The formula for geometric logic is if X is true, and X equals Y, then any statement that is true for X also applies to Y. For example, "We are helping Allstate Insurance reduce costs 10 percent" and "you are an insurance company like Allstate Insurance"; therefore, "we can help you reduce 10 percent of your costs."
- *Metaphors.* In chapter 4, we discussed the three different types of metaphors: educational, personal, and action based. The purpose

of each of these metaphors is to tell, teach, and enlighten the listener, with the ultimate goal of changing his or her opinion or behavior. While educational metaphors appeal to the conscious intellect, personal and action based metaphors can be tailored to the subconscious mind. Also, all three types can be connected, interwoven, and mixed together in any combination.

- *Suggestions.* Foreground suggestions are direct and explicit ("Consumer Reports gave our product the highest rating"). Background suggestions are indirect and their meaning is inferred ("One of their customers recently switched to our product").
- *Fallback position.* Every customer conversation is actually a negotiation between verbal dominance and submissive silence. Instead of giving ultimatums that force the customer to accept or reject your close, provide options from which customers can select and always have alternate suggestions prepared in advance.
- *Silence.* Silence is an important and useful linguistic structure. It indicates you are listening and waiting for a response. Silence can actually be used to gain dominance during conversations.

Here's an elevator pitch that incorporates these linguistic structures:

> Norman, hi, I'm Luke Skywalker with XYZ Technologies [fact]. It's a pleasure to meet you [softener]. I'm not sure if you are familiar with us [softener], but we work with AT&T [fact]. They've had to reduce their IT costs during these tough times [geometric logic]. I'm here because James Bond, the CIO of AT&T, is presenting a case study on how he cut his IT costs by 20 percent using our outsourcing solution [metaphor, background suggestion]. There'll be CIOs from some of our other customers, including General Electric and Johnson & Johnson, speaking as well [fact, background suggestion]. The session is tomorrow at 1 pm if you can make it [foreground suggestion, softener]? [Pause—silence, waiting for response.] That's too

bad [softener]. I'd be delighted to send you his presentation [fallback position, foreground suggestion]. Great. Just to confirm your e-mail address, that's Norman.bates@wonderful .com. Is there anyone else I should send it to [fallback position] [Pause—silence]. Okay, that's Ferris Bueller, your vice president of infrastructure. Thanks, Norman you'll be hearing from me shortly.

The most important linguistic structure used in this elevator pitch are the metaphors. Ideally, a metaphor will cause the mind to immediately recognize the importance of the information, accept the message, and follow the suggestion. The proof of a metaphor's success is evidenced by a change in the verbal and physical language the listener emits. This could range from an enthusiastic verbal response to a subtle readjustment of the body from a closed posture to an open posture.

In closed posture, the body is folded up on itself. Probably the most familiar closed posture is the arms crossed on the chest. More subtle closed positions are legs crossed, ankles crossed, hands interlocked on the table, and both hands touching the face. A closed posture is a natural position of skepticism that shifts to an open position as rapport is created. When people change to an open position, it may be as obvious as their uncrossing their arms. They may relax the tightness in the parts of the body that are folded: arms, hands, legs, ankles, feet, and even lips. They could also move their folded arms from their chest to their waist. Or they could switch positions, such as going from legs crossed with the right leg on top to legs crossed with the left leg on top. Watch for these subtle changes and make a mental note when they happen.

You Are a Walking, Talking Metaphor

The most important metaphor of the entire C-level executive meeting is you. You are a walking, talking metaphor. The way you dress, present yourself, and represent your product provides important symbolism to the customer. Your customer has standards and certain expectations about the way you will act, look, and speak. These standards vary greatly among customers, companies, industries, and places. Selling drilling equipment in Texas is different from selling computer chips in Silicon Valley or hotel supplies in Hawaii. Each requires a salesperson to use a different presence and demeanor to build credibility and gain rapport.

These qualities will greatly influence the executive's decision. For example, would you hire a personal trainer who was extremely out of shape? An interior designer who dressed sloppily or out of style? Would you visit a dentist who had terrible teeth and who used dilapidated equipment? Physical presence projects an important message to the customer.

Therefore, it makes sense to dress like your customers and express yourself in the manner they are comfortable with. The way you dress should show that your first concern is the customer's success, not your own self-interests. While we want to communicate success, we don't want the customer thinking he's being overcharged. That's why I frown on elaborate hairdos and expensive jewelry such as cufflinks and watches. Remember, a salesperson's dress and demeanor and how he treats the customer serve as a metaphor for their future relationship.

All salespeople are friendly, helpful, and attentive during the sales cycle because they know the customer is constantly evaluating them. It's after the sale is made and the commission paid when true service begins. A salesperson's humility is in fact a metaphor for service and selflessness. The ostentatious salesperson who is full of bravado will alienate far more customers than he wins over. The customer doesn't expect to see him once the deal closes. Meanwhile, the unpretentious salesperson naturally builds rapport. People expect he'll stay around after the deal closes.

People naturally want to be around positive people. In chapter 3, we discussed the Better Person Syndrome and how customers want to surround themselves with people who have the qualities they admire. Conversely, salespeople who constantly criticize the competition are less likely to win over executives. Think about yourself for a moment: do you like to be around people who are negative and demeaning?

Anchor Yourself to Success

I still get nervous when I meet with important executives or before I have to give a big presentation. In my opinion, nervousness is not only normal but positive because it drives you to better prepare yourself beforehand. However, once a meeting starts, you want your nervousness to stop. The tool I use to calm my nerves is a psychological anchor. Anchoring is the process of associating a premeditated feeling to an object.

Now it's time to do one of the most interesting exercises of the entire book. Think of the best day of your business career. Have a very specific day in your mind. Stop and think about it. Remember how great you felt. Perhaps it was a day you received an award or were promoted. Whatever it is, try to relive the feelings, hear the sounds, and re-create a picture of it in your mind. While holding these thoughts, take your right hand and gently pinch the back of your left hand and hold it while you think of the memory until the back of your pinched hand starts to tingle, usually around thirty seconds. Stop reading and concentrate on your memory. You have now created a psychological anchor.

Would you be nervous speaking in front of one thousand salespeople? Well, I am. That's why I use anchors all the time. Now go ahead and pinch the back of your hand again. Did you feel the tingle again and a reassuring sensation? If not, repeat the entire process very slowly with single-minded concentration.

There's no reason to be nervous when you meet with C-level executives. Regardless of how many people surround someone and how much fortune, fame, and power you think a person has, everyone is lonely in his or her own way. Loneliness isn't only about being alone. It is when you feel disconnected, isolated, alienated, unwanted, inadequate, self-conscious, unloved, and scared. Keep this idea in mind. The next executive you meet needs a friend.

The most important words you speak are the words you say to yourself. Now it's time for the nineteenth and final exercise of the book. When we talk to ourselves internally, it's usually in the context of our shortcomings. Personally, I am more likely to tell myself that I am a failure at something than I am great at something else. However, the congruence you emanate to anyone you speak with is based upon a positive perception of yourself. This exercise takes just a few seconds. Read the following statement slowly out loud, pause, and then repeat it again twice: "I am a success." Perhaps the only person who remains to be convinced you are a success is you.

C-Level Executive Meeting Preparation Checklist

The diligence with which you prepare yourself and your colleagues for the C-level sales call will directly influence the success of your meeting. However, it's an imperfect world and you will never have 100 percent of the information you would like to have about the executive you will be meeting with. In this case, you need to theorize about the missing pieces of information based upon your past meetings with executives and summon your sales intuition. Use this checklist to help you prepare for your next meeting with the bully with the juice, emperor, or other company leader.

What is our goal for the meeting?
What is the outcome by which we will know we have achieved our goal?
What problem is the executive trying to solve, worded in the business operations language?

What is the cause of the executive's problem?

What goal will the executive achieve when the problem is solved?

What are all the possible solutions the executive can use to solve his problem?

What is our solution to solve the problem, worded in the business operations language?

What is our value to the executive?

    Strategic value:

    Operational value:

    Political value:

    Psychological value:

What benefactions are behind his motives?

    Pain avoidance:

    Well-being:

    Self-preservation:

    Self-gratification:

What customer metaphors will we use to explain our value?

What is our account position, and who is in the fortress?

Which tactics will we use to penetrate the fortress?

Is this a renewal, persuasion, or creation sales cycle?

Is the executive a consolidator, consulter, responder, or bureaucrat buying type?

Who is our coach, and is he a frenemy, well-wisher, weak spy, strong spy, or guide?

Who is the bully with the juice, and what is our relationship with this person?

Who is the emperor, and what is our relationship with this person?

Is the executive a Visual, Auditory, or Kinesthetic?

What is the executive's source of stress (informational, peer
  pressure, or corporate citizenship)?
How does our solution defuse this stress?
What are the executive's group decision-making roles?

> Information role:
> Character role:
> Authority role:
> Company role:

Are we in a dominant, equal, or submissive position to the
  executive?
What familial role do we plan to assume during the call?
What intersecting activities do we share with the executive?
What selling style will we use?

Dominance	1	2	3	4	5
Hyperactivity	1	2	3	4	5
Pride	1	2	3	4	5
Confrontation	1	2	3	4	5
Transparency	1	2	3	4	5
Curiosity	1	2	3	4	5
Empathy	1	2	3	4	5

How will we structure our presentation?

> Pattern interruption:
> Key customer metaphors:
> Differentiating explanations:
> Closing background and foreground suggestions:
> Strategy slide:
> Money slide:

List the top twenty-five questions we would like to ask the
executive.

List the top twenty-five questions we should prepare for.

Has the executive spoken the confidential C-level language with us in the past and what did he confide?

What is the executive's ultimate fantasy?

Unfortunately, we have been trained to think of customers and ourselves as rational decision makers who use logic and reason exclusively. When you sell based solely upon logic, you are destined to be outsold. The successful C-level influencer is the salesperson who understands and appeals to the emotional, political, conscious, and subconscious executive decision maker. When you take the time to think about all the items on the checklist, you are thinking logically about the psychological reasons the C-level executive buys—something your competition is incapable of doing or won't take the time to think about.

What I Have Learned from Five Thousand C-Level Executives

While this book is based directly upon five hundred C-level executive interviews, I estimate that I have met with more than five thousand C-level executives over the course of my career. I would like to end the book by reiterating three essential lessons I have learned from all of these meetings.

The most important concept is that human nature is the ultimate decision maker for every major C-level executive decision. While the executive may have publicly recited a laundry list of rational reasons to justify the decision he made, he truthfully revealed in private that emotions, politics, and self-interests were responsible for the selection in the end.

> All things being equal, I'll go with the company that the salesperson established a relationship better—someone I felt comfortable with—because at that point it comes down to trust, in the guy calling

on you and his company. Is it a fellow I know I can do business with? Someone I might have some camaraderie with? When we're done with the business day can we enjoy the evening without him trying to sell me at ten o'clock at night?

CHIEF INFORMATION OFFICER

Your biggest enemy is time, not the competition. There are only 90 days in a quarter and 365 days in a year. It takes a winning sales strategy to defeat time. A brute force frontal strategy based upon features, functions, and benefits will fail, causing you to waste your precious time. An indirect strategy based upon understanding your value in solving the executive's problem while influencing the politics and psychology of C-level executive decision making will always succeed.

Are you talking generically or specifically? Tell me how you are going to help our business. Tell me how you are going to help our factories. Tell me how you are going to help our employees. I've had salespeople come rolling in my office with some bright idea and say that it is really great. But until I understand you and until you understand me, I'm not going to buy.

CHIEF EXECUTIVE OFFICER

The conversations you have with C-level executives are quite complex. They consist of verbal and nonverbal messages that are sent consciously and subconsciously. While you have most likely been in sales for years, you have probably neglected to improve your most important competitive sales weapon—your mouth and the words you speak! Mastering sales linguistics, the psychological study of how customers use and interpret language, will help you penetrate the C-level executive suite and convince company leaders to buy.

Our competitors are burning cash; we're controlling our cash flow. Right now, we would not make any capital investment unless it has less than a twelve-month payback. If all the solutions we are evaluating have the same payback, it becomes a sales job as to who can sell best to our upper management. What you say and how you say it truly sets you apart.

CHIEF FINANCIAL OFFICER

Congratulations on finishing what you started! I'd enjoy hearing from you. You can contact me at steve.martin@heavyhitterwisdom .com.

Epilogue

If Sigmund Freud Was
Your Sales Manager

Sigmund Freud is the most famous figure in all of psychology. If he was your sales manager I think he would ask you one very important question, "Why are you in sales?" While your conscious mind might rationalize that you got into sales through a calculated career move or even happenstance, Freud would probably argue that your decision to become a salesperson was made many years ago. This is because your subconscious mind has had a plan for your entire life. You are simply fulfilling your destiny.

Your subconscious mind knows you better than yourself. It remembers how you sought acceptance and recognition since the earliest days of your childhood. Today, it understands you crave adventure and excitement and that you could never be happy working a routine nine-to-five desk job. It also recognizes that you work in sales not because you have to, but because you have to be free. And this fundamental drive is at the core of the human spirit.

Sigmund Freud would acknowledge that you are a very rare type of individual. Most people don't have the capacity to intentionally endure the emotional and mental stress that is a daily part of a sales career. They don't have the self-confidence to attempt to accomplish difficult goals or possess the inward drive and perseverance to reach the pinnacle of success. In reality, most people can't deal with uncertainty and don't have the propensity to take risks. They are satisfied living average lives working at ordinary jobs because they are afraid to know the truth about themselves. While they shirk from the limelight because they fear their lack of courage will be exposed, you are on a continual mission to prove to the world you're right.

You not only tolerate risk, you thrive on it. You are a person who loves to compete because you must know whether you are winning or losing. You also know how to accept the consequences of defeat and you have a unique emotional aptitude that enables you to bounce back from adversity. Your subconscious mind has known for a long time that the secret of sales, as well as life, is turning failure into success, being able to not only learn from your mistakes but make the best of bad situations.

Sigmund Freud would say your subconscious mind is smarter than you think. It recognized way in advance that sales was the only profession that was right for you. It determined that you needed to be surrounded by people like yourself—modern-day warriors who embark on daily battles to vanquish evil archrivals. It also realized how important it is for you to have earned their respect and admiration.

Even though your conscious mind may occasionally daydream about doing some other profession, your subconscious knows that you are very fortunate to be in sales. While others have chosen life's mundane path, sales provides you the opportunity to fulfill your deep-seated drives to leave your legacy and become the hero who was able to make the family's dreams come true. You should be thankful it selected a career that increases your self-worth and net worth at the same time. Most importantly, your subconscious mind purposely chose this line of work so you could measure the significance of your life. And as your subconscious mind already knows, you are destined for great things.

Notes

CHAPTER 1

1. J. Atwell, "Why Are More People Right-Handed?" *Scientific American*, http:// www.sciam.com/askexpert_question.cfm?articleID=00063C8D-61EF-1C72 -9EB7809EC588F2D7&catID=3&topicID=3 (accessed March 23, 2006).
2. Growing Child, "Brain Development Facts," http://www.growingchild.com/ brain.html (accessed May 1, 2006).
3. Child Development Institute, "Normal Stages of Human Development," http://www.childdevelopmentinfo.com/development/normaldevelopment .shtml (accessed May 1, 2006).
4. Matt Sedensky, "Valentine's Day Research Key for Hallmark," *Yahoo! News*, February 13, 2006, http://news.yahoo.com/s/ap/20060213/ap_on_bi_ge/ hallmark_valentines (accessed February 13, 2006).
5. Ibid.

CHAPTER 2

1. Jim Hallowes and Amy Hallowes, "Being Highly Sensitive," About.com, http:// healing.about.com/od/empathic/a/HSP_hallowes.htm (accessed September 3, 2005).

CHAPTER 3

1. Victoria Neufeldt, ed., *Webster's New World College Dictionary*, 3rd ed. (New York: Prentice Hall, 1996).
2. Rosemary Haefner, "Survey: Three-in-Four Workers Suffer Stress on the Job: 10 Ways to Beat It," CareerBuilder.com, http://channels.netscape.com/ careers/package.jsp?name=careers/pm/workerstress (accessed March 14, 2006).
3. Michelle Meredith, "Pain at the Pump: Government Gas Secrets," *Yahoo! News*, May 8, 2006, http://news.yahoo.com/s/kcra/20060508/lo_ kcra/3452610 (accessed May 8, 2006).
4. Randolph Schmid, "Study Probes the Mystery of Hit Songs," *Yahoo! News*,

February 9, 2006, http://news.yahoo.com/s/ap/20060209/ap_en_ot/musical_mystery&printer=1;_ylt=ApLQ410qyvH2jX25Nl3kjc9Y24cA;_ylu=X3oDMTA3MXN1bHE0BHNlYwN0bWE- (accessed February 9, 2006).

5. Ibid.

6. Lauren NeerGaard, "Research Shows Anticipating Pain Hurts," *Yahoo! News,* May 4, 2006, http://news.yahoo.com/s/ap/20060504/ap_on_he_me/science_of_dread (accessed May 4, 2006).

7. Robert Roy Britt, "Why Men Report More Sex Partners Than Women," *Yahoo! News,* February 17, 2006, http://news.yahoo.com/s/space/2006 0217/sc_space/whymenreportmoresexpartnersthanwomen (accessed February 17, 2006).

8. Ibid.

CHAPTER 4

1. *Merriam-Webster Dictionary,* s.v. "reconnoiter," http://www.m-w.com/cgi-bin/dictionary?book=Dictionary&va=reconnoiter (accessed June 14, 2005).

2. *United States Department of Defense Dictionary,* s.v. "coup de main," http://www.dtic.mil/doctrine/jel/doddict/data/c/01369.html (accessed June 12, 2005).

CHAPTER 5

1. Leonard David, "Planet's Population to Hit 6.5 Billion Saturday," *Yahoo! News,* February 26, 2006, http://news.yahoo.com/s/space/20060224/sc_space/planetspopulationtohit65billionsaturday (accessed February 26, 2006).

2. Biblos, "Proverbs 24:5," http://bible.cc/proverbs/24-5.htm (accessed February 26, 2008).

CHAPTER 6

1. Brainy Quote, "Albert Einstein Quotes," http://www.brainyquote.com/quotes/quotes/a/alberteins133991.html (accessed February 26, 2008).

2. BBC News, "Invention of Writing—Sumer," Ancient Technology Facts, http://ancientx.com/nm/anmviewer.asp?a=95&z=1 (accessed January 5, 2009).

3. Michael Tchong, "Teenage Behavior," Ubercool LLC, http://www.ubercool.com/teenage-behavior (accessed January 13, 2009).

CHAPTER 7

1. Calvin S. Hall, Gardner Lindzey, and John B. Campbell, *Theories of Personality,* 4th ed. (New York: John Wiley and Sons, 1997).

2. R. J. Brown, "P. T. Barnum," HistoryBuff.com, http://www.historybuff.com/library/refbarnum.htmlPT (accessed March 21, 2006).

3. Lindsey Tanner, "Study Says Millions Have 'Rage' Disorder," *Yahoo! News*, June 6, 2006, http://news.yahoo.com/s/ap/20060605/ap_on_sc/road_rage_disease (accessed June 5, 2006).

4. Dictionary.com, s.v. "soldier," http://dictionary.reference.com/search?q=soldier (accessed April 4, 2006).

5. *Orange County Register*, "Quote of the Day," October 9, 2005.

6. Star Parker, "Private Savings Accounts Don't Attract Less Educated," *Scripps Howard News Service*, March 13, 2006.

7. Ibid.

CHAPTER 8

1. Arnab Basu, Raj Devnath, Derek Gasser, Jeff Ho, Richard Huie-Buckius, Josh Jaffe, Umang Jain, Nirave Kadakia, Kelly Kennedy, Parham Khoshkbari, Mark Kunkel, Anil Lalwani, Sean Lavery, Anlei Lee, Mark Lee, Gary Multani, Vinod Nair, Sudhir Nakhwa, Rodrigo Palacios, Aamir Qureshy, Dutta Satadip, Souma Sengupta, Mandar Shinde, Suki Singh, Joshua Sivaslian, Raj Sivasubramanian, Jim Squires, Jan Tai, Russell Tillitt, Colleen Varley, Jin Yun, University of California, Berkeley, Haas Business School MBA Program (fall 2008).

2. Robert Roy Britt, "Lies Take Longer Than Truths," Live Science, http://www.livescience.com/technology/090125-lie-detector.html, January 25, 2009 (accessed January 25, 2009).

3. Reuters, "Switching Languages Can Also Switch Personality: Study," http://www.reuters.com/article/lifestyleMolt/idUSSP4652020080624 (accessed June 24, 2008).

CHAPTER 9

1. Dave Sharpe, "Effective Communication," Montana State University, www.montana.edu/wwwcommd/effectcomm.htm (accessed February 9, 2004).

Index

About the Author

STEVE MARTIN began his career programming computers. Through working with computers, he became acutely aware of the preciseness and structure of language. In addition, programming is built upon models—verbal descriptions and visual representations of how systems work and processes flow. Models enable repeatable and predictable experiences.

Early in his career, he was also introduced to the concepts of neurolinguistics, the study of how the human brain uses and interprets language. When he transitioned his career into sales, he realized that he could build models to create successful relationships based upon customers' language and thought processes. Without any sales experience to speak of, he was the number one salesperson in his company for the following four years.

Steve went on to be a top sales producer for a billion-dollar software company and was promoted into management to imprint his selling model on other salespeople within the organization. As vice president of sales, Steve successfully trained his salespeople on the sales strategies and communication skills that are necessary to close complex accounts.

Steve is the author of several critically acclaimed books. *Heavy Hitter Selling: How Successful Salespeople Use Language and Intuition to Persuade Customers to Buy* is recommended reading by Harvard Business School and has been featured in *Forbes* and *Selling Power* magazines. *Heavy Hitter Sales Wisdom: Proven Sales Warfare Strategies, Secrets of Persuasion, and Common-Sense Tips for Success* is considered mandatory reading by Customer Relationship Management and Sales and Marketing Management magazines. He is also the author of *The Real Story of Informix Software and Phil White: Lessons in Business and Leadership for the Executive Team,* which is recommended by the American Bar Association and SoftwareCEO.

A highly sought-after speaker and sales trainer, Steve is both entertaining and enlightening. He has presented to hundreds of organizations. His clients include

Activant Solutions

Acxiom

Advanced Voice Speech
   Technologies

Akamai

Allstate Insurance

Applied Materials

Apptis

Automotive Resources
   International

BakBone Software

BEA Systems (Oracle)

Berbee Information Networks
   (CDW)

Best Manufacturing

Bruker Corporation

Captive Software (EMC)

Central Life Sciences

Chamberlain Group

Convergys

Cornerstone on Demand

Dawn Food Products

DHL

Document Sciences (EMC)

Eaton Vance Investments

Echelon

Edgar Online

ESRI

Experian

FusionStorm Tchnology

Global Healthcare Exchange

Globoforce

Graybar

Heartland Payment Sustems

Honeywell

I4 Commerce (Paypal)

IBM

Iona Software

Konecranes

Learn.com

LogicalApps (Oracle)

LSI Logic

Mathsoft (PTC)

McAfee Software

Metavante

MSC Software

MySQL (Sun)

NEC

Network Hardware

Norwest Ventures CEO Summit

Nuance Communications

Open Solutions

Pegasystems

Physicians Formula

Picis

Pillar Data

Power Equipment Company

Purolator

QAD Software

Riverbed Technology

Rosetta Stone

Shaw Industries

ShoreTel

Standard Register

Sungard Systems

Taleo

Teamquest Software

Tech Data

Telelogic Software (IBM)

Third Brigade Software

Triad Financial

TriQuint Semiconductors

USI Insurance

UTI Worldwide Logistics

Vitria

Werner Enterprises

Wonderware Software

Workbrain Software (Infor)

Steve has had the privilege of helping more than fifty thousand salespeople become top revenue producers. When not working with his clients, he enjoys teaching in the University of California Berkeley, Haas Business School MBA Program.

Please visit www.heavyhitterwisdom.com for keynote and sales training information.